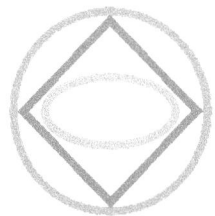

Symese – Universal Symbolic Script

Tim Lee

Any copy of this book issued by the publisher as a paperback is sold subject to the condition that it shall not by way of trade or otherwise be lent, resold, hired out or otherwise circulated without the publisher's prior written consent in any form of binding or cover other than that in which it is published and without a similar condition including these words being imposed on a subsequent purchaser.

ISBN
Paperback: 978-1-7635435-0-8
Hardcover: 978-1-7635435-2-2
Ebook: 978-1-7635435-1-5

© 2025 Scribblese Publishing, Sydney

First published in Australia in 2025 by Scribblese Publishing,
 2 Artlett St, Edgecliff, NSW 2027, Australia.

Cover design by Busybird Publishing.

Symese™ is a registered trademark of Tim Lee.

All Rights Reserved. No part of this publication may be reproduced or transmitted in any form or by any means, electronic or mechanical, including photocopy, recording or any other information storage and retrieval system, without prior permission in writing from the publisher.

Scribblese Publishing
2 Artlett St, Edgecliff
NSW 2027, Australia

Busybird Publishing
2/118 Para Road
Montmorency, Victoria
Australia 3094
www.busybird.com.au

To Rian and Ava,

You have kindled in my heart

the joy that comes from knowing that

we are not happy from being rich

but rich from being happy.

Symese – Universal Symbolic Script

© 2025 by Tim Lee

Foreword	1
Introduction	3
Typographical convention	4

Part I – Rationale and Framework

Chapter 1

Linguistic Context	5
Language and the human family	5
The streams of written language	6
The ideal of a universal script	6
The sound of silence	8

Chapter 2

Structure of Meaning	10
Outline of basic concepts	10
Basic concepts in mind maps	13

Part II – 1000+ Root Syms

Chapter 3

Basic Concepts	17

Chapter 4

Qualifiers	25

Chapter 5

Seed Shapes	30

Chapter 6

Abstract Concepts	35

Chapter 7

Basic Tangibles   39

Chapter 8

More Abstract Concepts   49

Part III – Augmented and Compound Syms, Practical Aspects of Usage

Chapter 9

More Qualifiers   56

Chapter 10

Compound Syms   64

Chapter 11

Symese in Practice   84
       Semantic simplicity   84
       Sample sentences   94

Appendices

Appendix A – Complete Set of Root Syms   98

Appendix B – Complete Set of Augmented Syms   119

Appendix C – Index of Root and Augmented Syms   187

Appendix D – Index of Headwords   229

Appendix E – Index of Compound Syms   248

Appendix F – Design Principles   261

Appendix G – Glossary   266

Appendix H – Index   267

Foreword

The stirrup. The wheel. The internet. Electricity. The compass. Which has been most important in advancing civilisation? Perhaps more important than any of them is writing.

Without writing, most human beings might still be hunter-gatherers on fertile savannahs. Writing enabled the development of complex societies; it gave rise to mass education; it created historical records. There were advanced cultures which developed without writing. The Incas of Peru and the Aztecs of Mexico, for instance, had powerful empires. But in both of them symbolic systems evolved to pass on knowledge.

A problem has bedevilled this invaluable tool. The incredible number of mutually incomprehensible languages throughout history is reflected in the diversity of scripts. The Latin script is just one of many. It competes with Cyrillic, Chinese, Japanese, Korean, Thai, Hindi, Telugu, Armenian, Georgian, Arabic, Hebrew, Greek and many others.

And these are just contemporary scripts. Many ancient scripts faded away when their societies collapsed or were conquered. Cretan Linear A and Linear B, Sumerian cuneiform, Egyptian hieroglyphics, Scandinavian runes, Indus script, and Elamite cuneiform have all perished.

The great dream of mankind since the destruction of the Tower of Babel has been to communicate in one language or at least one script. In John Milton's epic poem *Paradise Lost*, Adam and Eve speak to God in Hebrew, which mediaeval scholars believed to be the original language of mankind. The cacophony following the dispersion of the builders of Babel was regarded as a tragedy – but restoring unity was also derided as folly. In *Gulliver's Travels*, Jonathan Swift satirised attempts to create an artificial universal language. The preposterous academics of Laputa believe that words should be abolished and that people would do better to carry objects around with them to brandish at their companions in conversation.

As Umberto Eco, the best-selling author of The *Name of the Rose*, says: "The story of the confusion of tongues, and of the attempt to redeem its loss through the rediscovery or invention of a language common to all humanity, can be found in every culture."

It is in this context that you should read Tim Lee's heroic endeavour to compose a cross-cultural universal script which can be read intuitively. It is the latest step in centuries of attempts to reverse the curse of Babel.

I used the word "heroic" to describe the creation of *Symese*. The 17th century polymath Leibniz dreamed of a universal script and theorised about it, but Tim has done it.

The creation of an entirely new script is a rare event. Academics rhapsodize about how an illiterate Alaskan genius, Uyaquq, invented a script to communicate in his central Alaskan language Yup'ik. The Cherokee genius Sequoyah became famous for inventing a script for his native tongue which survives today.

But Tim Lee is even more ambitious. Uyaquq and Sequoyah created scripts for their own languages. Symese could become a medium of communication uniting all cultures. In quest of this noble aim, Tim's claim to have developed a rigorously logical and intuitive system of communication deserves to be examined.

Michael Cook
Author & Journalist

INTRODUCTION

Is it possible to express ourselves with symbols independent of their sounds in spoken language? To denote basic concepts using a reasonably small set of symbols, with a pictographic link to what each represents, that can be augmented or combined into compound symbols to represent more complex concepts?

Yes, it is!

This book presents an outline blueprint for *Symese*, a universal symbolic script that is simple but not simplistic. It has an elegance and coherence lacking in modern pictographic-rooted scripts whose glyphs (symbols or icons), stylised and expanded over time to denote sophisticated concepts, have lost much of their pictographic lineage.

My quest to develop a universal symbolic script has been inspired by how the Chinese script bridges many spoken dialects and appear even in other languages like Korean and Japanese. Notwithstanding syntactical and semantic differences in the use of Chinese characters across dialects and languages, can we achieve today on a global scale what ancient civilisations did at a local level?

Yes, we can!

PART I – CONTEXT, RATIONALE AND STRUCTURE

- Chapter 1 establishes the context and rationale for this script.
- Chapter 2 places some basic concepts within a logical framework.

PART II – 1000+ ROOT SYMS

- Chapter 3 presents an initial set of symbols for basic concepts.
- Chapter 4 introduces qualifiers to augment this set.
- Chapter 5 explores syms based on common geometric shapes.
- Chapter 6 presents an initial set of syms for abstract concepts.
- Chapter 7 explores syms based on shapes of tangible objects.
- Chapter 8 expands the set of syms for abstract concepts.

PART III – AUGMENTED AND COMPOUND SYMS, PRACTICAL ASPECTS OF USAGE
- Chapter 9 adds more qualifiers to augment root syms.
- Chapter 10 introduces compound syms and word parcels.
- Chapter 11 outlines how Symese might be used in practice.

TYPOGRAPHICAL CONVENTION

A word or phrase is set in **bold** type for a linguistic term or one with a specific meaning in this book (as outlined in the G̲l̲o̲s̲s̲a̲r̲y̲) and in *italics* for a term represented by a glyph.

Part I – Rationale and Framework

Chapter 1

Linguistic Context

Language and the human family

Language takes us beyond the "I" of who we are to the "we" of family and community and – with a universal language, if there be such a thing – the "we" of the human family. It allows a meeting of minds and hearts without subsuming our individuality, leaving us free to agree or disagree or agree to disagree. It can be twisted into a spear to impose our will on another or forged into a shield to deflect such deception.

There is a science and an art to communication. The science of a language – structural aspects like **syntax** and **semantics** – helps us to be precise in what we say. The art helps us to understand one another at the heart level – its balance and beauty. A language flows from its historical and cultural context and feeds into that context. Its embedded tapestry of cultural virtue and vice is both a strength and a weakness.

Men and women naturally form tribes that compete with other tribes for scarce resources. Along the way, we discover that cooperation can be more beneficial than competition on every level, that ingenuity in synergy is our most important human resource. The creative tension between competition and cooperation gives rise to tribes and nations. A language reflects and reinforces a group's resilience and resourcefulness.

In the Biblical story of Babel, one universal spoken language splintered into myriad tongues when God thwarted the people's attempt to reach the heavens as gods, throwing them into confusion. There is no prospect of the more than 7,000 spoken languages in the world, each with its own cultural context, ever merging into a single language. With written language, however, icons on traffic signs and emojis in social media are already a universal script of sorts within their respective domains.

THE STREAMS OF WRITTEN LANGUAGE

Written language developed along two streams – **phonographic** (syllabic/phonetic) and **pictographic** (logographic/ideographic). In the first stream, alphabets denote the sound of syllables or parts of words, as in English, Greek and Arabic. In the second stream, glyphs represent whole words or concepts. Chinese and **hieroglyphics** are nominally pictographic with phonetic elements. Hieroglyphs are a mix of **pictograms** and **rebus words** that use glyphs for their phonetic value. Most Chinese characters consist of a pictographic-rooted radical and a phonetic component.

No modern language is purely pictographic, unlike some ancient scripts like the Rongorongo of Easter Island, which consists of "stylized outlines of objects or creatures, with... some 120 basic elements, combined to form between 1500 and 2000 compound signs."[1] Phonographic scripts have the advantage of a simple framework in which a small set of alphabets (24 in Greek, 26 in English, 28 in Arabic) are combined into thousands of words, providing a direct link to spoken language.

Pictographic scripts bridge the tangible and intangible with glyphs derived from images. As proto-pictographic scripts (consisting of a few hundred symbols representing a basic set of objects and concepts) developed, they were stylised and expanded to represent sophisticated concepts, with their **pictographic roots** all but indiscernible.

THE IDEAL OF A UNIVERSAL SCRIPT

Can a universal script be developed using symbols to denote concepts independent of their sounds in spoken language? This idea is at least four hundred years old. "Some people, beginning with the philosopher and mathematician Leibniz in the 17th century, even like to imagine that we can invent an entire written language for universal communication... independent of any of the spoken languages of the world, dependent only upon the concepts essential to high-level philosophical, political and scientific communication. If music and mathematics can achieve it, so the thought goes – why not more generally?"[2] Of his *characteristica universalis*[3], Leibniz wrote:

---

[1] The Story of Writing, Andrew Robinson, Thames & Hudson 1995, ch. 8
[2] The Story of Writing, Andrew Robinson, Thames & Hudson 1995, Introduction
[3] https://en.wikipedia.org/wiki/Characteristica_universalis

> *And although learned men have long since thought of some kind of language or universal characteristic by which all concepts and things can be put into beautiful order, and with whose help different nations might communicate their thoughts and each read in his own language what another has written in his, yet no one has attempted a language or characteristic which includes at once both the arts of discovery and judgement, that is, one whose signs and characters serve the same purpose that arithmetical signs serve for numbers, and algebraic signs for quantities taken abstractly. Yet it does seem that since God has bestowed these two sciences on mankind, he has sought to notify us that a far greater secret lies hidden in our understanding, of which these are but the shadows.*

Blissymbols[1] is perhaps the nearest thing there is to a modern pictographic script. Inspired by Chinese characters and Leibniz's ideographic language project, it is a "constructed language conceived as an ideographic writing system called Semantography consisting of several hundred basic symbols, each representing a concept, which can be composed together to generate new symbols that represent new concepts... Semantography was published by Charles K. Bliss in 1949 and found use in the education of people with communication difficulties."

A more recent invention is iConji[2], a set of apps built around 1,200 icons "culled from base words used in common daily communications, word frequency lists, often-used mathematical and logical symbols, punctuation symbols, and the flags of all nations", developed as a digital form of visual communication. An artistic community was formed to grow the icon set.

iConji falls short of the ideal of a universal symbolic script in two respects. Firstly, it is essentially emojis on steroids without a logical structure of meaning. Secondly, it requires a computer app to write with. Blissymbols, on the other hand, must be learnt as a system of writing by hand to be useful as a language in its own right. It is akin to mental arithmetic while iConji is more like using a calculator for simple sums – a hindrance more than a help. Unlike basic arithmetic, Blissymbols has not proven to be elegant and intuitive enough to attract a critical mass of learners. Modern developments like the emojis used for text messaging do not constitute a self-contained language. None of these systems meet the criteria for a universal script. What might these criteria be?

---

[1] https://en.wikipedia.org/wiki/Blissymbols
[2] https://en.wikipedia.org/wiki/IConji

Without the advantage of historical evolution within a cultural context, a universal script must be simple enough for a non-linguist to learn without undue effort yet versatile enough to express a viable range of concepts. It would need a core set of glyphs that can be compounded to represent derivative concepts. There would need to be a curated crowd-sourced project to collate and incorporate useful structural and semantic features of other languages. As dialects arise, they will need to retain enough core features for the script to serve as a bridge across **natural languages**.

In her book *In the Land of Invented Languages*[1], Arika Okrent explores some of the 900 languages invented over the last millennium and notes that "the urge to invent languages is as old and persistent as language itself." She suggests that the language inventors have failed because "language refuses to be cured… it succeeds, not in spite of, but because of, the very qualities that the language inventors have tried to engineer away."

My quest has been inspired by how the Chinese script bridges many spoken dialects and appear even in other languages like Korean and Japanese. Notwithstanding syntactical and semantic differences in the use of Chinese characters across dialects and languages, can we achieve today on a global scale what ancient civilisations did at a local level?

Without attempting to emulate past attempts to invent new languages, I have developed a framework of pictographic logic as the basis for a universal symbolic script with the potential to evolve into a living language. Join the initiative to develop Symese further by subscribing or leaving a comment on my website: https://www.symese.com.

THE SOUND OF SILENCE

In the evolution of language, which came first – primal utterances that became the rudiments of a spoken language or caveman symbols that made up a proto-pictographic script – the noise of words or the sound of silence, the music or the lyrics? Linguistic researchers are unable to find compelling evidence either way. The fact that no purely pictographic script has survived the ages contrasts with the thousands of spoken languages and hundreds of phonographic scripts in existence. This reflects the elegance of the alphabet – in which a small set of symbols are combined into many thousands of words – an elegance that no pictographic script can match.

---

[1] In the Land of Invented Languages, Arika Okrent, Random House 2009, ch. 2

The lack of a direct link to the spoken word explains both the complexity and the beauty of a pictographic-rooted language like Chinese. In a stylised pictogram like 人 *(person),* 大 *(big)* and 天 *(sky),* we can discern the outline of a *person* on two legs, a horizontal stroke (outstretched arms) added to denote *big* and a second horizontal stroke (the expanse above) added to denote *sky*. The pictographic roots of other characters like 上, 下, 口 and 中 *(up, down, mouth* and *middle)* are also fairly obvious. To deal with the difficulty of representing abstract concepts, the pictograms were increasingly stylised and a phonetic component was introduced. The pictographic roots of most Chinese characters are a lot less evident than in the examples here.

Is it possible to construct a simple system of symbols with a pictographic link to the concept denoted by each symbol? To denote basic concepts with a few hundred symbols that can be augmented or combined into thousands of compound symbols to represent more complex concepts? To develop a script whose logic is self-evident and elegant enough to attract a critical mass of users? To capture the poetry of words in the sound of silence?

My initial set of a thousand base symbols is the core of a universal symbolic script, a system that is simple but not simplistic. It has an elegance and coherence lacking in modern pictographic-rooted scripts whose glyphs, stylised and expanded over time to denote sophisticated concepts, have lost much of their pictgraphic lineage.

Chapter 2
Structure of Meaning

Our language evolves as we grow – individually and as a community. We come into this world as a bundle of senses and cravings, learning first to communicate our physical and emotional needs with sounds and gestures while learning our mother tongue. We form relationships with people around us. As we journey through childhood, adolescence and adulthood, our language evolves to deal with an ever-wider circle of objects and concepts – our senses, body parts, everyday objects, work, leisure and thought. How might elements of a basic sense of reality be expressed in a pictographic script?

Outline of basic concepts

Let us start with *I* and *you*, *he/she* and *it*, *person* and *thing*, *mother* and *father*, *daughter* and *son*:

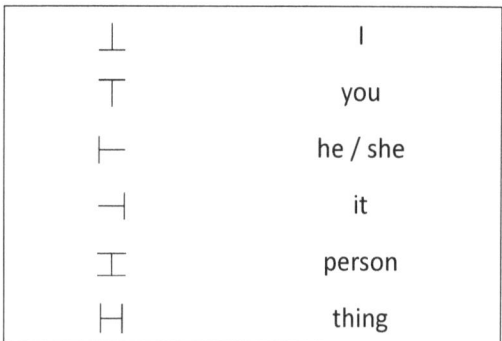
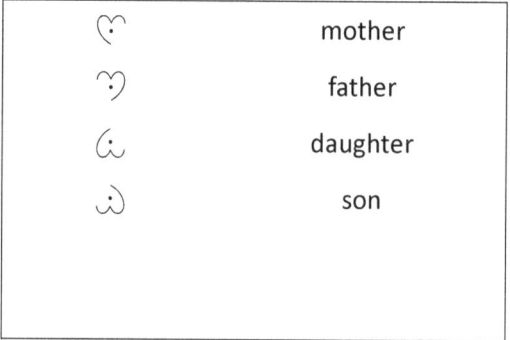

We perceive our body parts and objects around the house, and express them as:

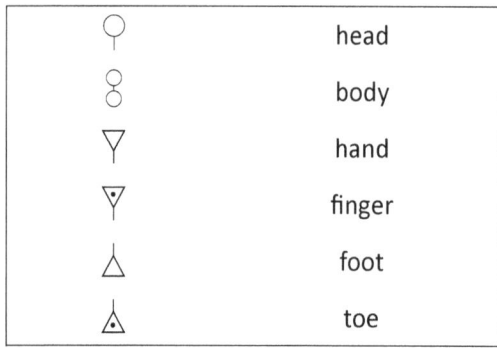

Some geometric shapes offer an easy pictographic link to syms to do with our senses:

⬯	sight		▱	smell
⊙	eye		▱	nose
( )	hearing		▱	taste
(⬯)	ear		▱	tongue
(·)	sound			
(∘)	silence			

Basic shapes are also used to denote position or state:

⌒	close		∩	big
⌣	open		∪	small
(	back		⊂	slow
)	front		⊃	fast

△	solid		=	top
▽	liquid		⌣	bottom
◁	be still		|(	before
▷	move		)|	after

⊓	on		∧	high
⊔	off		∨	low
⊏	in		<	seldom
⊐	out		>	often

△	many		⊼	over
▽	few		⊻	under
◁	stop		⊬	towards
▷	start		⊢	away from

↑	up		⋏	there
↓	down		⋎	here
←	left		⋖	near
→	right		⋗	far

Other shapes are used to denote objects in nature:

♀	mammal		♀	tree
♂	bird		♀	branch
∝	reptile		♀	root
∞	fish		♀	leaf

These sample syms are built on a framework of symbols that include others with less obvious pictographic logic but are nevertheless part of a coherent whole.

Chapter 2 — Structure of Meaning

BASIC CONCEPTS IN MIND MAPS

Let us explore this architecture in mind maps, starting with the basic concepts *on* and *off*, *in* and *out*, *with* and *without*, *of* and *if*, *this* and *that*, *how* and *so that*, *around* and *amid*:

Root Concepts 1

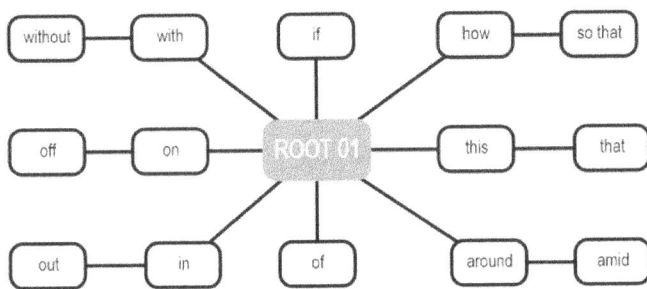

Other basic concepts are *at* and *so*, *between* and *among*, *while* and *during*, *since* and *until*, *within* and *beside*, *beyond* and *past*, *what* and *who/which*, *when* and *where*:

Root Concepts 2

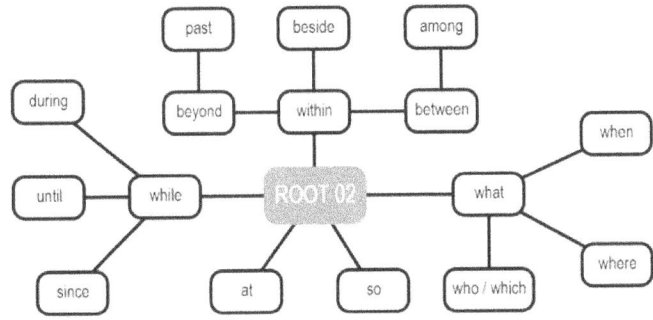

The concepts are grouped along the lines of their formulation as syms in the next chapter. Here are a few more semantic mind maps of these groupings:

Root Concepts 3

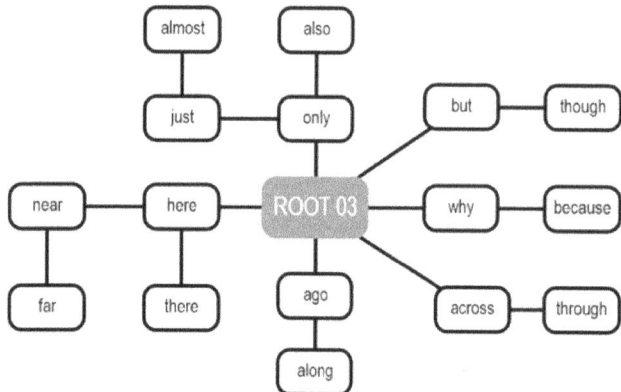

Root Concepts 4

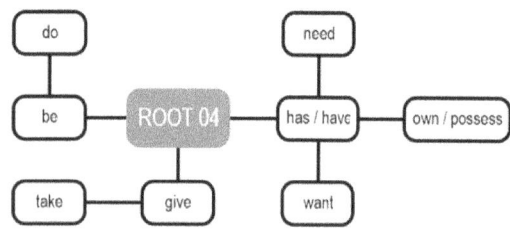

Root Concepts 5

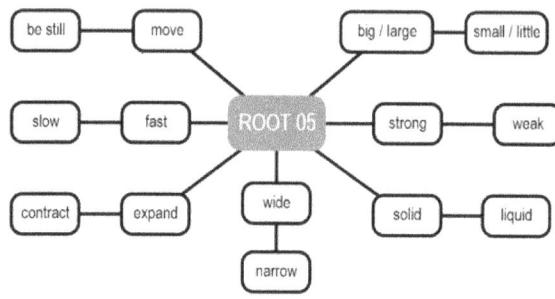

Chapter 2 — Structure of Meaning

Root Concepts 6

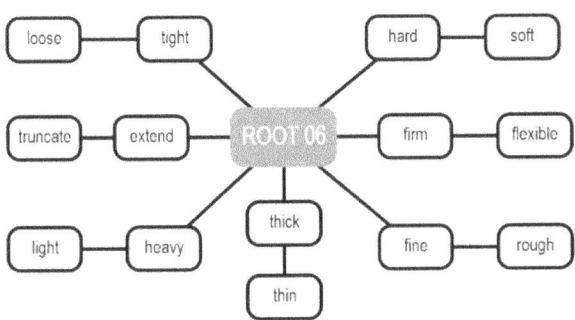

Root Concepts 7

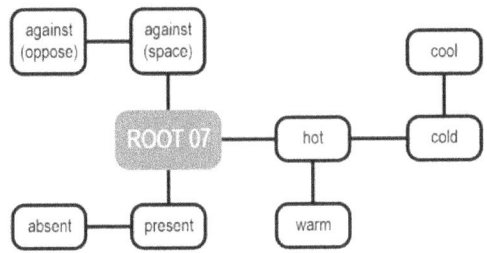

Root Concepts 8

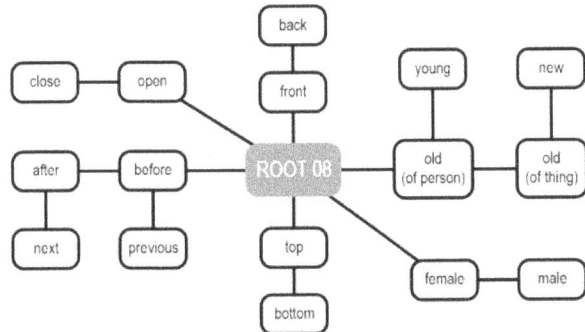

Root Concepts 9

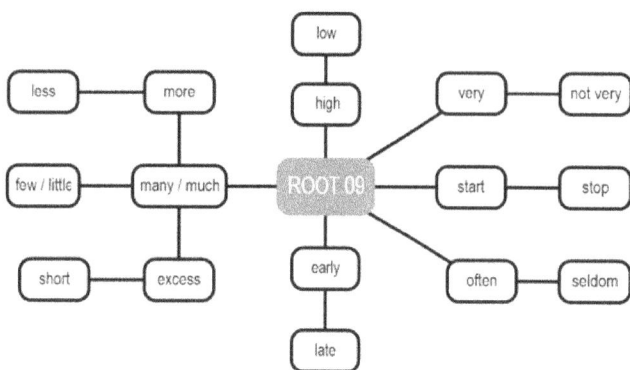

Root Concepts 10

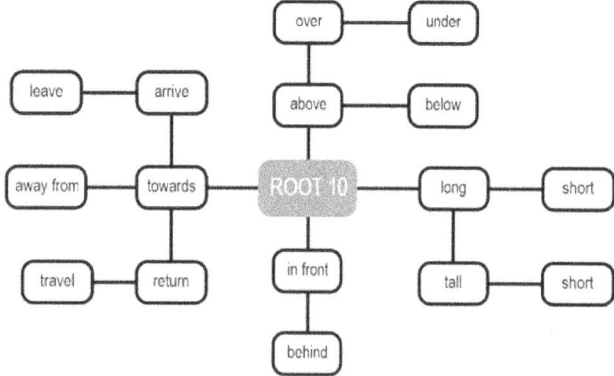

Part II – 1000+ Root Syms

Chapter 3
Basic Concepts

Unlike the many invented languages of the past, Symese does not attempt to

- catalog every conceivable concept in a "calculus of thought", as John Wilkins tried to do[1]
- distill a messy vocabulary into a pure language that precisely reflects reality, as the inventors of Loglan and Interlingua tried to do, with rules to facilitate logical thought[2]
- create a hybrid of several languages a la Esperanto
- emulate the complex richness of European languages like Spanish's many verb inflections, French's object genders and German's capitalisation of nouns.

Following a set of principles based on English vocabulary but consistent with **mentalese**, Symese has a set of **root syms** to represent basic concepts, with pictographic links that make sense. There is a coherence to the whole, and the syms are modified, augmented or combined into **derivative syms** or **compound syms**.

How many concepts are there that we might consider basic? A few hundred? A thousand? Linguists have compiled lists of the most common words in English, including a top 100, a top 500 and a top 1000. There is substantial overlap across these and similar lists, which I have merged and distilled, along with words from basic learners' dictionaries, into a relatively small set of basic concepts on which to build Symese.

Particles (articles, prepositions and conjunctions) are among the top 100 most common words. While particle-less (esp article-less) sentences can often be constructed without loss of meaning, particles are included in the list of root syms for completeness and to build derivatives on.

---

[1] In the Land of Invented Languages, Arika Okrent, Random House 2009, ch. 4
[2] In the Land of Invented Languages, Arika Okrent, Random House 2009, ch. 8

Let us associate some simple glyphs – basic straight and curved lines – with common concepts. We use the forward slash ╱ for *or* (as commonly understood), the backslash ╲ for *and*, ⌒ for *the* and ⌣ for *a/an*:

or	╱	the	⌒
and	╲	a / an	⌣

Taking the concepts from the ROOT 1 mind map in CHAPTER 2, we denote *on* and *off* by ⊓ and ⊔, *in* and *out* by ⊏ and ⊐, *with* and *without* by ⌐ and ⌙, *of* and *if* by ⌐⌐ and ⌙⌙, *this* and *that* by ⌐ and ⌐, *how* and *so that* by ⌐ and ⌐, *around* and *amid* by ⌐ and ⌐. To complete the symmetry, we add ⌐` and ⌐` for *common (shared)* and *common (frequent)*:

on	⊓	with	⌐
off	⊔	without	⌙
in	⊏	of	⌐⌐
out	⊐	if	⌙⌙

this	⌐	around	⌐
that	⌐	amid	⌐
how	⌐	common (shared)	⌐`
so that	⌐	common (frequent)	⌐`

In ROOT 2 we denote *between* and *among* by ▽ and △, *beside* and *past* by ▷ and ◁, *within* and *beyond* by ⌒ and ⌣, *since* and *until* by (and):

between	▽	within	⌒
among	△	beyond	⌣
beside	▷	since	(
past (conjunction)	◁	until	)

We denote *during* and *while* by ⌒ and ⌣, *at* and *so* by ⌒ and ⌣, *what* and *who/which* by ⌐ and ⌐, *when* and *where* by ⌐ and ⌐:

during	⌒	what	⌐
while (conjunction)	⌣	who / which	⌐
at	⌒	when	⌐
so	⌣	where	⌐

In ROOT 3 we denote *also* and *only* by ⌢` and ⌣` , *just* and *almost* by ∧` and ∨` , *why* and *because* by ⟨ and ⟩ , *but* and *though* by ⟨ and ⟩ , *across* and *through* by ⌢ and ⌣, *ago* and *along* by ⟨` and ⟩, *there* and *here* by ∧` and ∨` , *near* and *far* by ⟨` and ⟩` :

also	⌢`	why	⟨
only	⌣`	because	⟩
just (adv)	∧`	but	⟨
almost	∨`	though	⟩

across	⌢	there	∧`
through	⌣	here	∨`
ago	⟨`	near	⟨`
along	⟩	far	⟩`

In ROOT 4 we denote *do* and *be* by ⌣´ and ⌢´ , *take* and *give* by ⟩´ and ⟨´ , *has/have* and *own/possess* by ⌢´ and ⌣´ , *need* and *want* by ⟨´ and ⟩´ :

do (v)	⌣´	has / have	⌢´
be	⌢´	own / possess	⌣´
take (v)	⟩´	need (v)	⟨´
give	⟨´	want (v)	⟩´

These syms introduce the first **Design Principles** (DPs):

1. There is a logical link between sym and concept, eg an upward- or right-pointing shape is used to denote a more perceptible or active concept – ⊓ for *on*, ⊐ for *out* – and a similar downward- or left-pointing shape for its converse – ⊔ for *off*, ⊏ for *in*.

2. Where a shape has parts pointing in opposite directions, the direction of the left or upper part of the shape indicates the concept denoted, eg ⌣´ with its left part pointing up and ⟨´ with its upper part pointing right denote the more active concepts *do* and *give* while their mirror image syms ⌢´ and ⟩´ denote the more passive concepts *be* and *take*.

3. A symmetry of sym pairs is achieved by flipping or rotating the glyphs.

19

4. Particles and nouns are the default parts of speech and do not need superscripts to denote them as such – particles by virtue of their frequent occurrence in sentences and nouns for the reason that, consistent with the basic mental process of perceiving objects with our senses, they are used as tangible gateways to intangibles.

5. Superscript ` (adjective **qualifier** or AQ) is added for adjectives and adverbs and superscript ´ (verb qualifier or VQ) is added for verbs.

6. Where a word has divergent meanings, the most common parallel meanings are assigned to a sym, eg ⊓ denotes *on*, with the parallel meanings 'at a given time' and 'in contact with'. Similarly, ⊓ denotes 'next to' and 'in the manner of' as parallel meanings of *with*.

Starting from a blank canvas allows us to avoid much of the complexity embedded in the rich **etymology** of sophisticated languages. This legacy of richness is baggage in a script that transcends linguistic boundaries. Keeping the associations between sym and concept at a basic level makes the script less language-specific.

Moving on to basic qualities, in Root 5 we denote *big* and *small* by ∩` and ∪` , *slow* and *fast* by ⊂` and ⊃` , *solid* and *liquid* (as nouns) by △ and ▽, *be still* and *move* by ⊲´ and ⊳´ , *strong* and *weak* by A` and ∀` , *oppose* and *propose* by ⊲´ and ⊳´ , *wide* and *narrow* A` and ∀` , *contract* and *expand* by ⊄´ and ⊅´ :

big / large	∩`	solid (n)	△
small / little	∪`	liquid (n)	▽
slow (a)	⊂`	be still	⊲´
fast (a)	⊃`	move (v)	⊳´

strong	A`	wide	A`
weak	∀`	narrow (a)	∀`
oppose	⊲´	contract (shrink)	⊄´
propose	⊳´	expand	⊅´

Along the same lines, in Root 6 we denote *hard* and *soft* by ⌒` and ⌣` , *fine* and *rough* by ⊂` and ⊃` , *heavy* and *light* by △` and ▽` *tight* and *loose* by ◁` and ▷` , *firm* and *flexible* by A` and ∀` , *control* and *manage* by ⋐´ and ⋑´ , *thick* and *thin* by A` and ∀` , *truncate* and *extend* by ⋐´ and ⋑´ :

hard	⌒`	heavy	△`
soft	⌣`	light (opp heavy)	▽`
fine	⊂`	tight	◁`
rough	⊃`	loose	▷`

firm (a)	A`	thick	A`
flexible	∀`	thin	∀`
control (v)	⋐´	truncate	⋐´
manage	⋑´	extend	⋑´

This is the seventh DP:

7. **Modifiers** are added to basic shapes to denote related concepts, eg a dot or line is added to ⌒ and ⌣ to make ⌒` and ⌣` for *hard* and *soft*, △ and ▽ for *solid* and *liquid*, A` and ∀` for *strong* and *weak*, A` and ∀` for *wide* and *narrow*, △` and ▽` for *heavy* and *light*, A` and ∀` for *firm* and *flexible*, A` and ∀` for *thick* and *thin*.

In Root 7 a dot and/or line is added to ⌒ and ⌣ to make ⌒` and ⌣` for *hot* and *cold*, ⌒` and ⌣` for *warm* and *cool*. A dot and/or line is added to ⊂ and ⊃ to make ⊂` and ⊃` for *against (space)* and *against (oppose)*, ⊂` and ⊃` for *present* and *absent*:

hot (temperature)	⌒`	warm (a)	⌒`
cold (a)	⌣`	cool (a)	⌣`
against (space)	⊂`	present (opp absent)	⊂`
against (oppose)	⊃`	absent	⊃`

In Root 8 we denote *old (of person)* and *young* by ⌒` and ⌣` , *old (of thing)* and *new* by ⌒` and ⌣` , *female* and *male* by ⊂` and ⊃` , *previous* and *next* by ⊂` and ⊃` , *close* and *open* by ⌢` and ⌣` (shapes that look like closed and open lids), *back* and *front* by ◁` and ▷` , *top* and *bottom* by ⌢` and ⌣` , *before* and *after* by ⊂ and ⊃ :

Symese — Universal Symbolic Script

old (of person)	⌢`	female (a)	(:`
young	⌣`	male (a)	):`
old (of thing)	⌢̄`	previous	|(`
new	⌣̱`	next	)|`

close (a)	⌒`	top	⌢̄`
open (a)	⌣`	bottom	⌣̱`
back (opp front)	⟅`	before	|(
front (a)	⟆`	after	)|

This is the eighth DP:

8. Based on the convention (eg buttons on a tape recorder) of arrows pointing left and right to indicate backward and forward, we denote *back, be still, before, previous, present* and *near* by left-pointing shapes ⟅` , ⟅´ , |(, |(` , |(` and <` and the opposite concepts by their mirror image shapes.

In ROOT 9 we denote *high* and *low* by ∧` and ∨` , *seldom* and *often* by <` and >` , *very* and *not very* by ∧` and ∨` , *early* and *late* by <` and >` , *many/much* and *few/little* by △` and ▽` , *stop* and *start* by ◁´ and ▷´ , *more* and *less* by ⩓` and ⩔` , *short* and *excess* by ≪` and ≫` . The pictographic logic of these syms is discernible and in line with the DPs above:

high	∧`	very	∧`
low	∨`	not very	∨`
seldom	<`	early	<`
often	>`	late	>`

many / much	△`	more	⩓`
few / little	▽`	less	⩔`
stop (v)	◁´	short (opp excess)	≪`
start (v)	▷´	excess / too	≫`

Chapter 3 — Basic Concepts

In Root 10 we denote *above* and *below* by △ and ▽, *behind* and *ahead* by ◁` and ▷` , *tall* and *short* by A` and ∀` , *arrive* and *leave* by ◁´ and ▷´ , *long* and *short* by A` and ∀` , *return* and *travel* by ◁´ and ▷´ , *over* and *under* by ⊼ and ⊻ *towards* and *away from* by ⋉ and ⋊ :

above	△	tall	A`
below	▽	short (opp tall)	∀`
behind	◁`	arrive	◁´
ahead / in front	▷`	leave	▷´

long	A`	over	⊼
short (opp long)	∀`	under	⊻
return (v)	◁´	towards	⋉
travel (v)	▷´	away from	⋊

Continuing these logical groupings, we denote *rise* and *fall* by A´ and ∀´ , *come* and *go* by ◁´ and ▷´ , *light* and *darkness* by △ and ▽, *opposite of change* and *change* by ◁ and ▷, *shape* and *material* by ⬚△ and ⬚▽, *static* and *dynamic* by ◁` and ▷` , *surface* and *core* by ⬚△ and ⬚▽, *focus* and *dispersal* by ◁ and ▷ :

rise (v)	A´	light (opp darkness)	△
fall / drop (v)	∀´	darkness	▽
come	◁´	opp of change	◁
go	▷´	change (n)	▷

shape (n)	⬚△	surface (n)	⬚△
material	⬚▽	core (n)	⬚▽
static	◁`	focus (n)	◁
dynamic	▷`	dispersal	▷

Opposite of change is not a discrete concept in English but a logical one that arises from the symmetry of symbols in Symese. This introduces the ninth DP:

9. The symmetry of symbols fills conceptual gaps in natural languages.

We denote *up* and *down* by ↑` and ↓` , *left* and *right* by ←` and →` , *flip* and *turn* by ↕´ and ↔´ :

| up | ↑` | left (opp right) | ←` | flip (v) | ↕´ |
| down | ↓` | right (opp left) | →` | turn (v) | ↔´ |

We denote *about (relating to)* and *about (approximately)* by ⌒ and ⌣` , *number* by ε :

about (relating to)	⌒
about (approx)	⌣`
number (n)	ε

We denote *than* and *then* by ∽ and ∽` , *as* and *such* by ℓ and ℓ , *ready* and *available* by ℓ` and ∂` :

than	∽	ready	ℓ`
then	∽`	available	∂`
as	ℓ		
such	ℓ		

The mirror images of ε, ℓ and ∂ are excluded to avoid assigning syms that look like the numbers 3, 9 and 6 respectively, reserving numerals for use as numbers or in syms that require them as qualifiers. This is the tenth DP:

10. A numeral is used as a number or sym qualifier but not as a standalone sym. Besides 0-9, we also retain the conventional usage of the following common symbols:

| . | : | ' | ! | (| # | & | - |
| , | ; | " | ? |) | * | % | = |

CHAPTER 4
QUALIFIERS

Symese is designed to be an organic whole grown from **sym seeds** – a thousand-plus root syms and qualifiers that can be combined into thousands of **augmented** or **compound syms** to form a viable pictographic language. Design Principles (DPs) outlined in the previous chapters express the logic of Symese, forming a whole that is more than the sum of its parts.

Adding to the qualifiers introduced in CHAPTER 3 (superscript ` for adjectives or adverbs and ´ for verbs), we have ¯ for noun, ˣ for opposite, ¹ ² ³ etc for derivatives, ᴴ for device/substance and ˘ for essence/nuance. This introduces the eleventh DP:

11. Noun qualifier (NQ) superscript ¯ is used for a noun, opposite qualifier (OQ) superscript ˣ for the opposite of a concept, numeric qualifier (#Q) superscripts ¹ ² ³ etc for a derivative or extension of a concept, device/substance qualifier (DQ) superscript ᴴ for the device or substance formed from a concept and essence/nuance qualifier (EQ) superscript ˘ for the essence or nuance of a concept. The superscript is doubled or tripled where the root sym already has a superscript for the same part of speech.

AQ	Adjective / Adverb	`	#Q	Derivative	¹
VQ	Verb	´	DQ	Device / substance	ᴴ
NQ	Noun	¯	EQ	Essence / nuance	˘
OQ	Opposite	ˣ			

The following examples illustrate how these qualifiers are used to extend the range of definitions from basic concepts.

Removing the superscript in ∩` and ∪` for *big* and *small* makes ∩ and ∪ for *size* and *smallness*. Adding VQ makes ∩´ and ∪´ for *enlarge* and *shrink*, NQ makes ∩¯ and ∪¯ for *enlarging* and *shrinking* as nouns. Adding double AQ to ∩ makes ∩" for *enlarged* as adjective, adding NQ + AQ to ∪ makes ∪˵ for *shrinking* as adjective:

big / large	∩`	size	∩	small / little	∪`	smallness	∪
		enlarge	∩´			shrink	∪´
		enlarging (n)	∩¯			shrinking (n)	∪¯
		enlarged (a)	∩"			shrinking (a)	∪˵

Removing the superscript in ⊂ˋ and ⊃ˋ for *slow* and *fast* makes ⊂ and ⊃ for *slowness* and *speed*. Adding VQ makes ⊂′ and ⊃′ for *slow* and *speed* as verbs. Adding NQ makes ⊂⁻ and ⊃⁻ for *slowing* and *speeding* as nouns, NQ + AQ makes ⊂ˢ and ⊃ˢ for the adjectives:

slow	⊂ˋ	slowness	⊂		fast	⊃ˋ	speed (n)	⊃
		slow (v)	⊂′				speed (v)	⊃′
		slowing (n)	⊂⁻				speeding (n)	⊃⁻
		slowing (a)	⊂ˢ				speeding (a)	⊃ˢ

Removing the superscript in ∩ˋ and ∪ˋ for *hard* and *soft* makes ∩ and ∪ for *hardness* and *softness*. Adding VQ to ∩ and ∪ makes ∩′ and ∪′ for *harden* and *soften*. Adding NQ makes ∩⁻ and ∪⁻ for *hardening* and *softening* as nouns, adding NQ + AQ makes ∩ˢ and ∪ˢ for the adjectives. Adding double AQ to ∩ makes ∩″ for *hardened*:

hard	∩ˋ	hardness	∩		soft	∪ˋ	softness	∪
		harden	∩′				soften	∪′
		hardening (n)	∩⁻				softening (n)	∪⁻
		hardening (a)	∩ˢ				softening (a)	∪ˢ
		hardened (a)	∩″					

Removing the superscript in ⊓ˋ and ⊔ˋ for *wide* and *narrow* makes ⊓ and ⊔ for *width* and *narrowness,* adding VQ makes ⊓′ and ⊔′ for *widen* and *narrow* as verbs, adding NQ makes ⊓⁻ and ⊔⁻ for *widening* and *narrowing* as nouns, NQ + AQ makes ⊓ˢ and ⊔ˢ for the adjectives:

wide	⊓ˋ	width	⊓		narrow	⊔ˋ	narrowness	⊔
		widen	⊓′				narrow (v)	⊔′
		widening (n)	⊓⁻				narrowing (n)	⊔⁻
		widening (a)	⊓ˢ				narrowing (a)	⊔ˢ

This introduces the twelfth DP:

12. Where multiple superscripts are added to a sym, the topmost one indicates the primary derivative while the bottommost one indicates the part of speech. For example, NQ at the top and AQ at the bottom of ⊓ˢ indicate an adjective augmentation of the noun *widening*.

Removing the superscript in ⌐`  and ∀` for *thick* and *thin* makes ⌐ and ∀ for *thickness* and *thinness,* adding NQ makes ⌐⁻ and ∀⁻ for *thickening* and *thinning* as nouns, adding NQ + AQ makes ⌐˜ and ∀˜ for the adjectives. Adding #Q to ⌐ makes ⌐¹ for *fatness,* #Q + AQ makes ⌐¹` for *fat,* #Q + NQ and #Q + NQ + AQ make ⌐¹⁻ and ⌐¹˜ for *fattening* as noun and adjective:

thick	⌐`		
		thickness	⌐
		thickening (n)	⌐⁻
		thickening (a)	⌐˜
		fatness	⌐¹
		fat (a)	⌐¹`
		fattening (n)	⌐¹⁻
		fattening (a)	⌐¹˜

thin	∀`		
		thinness	∀
		thinning (n)	∀⁻
		thinning (a)	∀˜

Adding AQ to △ and ▽ for *solid* and *liquid* as nouns makes △` and ▽` for *solid* and *liquid* as adjectives, adding VQ makes for △´ and ▽´ for *solidify* and *liquify.* Adding #Q to ▽ makes ▽¹ for *chemical:*

solid (n)	△		
		solid (a)	△`
		solidify	△´

liquid (n)	▽		
		liquid (a)	▽`
		liquify	▽´
		chemical	▽¹

Removing the superscript in ⌐` and ∀` for *strong* and *weak* makes ⌐ and ∀ for *strength* and *weakness.* Adding VQ to ⌐ and ∀ makes ⌐´ and ∀´ for *strengthen* and *weaken,* adding NQ makes ⌐⁻ and ∀⁻ for *strengthening* and *weakening* as nouns, adding NQ + AQ makes ⌐˜ and ∀˜ for the adjectives. Adding EQ makes ∀ᵛ for *frailty,* EQ + AQ makes ∀ᵛ˙ for *frail:*

strong	⌐`		
		strength	⌐
		strengthen	⌐´
		strengthening (n)	⌐⁻
		strengthening (a)	⌐˜

weak	∀`		
		weakness	∀
		weaken	∀´
		weakening (n)	∀⁻
		weakening (a)	∀˜
		frailty	∀ᵛ
		frail	∀ᵛ˙

Removing the superscript in △` and ▽` for *heavy* and *light* makes △ and ▽ for *heaviness* and *lightness,* adding NQ to △ makes △⁻ for *weight,* adding #Qs makes △¹, △², and △³ for *gram, ounce* and *pound,* adding VQ to ▽ makes ▽´ for *lighten,* adding NQ makes ▽⁻ for *lightening* as noun, NQ + AQ makes ▽˜ for the adjective:

heavy ⌒`	heaviness ⌒ weight ⌒⁻ gram ⌒¹ ounce ⌒² pound (weight) ⌒³	light ⌣`	lightness ⌣ lighten ⌣´ lightening (n) ⌣⁻ lightening (a) ⌣˜	

Removing the superscript in ⌒` and ⌣` for *firm* and *flexible* makes ⌒ and ⌣ for *firmness* and *flexibility*, adding VQ makes ⌒´ and ⌣´ for *firm* and *flex* as verbs, adding NQ makes ⌒⁻ and ⌣⁻ for *firming* and *flexing* as nouns:

firm ⌒`	firmness ⌒ firm (v) ⌒´ firming (n) ⌒⁻	flexible ⌣`	flexibility ⌣ flex (v) ⌣´ flexing (n) ⌣⁻

Removing the superscript in ⌐` and ⌣` for *hot* and *cold* makes ⌐ and ⌣ for *heat* and *coldness*. Adding VQ makes ⌐´ and ⌣´ for *heat* and *freeze* as verbs, NQ makes ⌐⁻ and ⌣⁻ for *heating* and *freezing* as nouns, NQ + AQ makes ⌐˜ and ⌣˜ for the adjectives, double AQ makes ⌐῍ and ⌣῍ for *heated* and *frozen,* DQ makes ⌐ᴴ and ⌣ᴴ for *heater* and *freezer*. Adding EQ to ⌐ makes ⌐ᵛ for *temperature,* EQ + #Qs makes ⌐ᵛ₁ and ⌐ᵛ₂ for *centigrade* and *fahrenheit*. Adding DQ + #Q to ⌣ makes ⌣ᴴ₁ for *refrigerator:*

hot ⌐`	heat (n) ⌐ heat (v) ⌐´ heating (n) ⌐⁻ heating (a) ⌐˜ heated (a) ⌐῍ heater ⌐ᴴ temperature ⌐ᵛ centigrade ⌐ᵛ₁ fahrenheit ⌐ᵛ₂	cold ⌣`	cold (n) ⌣ coldness ⌣⁻ freeze ⌣´ freezing (n) ⌣⁻ freezing (a) ⌣˜ frozen ⌣῍ freezer ⌣ᴴ refrigerator ⌣ᴴ₁

Removing the superscript in ⌐` and ⌣` for *warm* and *cool* makes ⌐ and ⌣ for *warmth* and *coolness*. Adding VQ makes ⌐´ and ⌣´ for *warm* and *cool* as verbs, NQ makes ⌐⁻ and ⌣⁻ for *warming* and *cooling* as nouns, NQ + AQ makes ⌐˜ and ⌣˜ for the adjectives. Adding DQ makes ⌣ᴴ for *cooler (object):*

warm ⌐`	warmth ⌐ warm (v) ⌐´ warming (n) ⌐⁻ warming (a) ⌐˜	cool ⌣`	coolness ⌣ cool (v) ⌣´ cooling (n) ⌣⁻ cooling (a) ⌣˜ cooler (object) ⌣ᴴ

Chapter 4 — Qualifiers

Adding VQ to ⌒ and ⌣ makes ⌒´ and ⌣´ for *close* and *open* as verbs, adding NQ makes ⌒¯ and ⌣¯ for *closing* and *opening* as nouns, NQ + AQ makes ⌒˜ and ⌣˜ for the adjectives. Adding double AQ to ⌒ makes ⌒״ for *closed* as adjective:

close	⌒`	close (v)	⌒´	open	⌣`	open (v)	⌣´
		closing (n)	⌒¯			opening (n)	⌣¯
		closing (a)	⌒˜			opening (a)	⌣˜
		closed (a)	⌒״				

These syms introduce four new DPs:

13. DP 4 established noun as the default part of speech without the need for a superscript to denote it as such. As an extension of this, NQ is left out for the most basic noun extension of a base verb or adjective, a single NQ is added for the next most basic noun, a double or triple NQ is added for less basic nouns, eg *thickness* as the most basic noun extension of *thick* needs no NQ while *thickening* as the next most basic noun has a single NQ.

    The most basic nouns are those that use the same base word, the second most basic nouns are formed by adding a suffix like *-ness, -ty, -tion* or *-ing* indicating the action or quality of something, eg ⌒ for *heat* and ⌒¯ for *heating*.

14. A single AQ is added for the most basic adjective or adverb extension of a base noun or verb, a double or triple AQ is added for less basic adjectives or adverbs. The most basic adjectives are those that use the same base word or are formed by adding suffix *-ing* to a base word indicating the quality of something relating to its action, the next most basic adjectives are those formed by adding suffix *-ed* to a base word indicating the state of something, eg ⊃״ for *heated*. Adjectives formed by adding *-ed* are always denoted with double AQ.

15. A single VQ is added for the most basic verb extension of a base noun or adjective, a double or triple VQ is added for less basic verbs. The most basic verbs are those that use the same base word as the noun or adjective, eg ⌒´ for *firm* as verb.

16. For #Qs, ¹ is added for the most basic noun derivative of a base noun, verb or adjective and ², ³, ⁴ etc are added for less basic nouns.

CHAPTER 5
SEED SHAPES

The pictographic roots of some syms above are quite obvious. These include ↑ and ↓ *(up and down)*, ← and → *(left and right)*, ∧ and ∨ *(high and low)*, ⊼ and ⊻ *(over and under)*. Other syms that lend themselves naturally to certain concepts include the geometric shapes ◯, 〇, □, ⊙, ♡, ⌛ and ⋈ to denote *eye* (shape of eye), *ear* (shape of ear), *essence* (box), *sound* (sound wave), *love* (heart), *time* (hourglass) and *space* (hourglass on its side). In line with DP 10, a symbol that looks like a zero is excluded from our list of syms.

Adding modifiers to ◯ and 〇 denotes associated concepts:

sight	◯	appear	⌀´
eye	⊙	seem	⌀´
picture	⊚	image	⌀
view (v)	◯´	reflection	⌀
read (v)	⌀´		

hearing	〇	phone (n)	θ
ear	⊙	tablet (electrical)	⓪
record (v)	⊙´	noise	∅
		lull	⍉

Associated concepts for □ and ⊙ :

essence	□	sound	⊙
substance	⊡	silence	⊚
form (n)	⊡		

Associated concepts for ♡ :

love (agape)	♡	heart	♡	joy	♡
eros	♡	cry (v)	♡´	sorrow	♡
philia	♡	laugh (v)	♡´	excited	♡`
storge	♡	smile (v)	♡´	calm / placid	♡`

Chapter 5 — Seed Shapes

happy / glad	♡`	elated	◊`	mother	⌒
sad	⌒`	depressed	◊`	father	⌒
care (n)	⌒	kind	⌓`	daughter	⌒
concern (n)	⌒	gentle	⌓`	son	⌒

The first four syms fill in conceptual gaps in the English concept of love.

Associated concepts for ⊠ and ⋈ :

time (n)	⊠	past (time)		⊠
period / term	⊠̄	future	⊠	
duration	⊠	day	⊼
		night	⊻

moment	⋈	space (physical)	⋈
hour	⋈	place	⋈
second (time)	⋈	era	⋈̄
minute	⋈		

today	⊠̄	present / now		⊠	
tonight	⊠	last night		⊻
yesterday		⊠	tomorrow night	⊻	
tomorrow	⊠			

delay (n)			⋈	noon	⊼
immediate	⋈	`	midnight	⊻
not soon	⊠̄`		
soon	⊠̄`		

We denote *group* by ∥ , *every* and *any* by ⊦ and ⊤, *all* and *some* by ∥∥ and ≡, *yes* and *no/not* by + and ×, **with fairly obvious pictographic logic:**

group (n)	∥	all	⫽	yes	+
every	⫾	some	≡	no / not	×
any	⊤				

We denote *full* and *empty* by ⌒` and ⌣` , *pull* and *push* by {´ and }´ , *interest* and *curiosity* by ⌒ and ⌣, *opportunity* and *chance* by { and }, *enough* and *not enough* by ⌒` and ⌣` , *choose* and *randomise* by {´ and }´ :

full	⌒`	interest (topic)	⌒	enough	⌒`
empty (a)	⌣`	curiosity	⌣	not enough	⌣`
pull (v)	{´	opportunity	{	choose	{´
push (v)	}´	chance	}	randomise	}´

We denote *include* and *exclude* by ⌢´ and ⌣´ , *difficult* and *easy* by ⌢` and ⌣` , *indirect* and *direct* by |(` and )|` :

include	⌢´	difficult	⌢`	indirect	|(`
exclude	⌣´	easy	⌣`	direct (a)	)|`

We denote *base* and *lid/cover* by ⌒ and ⌓, *hide* and *reveal* by ⌒´ and ⌓´ , *enclosure* and *receptacle* by △ and ▽ *secret* and *exposure* by ⌒ and ⌓ :

base	⌒	enclosure	△
lid / cover	⌓	receptacle	▽
hide	⌒´	secret (n)	⌒
reveal	⌓´	exposure	⌓

We denote *pressure* and *release* by △ and ▽, *safety* and *risk* by ⌒ and ⌣ , *reaction* and *response* by (⊢ and ⊣) , *sudden* and *gradual* by ▷` and ◁` . Some of the pictographic links here are quite obvious, eg the shape of an umbrella in the sym for *safety*:

pressure	△	reaction	(⊢
release (n)	▽	response	⊣)
safety	⌒	sudden	▷`
risk (n)	⌣	gradual	◁`

Chapter 5 — Seed Shapes

We denote *recent, current, former* and *latter* by ⫽` , |D` , |⫽` and D|` , *area* and *zone* by ⌐ and ⌐| , *wait* and *proceed* by ⋖´ and ⊳´ , *follow* and *lead* by ⫽´ and |⊳´ :

recent	⫽`	area	⌐
current (time)	|D`	zone	⌐|
former	|⫽`		
latter	D|`		

wait	⋖´	follow	⫽´
proceed	⊳´	lead	|⊳´

It may seem somewhat arbitrary to assign particular syms to certain concepts, but a thread of logic runs through the system. This will become clearer as the system unfolds and we see how the root syms are modified, augmented and compounded. Changing a single assignment or set of assignments can ripple through and disrupt the coherence of the whole.

Of course, a script could be developed with a different framework, but that is a story for someone else to write. The semantic architecture may also be different for different languages. Notwithstanding my cursory knowledge of other languages, the logic of Symese is as close to mentalese as I can make it. Explore this framework with me while reserving your judgement on my pick of syms. If the assignment of a sym seems arbitrary, you will need to take it at face value as the coherence unfolds.

We denote *use* and *try* by ∾´ and ∾´ , *occur* and *result* by ∽´ and ∽´ , *accept* and *apply* by ∫´ and ∫´ , *provide* and *supply* by ∂´ and ∂´ , *do not* and *be not* by ⩫´ and ⩪´ , *take not* and *give not* by ⨎´ and ⨏´ :

use (v)	∾´	accept	∫´	do not	⩫´
try / attempt	∾´	apply	∫´	be not	⩪´
occur / happen	∽´	provide	∂´	take not	⨎´
result (v)	∽´	supply	∂´	give not	⨏´

These syms introduce another DP:

17. A line across certain sym shapes denotes its negative, eg a line across ∾´ (for *do*) makes ⩫´ (for *do not*).

Along the same lines, we denote *make* and *keep* by ≈´ and ᴓ´ , *receive* and *send* by ʂʂ´ and ʑʑ´ , *strategy* and *tactic* by ⁓⁓ and ⁓ , *source* and *produce* by ℰ´ and ℬ´ , *has/have not* and *own not* by ⋏´ and ⋎´ , *need not* and *want not* by ⋖´ and ⋗´ , *break* and *discard* by ≈´ and ᴓ´ . As an extension of DP 7, the sym shape is doubled to denote an associated concept, eg ∿´ for *do* is augmented to ≈´ for *make*:

make	≈´	strategy	⁓⁓	
keep	ᴓ´	tactic	⁓	
receive	ʂʂ´	source (v)	ℰ´	
send	ʑʑ´	produce (v)	ℬ´	

has / have not	⋏´	break (v)	≈´	
own not	⋎´	discard (v)	ᴓ´	
need not	⋖´			
want not	⋗´			

We denote *I/me* and *you* by ⊥ and ⊤ , *he/she/him/her* and *it* by ⊢ and ⊣ , *person/human* and *thing* by I and H , *item* and *list* by ∻ and ⊢⊣ , *you all* and *we/us* by ⊤̄ and ⊥̄ , *they/them* and *it all* by ⊩ and ⊣∣ , *general* and *particular* by ⌊` and ⌋` , *other* and *self* by ⌈ and ⌉.

Person is denoted by an uppercase I-shape, which is split into ⊥ and ⊤ for *I/me* and *you*. Similarly, *thing* is denoted by an uppercase H-shape, which is split into ⊢ and ⊣ for *he/she* and *it*. The pictographic roots of these syms are discernible and consistent with the DPs above:

I / me	⊥	person	I	
you	⊤	thing	H	
he / she / him / her	⊢	item	∻	
it	⊣	list (n)	⊢⊣	

you all	⊤̄	general	⌊`	
we / us	⊥̄	particular	⌋`	
they / them	⊩	other	⌈	
it all	⊣∣	self	⌉	

Chapter 6
Abstract Concepts

Moving on to more abstract concepts, we denote *question* and *answer* by ↑ and ↑ , *valid* and *right* by ↓˙ and ↓˙ , *from* and *to* by ⌐ and ⌐ , *by* and *for* by ← and → , *invalid* and *wrong* by ╪˙ and ╪˙ , *precise* and *accurate* by ↕˙ and ↕˙ , *imprecise* and *inaccurate* by ╪˙ and ╪˙ , *reason* and *except* by ◊ and ◊ , *to and fro* and *up and down* by ⟠ and ⟠ .

The logic of these syms is not as opaque as it may seem, eg the outline of part of a question mark in ↑ for *question*, the outline of a tick in ↓˙ for *right,* the syms for *question* and *valid* merged in ↕˙ for *precise,* the syms for *answer* and *right* merged in ↕˙ for *accurate.*

question (n)	↑	to	⌐
answer (n)	↑	by	←
valid	↓˙	for	→
right (opp wrong)	↓˙	invalid	╪˙
from	⌐	wrong (a)	╪˙

precise	↕˙	reason	◊
accurate	↕˙	except	◊
imprecise	╪˙	to and fro	⟠
inaccurate	╪˙	up and down	⟠

We denote *seek* and *find* by ⌒˙ and ⌒˙ , *possible* and *is/are* by ⟨˙ and ⟩˙ , *may/maybe* and *can* by ⟨˙ and ⟩˙ , *true* and *good* by ✓˙ and ✓˙ , *impossible* and *is/are not* by ⟨˙ and ⟩˙ , *may/maybe not* and *cannot* by ⟨˙ and ⟩˙ , *false* and *bad* by ✗˙ and ✗˙ . The logic of these assignments is consistent with DPs above, eg right-pointing syms for the more active *is/are* and *can* and left-pointing syms for the more passive *possible* and *may/maybe*:

seek	⌒˙	may / maybe	⟨˙
find (v)	⌒˙	can (able to)	⟩˙
possible	⟨˙	true	✓˙
is / are	⟩˙	good (a)	✓˙

impossible		false	
is / are not		bad	
may / maybe not			
cannot			

As augmentations of the syms above, we denote *expect* and *relate* by   and   , *probable/likely* and *should* by   and   , *option* and *will/shall* by   and   , *real* and *virtue* by   and   , *improbable/unlikely* and *should not* by   and   , *will/shall not* by   , *unreal* and *vice/malice* by   and   :

expect		option	
relate		will / shall (v)	
probable / likely		real	
should		virtue	

improbable / unlikely		unreal	
should not		vice	
will / shall not			

Similarly, we denote *quest* and *research* by   and   , *certain* and *must* by   ,   , *even* by   , *agree* and *moral* by   and   , *uncertain* and *must not* by   and   , *not even* by   , *disagree* and *immoral* by   and   :

quest		even (adv)	
research (n)		agree	
certain		moral (a)	
must			

uncertain		disagree	
must not		immoral	
not even (adv)			

We denote *centre* and *middle* by () and ◯, *role* and *function* by)(and ⋈, *success* and *achievement* by ⊖ and ⊕, *harmony* and *accord* by ⊕ and ⊕, *job* and *career* by ✕ and ✳, *duty* and *loyalty* ✕ and ✳, *topic* and *theme* by Ⅺ and Ⅱ, *sub* and *main* ⋈` and ⋈` :

Chapter 6 — Abstract Concepts

centre	( )	success	⊖	
middle (n)	◯	achievement	⊖	
role	)(	harmony	⊕	
function	⋈	accord	⊕	

job	✗	topic	⋊	
career	✳	theme	⋉	
duty	⋈	sub	⋈`	
loyalty	✳	main	⋈`	

Elements of various DPs can be discerned in these syms, along with a new one:

18. Extending part of a sym shape indicates an extension of a concept, eg extending the horizontal line in ⊖ for *success* makes ⊖ for *achievement*.

We denote *freedom* and *restriction* by ⊔ and ⊓, *scope* and *range* by ∃ and ∈, *direction* and *distance* by ✗ and ⋈ :

freedom	⊔	direction	✗	
restriction	⊓	distance	⋈	
scope	∃			
range (n)	∈			

We denote *unobscured* and *uncluttered* as the two primary divergent meanings of *clear* by ∺ and ⋋⋌, *matrix*, *powder*, *grain* and *magic* by ◇, ◈, ⊙ and ❊, *swap* and *replace* by ⊓´ and ⊔´ :

clear (unobscured)	∺`	grain (texture)	⊙	
clear (uncluttered)	⋋⋌`	magic	❊	
matrix	◇	swap (v)	⊓´	
powder	◈	replace	⊔´	

We denote *quality* and *quantity* by ⋈ and ⋉, *serious* and *important* by ∑` and ⋜`, *blunt* and *sharp* by ⋁` and ⋀`, *method* and *rule* by M and W, *check* and *proof* by ∑ and ⋜, *north, south, west* and *east* by ⇑, ⇓, ⇐ and ⇒ :

quality	⋈	blunt (a)	⋎`
quantity	N	sharp	⋀`
serious	Σ`		
important	Z`		

method	M	north	↑
rule (n)	W	south	↓
check (n)	Σ	west	←
proof	⋝	east	→

This completes our initial set of basic concepts and design principles.

CHAPTER 7
BASIC TANGIBLES

Taking in the 450 syms outlined so far may feel like cracking some tough nuts for a taste of an exotic fruit. With some symbols, it is not easy to see a link to the underlying concepts. You may be wondering what on earth the script might be useful for and Symese may look like a solution looking for a problem. Well, in some ways it is.

There is a story about a CEO in the 1970s being offered an email solution before most people had heard of the now-ubiquitous business tool. He half-jokingly asked if they could have "femail" instead of "hemail" but agreed to try it out for a month or two. In that time, he and his team found it useful beyond their expectations. My vision for Symese is as a tool that, once in use, feels so natural that one wonders why it took so long to see the light of day!

Symese may evolve into a living language or it may fill a niche as an auxiliary tool for cross-cultural communication, focussed on a set of basic concepts that can be augmented or combined into more complex ones. As with doodling and emojis, it is a thinking aid that taps the power of a visual gateway to thought, with back-to-basics semantics that cuts through layers of complexity embedded in natural languages, like the complex spelling and nuances of many English words.

With compound syms (CHAPTER 10), we will see how this elegance of logic and simple syntax can aid both thought and expression without encumbering the memory with thousands of glyphs. Applying pictographic logic to intangibles is difficult and may seem arbitrary. On the flip side, there is a natural feel to denoting tangible objects and related concepts with graphic symbols that look like outlines of the associated objects.

Taking up the task of defining tangibles, we denote *table, limit, shelf* and *cupboard* by ⊤ , ⊥ , ⊨ and ⊣ , *sibling* and *ladder* by ⊨ and ⊨ , *peer* and *step* by ╫ and ÷ , *wife* and *husband* by ⊥ and ⊥ (as a corollary of ⟨ and ⟩ for *female* and *male*), *marriage* and *friendship* by ⊥ and ⊥ , *bridge* and *tunnel* by ⊓ and ⊔ , *station* and *stage/phase* by ⋈ and ⋈ :

table / desk	⊤		sibling	⊨
limit (n)	⊥		ladder	⊨
shelf	⊨		peer	╫
cupboard	⊣		step (n)	÷

wife	⊏	bridge	H
husband	⊐	tunnel	⋈
marriage	⊐⊏	station	⋈
friendship	X	stage / phase	⋈

We denote *facet* and *layer* by F and ⌶ , *key* and *lock* by ⊔ and ⊓ , *path/route* and *way* by ⌶ and ⊤ , *line* and *row* by ⊥ and ⊤ , *chair, column* and *beam* by h , ⊢ and ⊢ , *work* and *earn* by ⊞′ and ⊞′ . In line with DP 10, the mirror image of ⊢ is excluded to avoid assigning a sym that looks like the number 4.

facet	F	path / route	⌶
layer (n)	⌶	way	⊤
key (n)	⊔	line	⊥
lock (n)	⊓	row	⊤

chair	h	work (v)	⊞′
column	⊢	earn	⊞′
beam (object)	⊢		

We denote *corner* and *tip* by ⌈ and ⌉ , *hole* and *gap* by ⌊ and ⌋ , *edge* and *hammer* by ⌐ and ⌐ , *screwdriver* and *tape* by ⌐ and ⌐ , *tap* and *pipe/tube* by ⌈ and ⌉ , *pocket* and *drain* by ⌊ and ⌋ , *vent* and *nail* by ⌐ and ⌐ , *screw* and *net* by ⌐ and ⌐ , using discernible outlines of the respective objects:

corner	⌈	edge	⌐
tip	⌉	hammer	⌐
hole	⌊	screwdriver	⌐
gap	⌋	tape (n)	⌐

tap (object)	⌈	vent	⌐
pipe / tube	⌉	nail	⌐
pocket	⌊	screw	⌐
drain	⌋	net	⌐

Chapter 7 — Basic Tangibles

We denote *staff/cane* and *stick* by ⌐ and ⌐, *pin* and *string* by ∪ and ∪, *board* and *tray* by ⊂ and ⊂, *handle* and *band* by ⊃ and ⊃, *pole* and *bat* by ⌐ and ⌐, *hook* and *knot* by ∪ and ∪, *platform* and *drawer* by ⊂ and ⊂, *brush* and *belt* by ⊃ and ⊃ :

staff / cane	⌐	board (n)	⊂
stick (n)	⌐	tray	⊂
pin (n)	∪	handle (n)	⊃
string (n)	∪	band (object)	⊃

pole	⌐	platform	⊂
bat (object)	⌐	drawer	⊂
hook	∪	brush (n)	⊃
knot	∪	belt	⊃

This is the nineteenth DP:

19. As an extension of DP 6, which established the principle of keeping the associations between sym and concept at a basic level to make the script less language specific, certain concepts are represented by a shared sym, eg *staff* and *cane* are denoted by a glyph that looks like a walking stick with a handle on the right, reflecting the prevalence of right-handedness.

We denote *leg* and *arm* by ∧ and ∨, *support* and *help/aid* by ≺´ and ≻´, *foot* and *hand* by △ and ▽, *train* and *play* by ◁´ and ▷´, *sole* and *palm* by △ and ▽, *knee* and *elbow* by ∧ and ∨, *toe* and *finger* by △ and ▽, *toenail* and *fingernail* by △ and ▽ :

leg	∧	foot	△
arm	∨	hand	▽
support (v)	≺´	train (v)	◁´
help / aid (v)	≻´	play (v)	▷´

sole (of foot)	△	toe	△
palm (of hand)	▽	finger	▽
knee	∧	toenail	△
elbow	∨	fingernail	▽

Modifying these syms, we denote *walk* and *run* by ⋋´ and ⋏´, *jump* and *kick* by ⋌´ and ⋆´, *catch* and *throw* by ·Y´ and Y·´, *hold* and *carry* by ·Y·´ and ¥´:

walk (v)	⋋´	catch (v)	·Y´
run (v)	⋏´	throw (v)	Y·´
jump (v)	⋌´	hold (v)	·Y·´
kick	⋆´	carry	¥´

Staying consistent with the logic of syms for basic concepts and objects, we move on to other tangibles and some abstract concepts. We denote *wing* and *fin* by ∧ and ∨, *tradition* and *trend* by ≪ and ≫, *fly* and *swim* by ⋏´ and Y´, *order* and *chaos* by ⋘ and ⋙:

wing	∧	fly (v)	⋏´
fin	∨	swim (v)	Y´
tradition	≪	order	⋘
trend	≫	chaos	⋙

We denote *peak* and *trough* by △ and ▽, *moderate* and *extreme* by ◁` and ▷`, *hill* and *valley* by △ and ▽, *condition/status* and *position* by ◁ and ▷, *sequence* and *arrangement* by ◇ and ◇, *measurement* and *set* by ✕ and ⋈:

peak (n)	△	hill	△	sequence (n)	◇
trough	▽	valley	▽	arrangement	◇
moderate	◁`	condition / status	◁	measurement	✕
extreme	▷`	position	▷	set	⋈

We denote *tool* and *device* by ⇧ and ⇩, *utensil* and *cutlery* by ⇦ and ⇨, *pencil* and *pen* by ⇧̄ and ⇩̄, *insert* and *remove* by ⇦´ and ⇨´, *machine* and *computer* by ⇧ and ⇩, *mechanism* and *engine* by ⇦ and ⇨, *spring* and *wire* by ⌒ and ⌒, *tail* by ε:

tool	⇧	pencil	⇧̄
device	⇩	pen	⇩̄
utensil	⇦	insert	⇦´
cutlery	⇨	remove	⇨´

machine	⇧	spring (object)	⌒
computer	⇩	wire	⌒
mechanism	⇦	tail	ε
engine	⇨		

We denote *shallow* and *deep* by ⊢` and ⊢` , *ancestor* and *descendant* by ⊥ and ⊤, *concept* and *factor* by ⊢ and ⊢, *adult* and *child* by ⊥ and ⊤, *old person* and *baby/infant* by ≡ and ≡ , *human* and *couple* by ≡ and ≡ , *entity* and *family* by ⊢ and ⊢ , *context* and *situation* by ⊩ and ⊫ :

shallow	⊢`	concept	⊢
deep	⊢`	factor	⊢
ancestor	⊥	adult	⊥
descendant	⊤	child	⊤

old person	≡	entity	⊢
baby / infant	≡	family	⊢
human	≡	context	⊩
couple	≡	situation	⊫

We denote *garment (above waist)* and *garment (below waist)* by ⊓ and ⊔, *inner garment* and *outer garment* by ⊐ and ⊏, *covering (head)* and *covering (foot)* by ⊓ and ⊔, *background* and *foreground* by ⊣ and ⊢, *sleep* and *rest* by ⊓´ and ⊔´ , *kneel* and *bow* by ⊐´ and ⊏´ , *stand* and *reach* by ⊢´ and ⊣´ , *sit* and *reside* by ⊢´ and ⊣´ :

garment (waist up)	⊓	covering (head)	⊓
garment (waist dn)	⊔	covering (foot)	⊔
inner garment	⊐	background	⊣
outer garment	⊏	foreground	⊢

sleep (v)	⊓´	stand (v)	⊢´
rest (v)	⊔´	reach (v)	⊣´
kneel	⊐´	sit	⊢´
bow (v)	⊏´	reside	⊣´

We denote *building, room* and *structure* by ⊟ , ⊟ and ⊕, *ceiling, floor* and *frame* by ⊟ , ⊟ and ⊟ , *window, door* and *wall* by ⊟, ⊟ and ⊟ :

building	⊟	ceiling	⊟	window	⊟
room	⊟	floor	⊟	door	⊟
structure	⊕	frame	⊟	wall	⊟

We denote *attic* and *basement* by ☰ and ☷, *shutter* and *gate* by ▐☐ and ☐▌, *roof* and *foundation* by ⌂ and ⌂, *home* and *house* by ⊲☐ and ☐⊳:

attic	☰		roof	⌂
basement	☷		foundation	⌂
shutter	▐☐		home	⊲☐
gate	☐▌		house	☐⊳

We denote *book, data, card* and *index* by ▯, ⌽, ▯ and ▯, *catalog, furniture* and *paper* by ▯, ▯ and ▯:

book	▯		catalog (n)	▯
data	⌽		furniture	▯
card	▯		paper	▯
index	▯			

We denote *bench* and *bed* by ▱ and ▱, *cart* and *carriage* by ⟦ and ⟧, *vehicle* and *transport* by △ and ▽, *car* and *bus* by ⟨ and ⟩, *flow* and *road/street* by ◁ and ▷, *aircraft* and *boat* by △ and ▽, *truck* and *train* by ⟨ and ⟩, *garment/clothes* by ✢:

bench	▱		vehicle	△
bed	▱		transport	▽
cart	⟦		car	⟨
carriage	⟧		bus	⟩

flow (n)	◁		truck	⟨
road / street	▷		train (n)	⟩
aircraft	△		garment / clothes	✢
boat	▽			

We denote *operate* and *maintain* by ◿´ and ◺´, *factory* and *depot* by ◿ and ◺, *network* and *field (subject)* by ⊞ and ⊠, *internet* and *industry* by ⊕ and ⊠:

operate	◿´		network	⊞
maintain	◺´		field (subject)	⊠
factory	◿		internet	⊕
depot	◺		industry	⊠

We denote *world* and *planet* by ⊖ and ⊖, *environment* and *space* by ⊕ and ⊕, *team* and *company* by ⊘ and ⊘, *community* and *business* by ⊗ and ⊗, *nature* and *season* by ⊕ and ⊕, *society* and *government* by ⊗ and ⊗ :

world / earth	⊖	team (n)	⊘	nature	⊕
planet	⊖	company (n)	⊘	season	⊕
environment	⊕	community (n)	⊗	society	⊗
space (astronomy)	⊕	business (n)	⊗	government	⊗

We denote *fire* and *water* by ⊖ and ⊖, *air* and *wind* by ⊕ and ⊕, *wood* and *metal* by ⊖ and ⊖, *earth* and *stone* by ⊕ and ⊕, *sky* and *land/ground* by ⊖ and ⊖, *private* and *public* by ⊕ and ⊕, *summer, winter, autumn* and *spring* by ⊖, ⊖, ⊕ and ⊕ :

fire	⊖	wood	⊖
water	⊖	metal	⊖
air	⊕	earth (soil)	⊕
wind	⊕	stone	⊕

sky	⊖	summer	⊖
land / ground	⊖	winter	⊖
private	⊕`	autumn	⊕
public	⊕`	spring (season)	⊕

We denote *office* and *administration* by ⊘ and ⊘, *politics* and *political party* by ⊗ and ⊗, *climate* and *weather* by ⊖ and ⊖, *vapour* and *gas* by ⊕ and ⊕, *rain* and *cloud* by ⊖ and ⊖, *mist/fog* and *smog* by ⊕ and ⊕, *plastic* and *oil* by ⊘ and ⊘, *sand* and *glass* by ⊗ and ⊗ :

office (n)	⊘	climate	⊖
administration	⊘	weather (n)	⊖
politics	⊗	vapour	⊕
political party	⊗	gas	⊕

rain (n)	⊖	plastic	⊘
cloud (n)	⊖	oil (n)	⊘
mist / fog	⊕	sand	⊗
smog	⊕	glass (material)	⊗

We denote *head* and *torso* by ♀ and ♂, *bubble* and *bulb* by ⊶ and ⊸, *brain* and *organ* by ♀̄ and ♂̇, *forehead* and *groin* by ♀̣ and ♂̣, *chin* and *neck* by ♀̱ and ♂̄ :

head (n)	♀	bubble	⊶
torso	♂	bulb	⊸

brain	♀̇	forehead	♀̄	chin	♀̱
organ	♂̇	groin	♂̣	neck	♂̄

We denote *scalp* and *buttock* by ♀̂ and ♂̂, *jaw* and *shoulder* by ♀̰ and ♂̰, *hair*, *beard* and *fur* by ♀̂̂, ♀̰̂ and ♂̂̂, *back of head* and *back of body* by |♀ and |♂, *face* and *chest* by ♀| and ♂|, *cheek* and *breast* by ♀|| and ♂|| :

scalp	♀̂	hair	♀̂̂
buttock	♂̂	beard	♀̰̂
jaw	♀̰	fur	♂̂̂
shoulder	♂̰		

back of head	|♀	face	♀|	cheek	♀||
back of body	|♂	chest	♂|	breast	♂||

We denote *horizon* and *perspective* by ⊖ and ♀, *sun* and *moon* by ☉ and ☿, *link* and *joint* by ⚭ and ⦵, *bond* and *hinge* by ⚭ and ⦵, *aim* and *spiral* by ⊙ and ◎, *body* and *corpse* by 8 and ∞, *toy* and *bicycle* by 8 and ⚯, *lens* and *roll* by ∞ and ∞, *either* and *neither* by 8 and 8 :

horizon	⊖	link (n)	⚭
perspective	♀	joint	⦵
sun	☉	bond	⚭
moon	☿	hinge	⦵

aim (n)	⊙	bicycle	⚯
spiral (n)	◎	lens	∞
body	8	roll (n)	∞
corpse	∞	either	8
toy	8	neither	8

Chapter 7 — Basic Tangibles

We denote *tree, branch, root* and *leaf* by ♀ , ♀ , ♀ and ♀ , *fruit, nut, seed* and *vegetable* by ♀ , ☿ , ♀ and ♀ , *fungus, grain, grass* and *moss* by ⌀ , ⌽ , ♀ and ⌀ , *flower, herb, spice* and *bud* by ♀ , ♀ , ☿ and ♀ :

tree	♀	fruit	♀	
branch	♀	nut	☿	
root	♀	seed	♀	
leaf	♀	vegetable	♀	

fungus	⌀	flower	♀	
grain (plant)	⌽	herb	♀	
grass	♀	spice	☿	
moss	⌀	bud	♀	

We denote *flesh, fat, muscle, tissue* and *bone* by 8 , 8 , 8 , 8 and 8 , *blood, white* and *red blood cell* by ∞ , ∞ and ∞ , *cell (bio)* and *organism* by ∞ and ∞ , *sense* and *instinct* by ♋ and ♡ , *skin* and *touch* by ♋ and ♡ , *conscious* and *subconscious* by ♋` and ♡` :

flesh	8	blood	∞	
fat (bio)	8	white blood cell	∞	
muscle	8	red blood cell	∞	
tissue	8	cell (bio)	∞	
bone	8	organism	∞	

sense (n)	♋	conscious	♋`	
instinct	♡	subconscious	♡`	
skin	♋			
touch (n)	♡			

We denote *spirit, life* and *health* by ☿ , ☿ and ☿ *gender* and *sex* by ☿̇ and ♀ , *desire* and *pleasure* by ·☿ and ☿· , *courage/bravery* and *character* by ☿̄ and ☿̱ , *inspiration* and *aspiration* by |☿ and ☿| , *ego, death* and *fear* by ⋈ , ⋈ and ⋈ , *distress* and *pain/ache* by ⋈ and ⋈| , *hate/hatred* and *anger* by ·⋈ and ⋈· :

spirit	⌀	desire (n)	·⌀
life	⌀	pleasure	⌀·
health	⌀	courage / bravery	̄⌀
gender	⌀̇	character	⌀⌀
sex (gender)	♀		

inspiration	I⌀	distress (n)	II⌀
aspiration	⌀I	pain / ache	⌀II
ego	⌀	hate / hatred	·⌀
death	⌀	anger	⌀·
fear (n)	⌀		

We denote *animal* and *illness/disease* by 8 and 8, *micro-organism* and *insect* by ∞ and ∞, *lifeform* and *plant* by 8 and ∞, *giant* and *beast* by 8 and 8, *mammal, bird, reptile* and *fish+ (a generic term that includes all non-reptilian marine animals)* by ♀, ♂, ∝ and ∞ :

animal	8	lifeform	8	mammal	♀
illness / disease	8	plant	∞	bird	♂
micro-organism	∞	giant	8	reptile	∝
insect	∞	beast	8	fish+	∞

This completes our set of objects and related concepts, which includes some intangibles whose sym shapes are modifications of those for tangibles.

CHAPTER 8
MORE ABSTRACT CONCEPTS

Construction of the 800 syms so far reveals some of the elegant logic and coherence of Symese. Building on this logic and coherence, we move on to more abstract concepts in this chapter, rounding off our set of a thousand-plus root syms.

Staying consistent with the logic of syms for basic concepts and objects, we denote *same* and *similar* by ⁄` and \` , *different* and *unlike* by ⨯` and ⨯` , *complex* and *simple/basic* by ≡` and ≡` *together* and *apart* by ‖` and ‖` . The underlying logic is not hard to discern:

same / alike	⁄`	complex	≡`
similar / like	\`	simple / basic	≡`
different	⨯`	together	‖`
unlike	⨯`	apart	‖`

We denote *word* and *letter* by ⌞· and ·⌟, *regular (even)* and *regular (norm)* by ⌈·` and ⌐⌉` , *standard (norm)* and *standard (class)* by ⌐·⌉` and ⌊·⌋` , *indication* and *sign* by ⌐· and ·⌐, *description* and *name* by ·⊥ and ⊥·, *science* and *technology* by ·⊤ and ⊤·, *literature* and *poetry* by ⊢· and ⊢·, *craft* and *art* by ⊣· and ⊣· :

word	⌞·	standard (a - norm)	⌐·⌉`
letter (character)	·⌟	standard (a - class)	⌊·⌋`
regular (even)	⌈·`	indication	⌐·
regular (norm)	⌐⌉`	sign	·⌐

description	·⊥	literature	⊢·
name (n)	⊥·	poetry	⊢·
science	·⊤	craft	⊣·
technology	⊤·	art	⊣·

Along similar lines, we denote *subject* and *object* by ⊓ and ⊔, *project* and *delivery* by ⊏ and ⊐, *preparation* and *execution* by ⊬ and ⊢⊣, *process* and *program* by ‡ and ‡, *balance (parity)* and *balance (harmony)* by ⌑ and ⌒, *match* and *compare* by ⟦´ and ⟧´ , *collection* and *unit* by ⌒ and ⌒, *develop* and *build* by ⟦·´ and ·⟧´ :

49

Symese — Universal Symbolic Script

subject	⊟	preparation	⊓	
object (n)	⊔	execution (task)	⊔	
project (n)	⟦	process (n)	⟨	
delivery	⟧	program (n)	⟩	

balance (parity)	⊓	collection	⊓·	
balance (harmony)	⊔	unit	⊔·	
match (v)	⟦´	develop	⟦·´	
compare	⟧´	build	·⟧´	

We denote *model* and *example* by ⊓ and ⊔, *code* and *symbol* by ⊢ and ⊣, *category* and *type* by ⊓ and ⊔, *compound* and *mixture/mix* by ⊢ and ⊣, *whole* and *section/part* by ⊓ and ⊔, *template* and *pattern* by E and ∃, *complete* and *incomplete* by ⊓` and ⊔`, *design* and *system* by ⊢ and ⊣ :

model (n)	⊓	category	⊓	
example	⊔	type	⊔	
code	⊢	compound	⊢	
symbol	⊣	mixture / mix	⊣	

whole	⊓	complete (a)	⊓`	
section / part	⊔	incomplete	⊔`	
template	E	design (n)	⊢	
pattern	∃	system	⊣	

We denote *major* and *minor* by ⌢` and ⌣`, *automatic* and *manual* by ⟨` and ⟩` :

major	⌢`	automatic	⟨`	
minor	⌣`	manual (a)	⟩`	

We denote *claim* and *refer* by ⌒´ and ⌒´, *review* and *recap* by ⌢´ and ⌣´, *please* and *thank* by ९´ and ₽´, *sorry* and *again* by ᑯ` and ᑲ` :

claim (v)	⌒´	please	९´	
refer	⌒´	thank	₽´	
review (v)	⌢´	sorry	ᑯ`	
recap (v)	⌣´	again	ᑲ`	

Chapter 8 — More Abstract Concepts

We denote *win* and *lose* by ⟯´ and ⟰´ , *adapt* and *access* by ∝´ and ∾´ , *digital* and *analog* by ⟊ and ⋈, *will* and *mind* by ⟊ and ∾ :

win (v)	⟯´	digital	⟊
lose	⟰´	analog	⋈
adapt	∝´	will (n)	⟊
access (v)	∾´	mind	∾

We denote *buy* and *sell* by △⎯´ and ⎯△´ , *hire in* and *hire out* by ▽⎯´ and ⎯▽´ , *cost* and *price* by ◁ and ▷ , *account* and *transaction* by ◁ and ▷ , *shop* and *trade* by △△ and ▽▽, *economy* and *market* by ◁ and ▷ :

buy / purchase	△⎯´	cost (n)	◁	shop (n)	△△
sell	⎯△´	price (n)	▷	trade (n)	▽▽
hire in	▽⎯´	account	◁	economy	◁
hire out	⎯▽´	transaction	▷	market (n)	▷

We denote *funnel* and *filter* by ⋀ and ⋁ , *divergence* and *convergence* by ≺ and ≻ , *issue/matter* and *detail* by ∧ and ∨ , *visit* and *escape* by < and > , *secure* and *insecure* by ⩑` and ⩒` , *tame* and *wild* by ⩐` and ⩏` :

funnel (n)	⋀	issue / matter	∧	secure (a)	⩑`
filter (n)	⋁	detail (n)	∨	insecure	⩒`
divergence	≺	visit (n)	<	tame	⩐`
convergence	≻	escape (n)	>	wild	⩏`

We denote *specific* and *various* by ∽` and ∾` , *serve* and *share* by §´ and ∫´ , *practice* and *plan* by ∾ and ∽ , *value* and *money* by $ and ₵ :

specific	∽`	practice	∾
various	∾`	plan (n)	∽
serve	§´	value (n)	$
share (v)	∫´	money	₵

We denote *special* and *ordinary/usual* by ∞` and ∞` , *subtle* and *obvious* by ∫` and ∫` , *clean* and *dirty* by ♁` and ♂` , *element* and *feature* by ◁ and ▷:

special	⌢ `		clean (a)	○ `
ordinary / usual	⌣ `		dirty	○̄ `
subtle	8 `		element	⊂
obvious	β `		feature (n)	⊃

We denote *justice* and *law* by ⋈ and ⋈, *meaning* and *purpose* by Σ and Ƨ, *master* and *slave* by ⋈ and ⋈, *discern* and *consider* by Σ´ and Ƨ´ :

justice	⋈		master	⋈
law	⋈		slave	⋈
meaning	Σ		discern	Σ´
purpose	Ƨ		consider	Ƨ´

We denote *force* and *energy* by ⋀ and ⋁, *potential* and *power* by ≲ and ≳, *permission* and *decision* by ⋊⋉ and ✕ :

force (n)	⋀		permission	⋊⋉
energy	⋁		decision	✕
potential	≲			
power	≳			

We denote *purity* and *beauty* by ⋌⋋ and ⋎⋏, *principle* and *theory* by ⋙ and ⋘, *problem* and *solution* by ⋋ and ⋎, *cooperate* and *compete* by ⋌⋋´ and ⋎⋏´ :

purity	⋌⋋		problem	⋋
beauty	⋎⋏		solution	⋎
principle	⋙		cooperate	⋌⋋´
theory	⋘		compete	⋎⋏´

We denote *blade* and *fight* by ⋊⋉ and ⋊⋉, *defence* and *attack* by ⋊⋉ and ⋊⋉, *scissors* and *weapon* by ⋊⋉ and ⋊⋉, *peace* and *war* by ⋊⋉ and ⋊⋉. Some of these syms have obvious pictographic roots:

blade	⋊⋉		scissors	⋊⋉
fight (n)	⋊⋉		weapon	⋊⋉
defence	⋊⋉		peace	⋊⋉
attack (n)	⋊⋉		war	⋊⋉

Chapter 8 — More Abstract Concepts

We denote *grow* and *revert* by ⌒´ and ⌣´ , *regress* and *progress* by ⊂´ and ⊃´ , *advantage* and *disadvantage* by ⊓ and ⊔ , *discontinue* and *continue* by ⊏ and ⊐ :

grow	⌒´	advantage	⊓
revert	⌣´	disadvantage	⊔
regress	⊂´	discontinue	⊏´
progress (v)	⊃´	continue	⊐´

We denote *perception*, *impression* and *cognition* by ◇ , ◈ and ⊚ , *feel*, *think*, *understand* and *imagine* by ◇´ , ◈´ , ◇´ and ⊗´ , *empathy*, *insight*, *idea* and *analysis* by ⇔ , ⇔ , ⬨ and ⬦ , *experience* and *knowledge* by ⇔ and ⬥ , *wise* and *clever* by ⇔` and ⊗` :

perception	◇	feel (v)	◇´
impression	◈	think	◈´
cognition	⊚	understand	◇´
		imagine	⊗´

empathy	⇔	experience	⇔
insight	⇔	knowledge	⬥
idea	⬨	wise	⬥`
analysis	⬦	clever	⊗`

We denote *advice* and *doubt* by ⬨ and ⊗ , *guess* and *wonder* by ⬨ and ⊗ , *consult* and *mystery/enigma* by ⊗´ and ⊗ , *trust* and *belief* by ⇔ and ⬨ , *resource* and *hope* by ⇔ and ⇔ , *assume* and *deduce* by ⬨´ and ⬨´ , *pride* and *humility* by ⇔̄ and ⇔ , *diffident* and *confident* by |⇔` and ⇃|` , *remember* and *forget* by ⬨̄´ and ⬨´ , *learn* and *teach* by |⬨´ and ⬨|´ :

advice	⬨	mystery / enigma	⊗
doubt (n)	⊗	trust (n)	⇔
guess (n)	⬨	belief	⬨
wonder (n)	⊗	resource	⇔
consult	⊗´	hope (n)	⇔

assume	⬨´	confident	⇃	`
deduce	⬨´	remember	⬨̄´
pride	⇔̄	forget	⬨´
humility	⇔	learn		⬨´
diffident	|⇔`	teach	⬨|´

53

We denote *smell*, *nose* and *breath* by ⌐, ⌐ and ⌐, *perfume* and *stench* by ⌐ and ⌐, *taste*, *tongue* and *saliva* by ⌐, ⌐ and ⌐, *antidote* and *poison/toxin* by ⌐ and ⌐:

smell (n)	⌐		taste (n)	⌐
nose	⌐		tongue	⌐
breath	⌐		saliva	⌐
perfume	⌐		antidote	⌐
stench	⌐		poison / toxin	⌐

We denote *music*, *melody*, *tempo* and *rhythm* by ♀, ♀, ♭ and ♂, *pitch*, *tone*, *volume* and *cadence* by ♂, ♀, ♭ and ♀:

music	♀		pitch (sound)	♂
melody	♀		tone (sound)	♀
tempo	♭		volume (sound)	♭
rhythm	♂		timbre	♀

We denote *voice*, *mouth* and *talk/speech* by ♡, ♡ and ♡, *culture* and *language* by ♡ and |♡|, *statement*, *comment* and *report* by ♡, ♡ and ♡, *call*, *tell* and *message* by |♡´, ♡´ and |♡|, *story*, *opinion* and *conversation* by ♡, ♡ and ♡, *explanation*, *information* and *instruction* by |♡, ♡| and |♡|, *lip* and *tooth* by ♡ and ♡:

voice	♡		statement	♡
mouth	♡		comment (n)	♡
talk / speech	♡		report (n)	♡
culture	♡		call (v)	|♡´
language	|♡|		tell (v)	♡´

message	|♡|		explanation	|♡
story	♡		information	♡|
opinion	♡		instruction	|♡|
conversation	♡		lip	♡
			tooth	♡

We denote *appetite*, *stomach* and *thirst* by ⌒, ⌒ and ⌒, *food* and *defecation* by ⌒ and ⌒, *consumption* and *meal* by ⌒ and |⌒|, *drink*, *urination* and *refreshment* by ⌒, ⌒ and ⌒, *small* and *large intestines* by ⌒ and ⌒:

Chapter 8 — More Abstract Concepts

appetite	⌒	food	⌒̄
stomach	⊙̯	defecation	⌣
thirst	⊗̯	consumption	⌒̲

meal	|⌒|	refreshment	⊗̄
drink (n)	⊗̄	small intestines	⊖
urination	⊗̲	large intestines	⌒⌒

We denote *bucket/basin, cup* and *pot* by ▽, ▽ and ▽, *glass/tumbler* and *bell* by ⍽ and ⍍, *dish/plate* and *bowl* by |⌒| and |▽| :

bucket / basin	▽	glass / tumbler	⍽	dish / plate	|⌒|
cup	▽	bell	⍍	bowl	|▽|
pot	▽				

We denote *royalty, king* and *queen* by ◌, ◌ and ◌, *palace, castle/fortress* and *kingdom* by ⊟, ⊞ and ⊕, *rich* and *poor* by ⌒` and ⌣`, *process food* and *cook* by ᠎Ɛ´ and β´ :

royalty	◌	palace	⊟
king	◌	castle / fortress	⊞
queen	◌	kingdom	⊕

rich (a)	⌒`	process food	Ɛ´
poor (a)	⌣`	cook (v)	β´

We denote *block, box, bag, parcel, package* and *content* by ▫, △, ⊙, △, △ and △ :

block (n)	▫	parcel	△
box	△	package	△
bag	⊙	content	△

We denote *star, universe* and *infinity* by ✧, ✧ and ✧, *transcendence, eternity* and *god* by ⌶, ⌶ and ⌾ :

star	✧	transcendence	⌶
universe	✧	eternity	⌶
infinity	✧	god	⌾

This completes our set of root syms.

Part III – Augmented and Compound Syms, Practical Aspects of Usage

Chapter 9
More Qualifiers

In addition to the qualifiers outlined so far, there are superscripts for maxi, mini, person, place and group:

AQ	Adjective / Adverb	\	~Q	Essence / nuance	ˇ
VQ	Verb	/	=Q	Maxi	∧
NQ	Noun	−	-Q	Mini	∪
OQ	Opposite	x	IQ	Person	I
#Q	Derivative	1	PQ	Place	v
DQ	Device / substance	H	GQ	Group	‖

This is the twentieth DP:

20. =Q and -Q indicate a bigger (or otherwise more advanced case) and smaller (or otherwise less advanced case) – for example, added to *house* to make *mansion* and *hut* respectively. IQ indicates person – added to *male* to make *man*. PQ indicates a place of – added to *money* to make *bank*. GQ indicates group – added to *person* to make *crowd*. The syms for these examples can be found in the following tables.

Here are some augmented definitions using qualifiers in the table above:

close (v)	⌒ ′	open (v)	⌣ ′	
closing (n)	⌒ −	opening (n)	⌣ −	
closing (a)	⌒ ˇ	opening (a)	⌣ ˇ	
closed (a)	⌒ ″			

back (n)	(	backing (a)	(ˇ	retreat (v)	(1
back (v)	(′	backward	(ˇ	retreating (n)	(1
backing (n)	(−	retreat (n)	(1	retreating (a)	(1

Chapter 9 — More Qualifiers

front (n)	⌒	forward (a)	⌒ˢ	advancing (n)	⌒¹
front (v)	⌒ʹ	advance (n)	⌒¯¹	advancing (a)	⌒¹̄
fronting (a)	⌒¯	advance (v)	⌒ʹ¹	advanced (a)	⌒¹̈

age	⌢	aging (a)	⌢¯	youthfulness	⌣¯
age (v)	⌢ʹ	old age	⌢¯	young person	⌣ᴵ
aging (n)	⌢¯	youth	⌣		

female (n)	⟮	male (n)	⟯	
woman	⟮ᴵ	man	⟯ᴵ	
lady	⟮ᴵₛ	gentleman	⟯ᴵₛ	

base (v)	⌓ʹ	basis	⌓ˢ	
basing (n)	⌓¯	base (place)	⌓ᵛ	
based (a)	⌓¨			

cover (v)	⌓ʹ	covered (a)	⌓¨	uncover	⌓ˣ
covering (n)	⌓¯	shell	⌓¹	uncovering (n)	⌓ˣ̄
covering (a)	⌓¯			uncovered (a)	⌓ˣ̈

my / mine	⊥ˋ	his / her(s)	⊢ˋ
your(s)	⊤ˋ	its	⊣ˋ

personal	⊥ˋ	personality	⊥ˢ
impersonal	⊥ˣ	crowd	⊥"

switching on (n)	⊓¹	switching off (n)	⊔¹
switch on	⊓ʹ	switch off	⊔ʹ

measure	✕ʹ	gauging (n)	✕ᴴ̄
measuring (n)	✕¯	gauge (v)	✕ᴴʹ
measuring (a)	✕¯	level (measure)	✕¹
measured	✕¨	superset	⋊⌒
gauge (n)	✕ᴴ	subset	⋊⌣

57

We also have superscript qualifiers for plural, repeat and upper case, and non-superscript qualifiers for more, most, past and future tense:

AQ	Adjective / Adverb	\		=Q	Maxi	∧		UQ	Upper case	∧	
VQ	Verb	/		-Q	Mini	∪		+Q	More	⟨	
NQ	Noun	−		IQ	Person	I		*Q	Most	⟩	
OQ	Opposite	x		PQ	Place	∨		<Q	Past tense	⟨	
#Q	Derivative	1		GQ	Group	‖		>Q	Future tense	⟩	
DQ	Device / substance	H		SQ	Plural	+					
EQ	Essence/nuance	∽		RQ	Repeat	‡					

This is the twenty-first DP:

21. SQ indicates plural where the noun number is relevant — added, for example, to *age* to make *ages*. RQ indicates repeated action — added to *try* to make *retry*. UQ indicates upper case — added to *earth* to make *Earth*. +Q and *Q indicate more and most — added to *good* to make *better* and *best,* with the redundant adjective superscript left out. <Q and >Q indicate past and future tenses — added to *close* to make *closed* and *will close,* with the redundant verb superscript left out:

ages	⌒⁺		retrying (n)	∿‡	
people	I⁺		Earth	⊖^	
retry (n)	∿‡		God	⌸^	
retry (v)	∿‡				

better	∨⟨		closed (v)	⌒⟨	
best	∨⟩		will close	⌒⟩	
worse	×⟨		opened	⌣⟨	
worst	×⟩		will open	⌣⟩	

Chapter 9 — More Qualifiers

Adding AQ to ⊠ for *day* makes ⊠` for *daily,* GQ makes ⊠" for *calendar,* EQ makes ⊠ⁿ for *date,* #Q makes ⊠¹, ⊠² and ⊠³ for *week, month* and *year*. Adding AQ to ⊠¹, ⊠² and ⊠³ makes ⊠¹`, ⊠²` and ⊠³` for *weekly, monthly* and *yearly,* SQ makes ⊠¹₊, ⊠²₊ and ⊠³₊ for *fortnight, two months* and *two years*:

daily	⊠`	week	⊠¹
calendar	⊠"	month	⊠²
date (n)	⊠ⁿ	year	⊠³
date (v)	⊠ⁿ	decade	⊠⁴
dated (a)	⊠ⁿ	century	⊠⁵
		millennium	⊠⁶

weekly	⊠¹`	fortnight	⊠¹₊
monthly	⊠²`	two months	⊠²₊
yearly / annual	⊠³`	two years	⊠³₊

Adding #Qs to ♀ for *garment (waist up)* makes ♀¹ and ♀² for *shirt* and *blouse*, to ♂ for *garment (waist down)* makes for ♂¹ and ♂² for *trousers* and *skirt*, to ⊡ for *inner garment* makes ⊡¹ for *underpants*, to ⊡ for *outer garment* makes ⊡¹ for *dress*, to ⊓ for *covering (head)* makes for ⊓¹ and ⊓² for *hat* and *cap*, to ⊔ for *covering (foot)* makes ⊔¹ and ⊔² for *shoe* and *boot*:

shirt	♀¹	coat	♀⁴	trousers	♂¹
blouse	♀²	jacket	♀⁵	skirt	♂²
vest	♀³	jumper	♀⁶	shorts	♂³

underpants	⊡¹	singlet	⊡³
bra	⊡²	dress	⊡¹

hat	⊓¹	shoe	⊔¹	sneaker	⊔³
cap	⊓²	boot	⊔²	sandal	⊔⁴
				sock	⊔⁵

Adding #Qs to ▽ for finger makes ▽¹ and ▽² for *thumb* and *index finger*, to ☰ for *room* makes ☰¹ and ☰² for *lounge* and *kitchen*, to ⊖ for *world* makes ⊖¹ and ⊖² for *continent* and *region*, to ⊖ for *water* makes ⊖¹ and ⊖² for *ocean* and *sea*:

thumb	▽¹	ring finger	▽⁴
index finger	▽²	little finger	▽⁵
middle finger	▽³		

lounge	☰¹	bedroom	☰⁴
kitchen	☰²	bathroom	☰⁵
dining room	☰³	toilet	☰⁶

continent	⊖¹	city / town	⊖⁵
region	⊖²	suburb / district	⊖⁶
country / nation	⊖³	village	⊖⁷
state (n)	⊖⁴	national	⊖³~

ocean	⊖¹	river	⊖⁵
sea	⊖²	stream	⊖⁶
lake	⊖³	creek	⊖⁷
pond	⊖⁴	marine	⊖²~

Embedded qualifiers are a corollary of numeric qualifier superscripts introduced in DP 11:

AQ	Adjective / Adverb	\	=Q	Maxi	∧	UQ	Upper case	∧
VQ	Verb	/	-Q	Mini	∪	+Q	More	⟨
NQ	Noun	–	IQ	Person	ɪ	*Q	Most	⟨
OQ	Opposite	x	PQ	Place	v	<Q	Past tense	(
#Q	Derivative	1	GQ	Group	‖	>Q	Future tense	)
DQ	Device / substance	H	SQ	Plural	+	~Q	Embedded	⬨
EQ	Essence/nuance	∽	RQ	Repeat	ǂ			

Chapter 9 — More Qualifiers

22. Some numeric qualifiers are embedded within the sym, eg adding Embedded Qualifier (~Q) to ▱ for *smell* makes ▱, ▱ and ▱ for *sweet, salty* and *sour smell*, to ◠ for *taste* makes ◠, ◠ and ◠ for *sweet, salty* and *sour taste:*

sweet smell	▱	hot (spicy) smell	▱
salty smell	▱	pungent smell	▱
sour smell	▱	savoury smell	▱
bitter smell	▱		

sweet taste	◠	sweet	◠`
salty taste	◠	salty	◠`
sour taste	◠	sour	◠`
bitter taste	◠	bitter	◠`
hot (spicy) taste	◠	hot (spicy)	◠`
pungent taste	◠	pungent	◠`
savoury taste	◠	savoury	◠`

We denote colours by enclosing a glyph or ~Q in a circle — ⊙ for *white*, for ⊖ *black*, ⊘ for *colour*, ⊙ for *grey*, ⊕ for *spectrum*, ⊕˘ for *rainbow*, ⊗` for *colourless*, ②, ③, ④, ⑤, ⑥, ⑦ and ⑧ for *red, orange, yellow, green, blue, purple,* and *brown.* The numerals 2-8 are assigned to the three primary and three secondary colours plus the common colour brown.

Some hues are a blend of colours and are assigned dual ~Qs, eg *cyan* (a blend of blue and green) is denoted by ㊆ and *maroon* (a blend of blue and purple) by ㊆. A vertical line is added on the left or right for a lighter or darker hue, eg |② and ②| for *pink* and *dark red*, |⑤ and ⑤| for *light green* and *dark green*, |⑥ and ⑥| for *light blue* and *dark blue*, ⑦| for *violet*:

white	⊙	spectrum	⊕
black	⊖	rainbow	⊕˘
colour	⊘	colourless	⊗
grey	⊙		

red	②	brown	⑧	light green	|⑤
orange (colour)	③	cyan	㊆	dark green	⑤|
yellow	④	maroon	㊆	light blue	|⑥
green	⑤	pink	|②	dark blue	⑥|
blue	⑥	dark red	②|	violet	⑦|
purple	⑦				

We denote shapes and other concepts by enclosing a glyph in square brackets – [·]˵ for *pointed*, [:]˵ for *spotted*, [–]ˋ for *horizontal*, [ı]ˋ for *vertical* etc:

pointed	[·]˵
point	[·]
spotted	[:]˵

horizontal	[–]ˋ
vertical	[ı]ˋ

curve (n)	[∾]	curved	[∾]˵	curling (n)	[∾]ᴴ
curve (v)	[∾]´	curl (n)	[∾]ᴴ	curled	[∾]ᴴ˵
curving (n)	[∾]⁻	curl (v)	[∾]ᴴ´		

circle	[o]	cycle (n)	[o]˵
circling (n)	[o]⁻	cyclical	[o]ˇ
circled (a)	[o]˵	wheel	[o]ᴴ
circular	[o]ˋ	wheeling (n)	[o]ᴴ⁻

square (n)	[□]	squaring (n)	[□]⁻
square (a)	[□]ˋ	squared (a)	[□]˵

triangle	[△]	triangulate	[△]´
triangular	[△]ˋ	triangulating (n)	[△]⁻

We denote other abstract concepts by enclosing a glyph in pointed brackets – ⟨+⟩ for *addition*, ⟨−⟩ for *subtraction*, ⟨×⟩ for *multiplication* etc:

addition	⟨+⟩	adding (n)	⟨+⟩⁻
add	⟨+⟩´	added	⟨+⟩˵

subtraction	⟨−⟩
subtract	⟨−⟩´
subtracting (n)	⟨−⟩⁻

multiplication	⟨×⟩
multiply	⟨×⟩′
multiplying (n)	⟨×⟩⁻

division	⟨÷⟩	divided	⟨÷⟩\\
divide	⟨÷⟩′	dividing (n)	⟨÷⟩⁻

half	⟨½⟩
one-third	⟨⅓⟩
quarter	⟨¼⟩

once	⟨1⟩
twice	⟨2⟩
thrice	⟨3⟩

A more complete list of augmented definitions can be found in APPENDIX B.

CHAPTER 10

COMPOUND SYMS

A key feature of Symese and pictographic-rooted languages like Chinese is the blending of glyphs to make compound words. The 4,500 root and augmented syms defined above can be combined into thousands of compound syms to form a viable pictographic language.

DP 6 dealt with the advantage of starting from a blank canvas in avoiding the complexity of sophisticated languages by keeping the associations between sym and concept at a basic level. Another aspect of keeping the language structure simple and logical is to place a noun before its qualifying adjective. This introduces the twenty-third DP:

23. A noun sym is placed before its qualifying adjective sym, eg ⊥ for *child* + ⸜ ` for *female* = ⊥ ⸜ ` for *girl*, ⊥ + ⸝ ` = ⊥ ⸝ ` for *boy*. ☰ for *old person* + ⸜ ` = ☰ ⸜ ` for *old woman* , ☰ + ⸝ ` = ☰ ⸝ ` for *old man*:

child	⊥
female (a)	⸜ `
male (a)	⸝ `

girl	⊥	⸜ `
boy	⊥	⸝ `

old person	☰
female (a)	⸜ `
male (a)	⸝ `

old woman	☰	⸜ `
old man	☰	⸝ `

Here are more examples of compound syms:

sibling	⊥⊥
female (a)	⸜ `
male (a)	⸝ `

sister	⊥⊥	⸜ `
brother	⊥⊥	⸝ `

| mother | ෆ |
| before | |(|

grandmother	ෆ	|(`
great-grandmother	ෆ	|(‡

Chapter 10 — Compound Syms

father	～୨			
before	⟨(	grandfather	～୨	⟨(`
		great-grandfather	～୨	⟨(‡
daughter	૯.			
after	)⟨	granddaughter	૯.	)⟨`
		great-granddaughter	૯.	)⟨‡
son	ω			
after	)⟨	grandson	ω	)⟨`
		great-grandson	ω	)⟨‡
big	∩`			
very	∧`	very big	∩`	∧`
		huge / enormous / massive	∩`	∧‡
small	∪`			
very	∧`	very small	∪`	∧`
		tiny / minute / miniscule	∪`	∧‡

For compound syms that use non-adjectives to qualify nouns, we introduce word parcel qualifiers, where glyphs placed between a word-parcel open qualifier and word-parcel close qualifier denote a single concept. This is the twenty-fourth DP:

24. PO (parcel open) and PC (parcel close) are square brackets that enclose two or more glyphs denoting a single concept. Having appropriated [and] for use as qualifiers, we denote square brackets in common usage by ⟦ and ⟧ :

AQ	Adjective / Adverb	`	-Q	Mini	∪	*Q	Most	⟨
VQ	Verb	´	IQ	Person	I	<Q	Past tense	(
NQ	Noun	−	PQ	Place	∨	>Q	Future tense	)
OQ	Opposite	x	GQ	Group	‖	~Q	Embedded	⟨1⟩
#Q	Derivative	1	SQ	Plural	+	PO	Parcel open	⟦
DQ	Device / substance	H	RQ	Repeat	‡	PC	Parcel close	⟧
EQ	Essence/nuance	∽	UQ	Upper case	∧			
=Q	Maxi	∩	+Q	More	⟨			

65

Symese — Universal Symbolic Script

mother	♡
father	♍

parent	[♡	♍]	

sibling	Ⅱ
mother	♡
father	♍
daughter	ᘓ
son	ᘌ

uncle / aunt (maternal)	[Ⅱ	♡]		
uncle / aunt (paternal)	[Ⅱ	♍]		
niece	[ᘓ	Ⅱ]		
nephew	[ᘌ	Ⅱ]		
cousin sister	[ᘓ	Ⅱ	♡	♍]
cousin brother	[ᘌ	Ⅱ	♡	♍]

heat (n)	⌒̄
body	8
very	∧ `

fever	[⌒̄	8	∧ `]

pull (v)	-(´
difficult	⌒̄ `

drag	-(´	⌒̄ `

cover (n)	⊽
face	ⓠ
hand	▽
bird	ᘒ
fish+	∞
bed	⊟
pillow	⊟[1]
quilt	⊟[3]

mask	[⊽	ⓠ]
glove	[⊽	▽]
feather	[⊽	ᘒ]
scale	[⊽	∞]
bedsheet	[⊽	⊟]
pillow case	[⊽	⊟[1]]
quilt cover	[⊽	⊟[3]]

Chapter 10 — Compound Syms

move (v)	D'	
circular	$[o]`$	
to and fro	$\rightarrow\!\diamond$	
up and down	$\diamond\!-$	
energy	$\vee\!\vee$	

rotate	D'	$[o]`$
shake	$[D'$	$\rightarrow\!\diamond\,]$
vibrate	$[D'$	$\rightarrow\!\diamond\,]^{\cup}$
flux / oscillate	$[D'$	$\diamond\!-\,]$
exercise	$[D'$	$\vee\!\vee\,]$

driver	$D\frac{1}{x}$	
car	$\lhd$	
bus	Σ	
aircraft	$\boxtimes$	
boat	$\boxdot$	
truck	$\lhd$	
train (n)	Σ	

car driver	$[D\frac{1}{x}$	$\lhd\,]$
bus driver	$[D\frac{1}{x}$	$\Sigma\,]$
pilot	$[D\frac{1}{x}$	$\boxtimes\,]$
boat driver	$[D\frac{1}{x}$	$\boxdot\,]$
truck driver	$[D\frac{1}{x}$	$\lhd\,]$
train driver	$[D\frac{1}{x}$	$\Sigma\,]$

liquid (n)	$\triangledown$	
pen	$\underline{\triangledown}$	

ink	$[\triangledown$	$\underline{\triangledown}\,]$

liquify	$\triangledown'$	
heat (n)	$\overline{\cap}$	

melt	$[\triangledown'$	$\overline{\cap}\,]$

gram	$\triangle^{1}$	
ten times	$\langle 10 \rangle$	
one-tenth	$\langle \overline{10} \rangle$	

kilogram	$[\triangle^{1}$	$\langle 10 \rangle^{2}\,]$
metric ton	$[\triangle^{1}$	$\langle 10 \rangle^{5}\,]$
milligram	$[\triangle^{1}$	$\langle \overline{10} \rangle^{2}\,]$

in	$\sqsubset$	
building	$\boxminus$	
out	$\sqsupset$	
building	$\boxminus$	

indoor	$[\sqsubset$	$\boxminus\,]$
outdoor	$[\sqsupset$	$\boxminus\,]$

metre	A^1					
ten times	$\langle 10 \rangle$		kilometre	[A^1	$\langle 10 \rangle^2$	]
one-tenth	$\langle \overline{10} \rangle$		centimetre	[A^1	$\langle \overline{10} \rangle^1$	]
			millimetre	[A^1	$\langle \overline{10} \rangle^2$	]

top	木				
soft	∪)ˋ		cream	木	∪)ˋ
ice	⊖¹		ice-cream	[木	∪)ˋ ⊖¹]

day	⊠			
early	<ˋ		morning	⊠ <ˋ
late	>ˋ		evening	⊠ >ˋ
before	|(		dawn	⊠ |(ˋ

week	⊠¹			
start (n)	▷		start of week	[⊠¹ ▷]
end (n)	◁ˢ		weekend	[⊠¹ ◁ˢ]

calendar	⊠"		
pen	⊻		diary [⊠" ⊻]

night	⊠		
before	|(		dusk ⊠ |(ˋ

noon	⊠		
before	|(		forenoon ⊠ |(ˋ
after	)|		afternoon ⊠)|ˋ

period	⊠̄		
yearly	⊠³		anniversary ⊠̄ ⊠³

Chapter 10 — Compound Syms

time (n)	⊠
all	|||
yes	+
no	×
infinity	◇

always	[⊠	|||]
ever	[⊠	+]
never	[⊠	×]
forever	⊠	◇'

answer (n)	↑
hint (n)	◇¹

clue	[↑	◇¹]

good (a)	∨'
very	∧'

very good	∨'	∧'
excellent	∨'	∧‡

bad	⌄'
veryx	∧'

very bad	⌄'	∧'
terrible / horrible	⌄'	∧‡

take (v)	ς'
out	⊐

extract	[ς'	⊐]

give	⊃'
price (n)	₽

pay	[⊃'	₽]

make	≈'
better	∨s

improve	[≈'	∨s]
enhance	[≈'	∨s]¹

destroy	≈⌒
life	⊘
malice	⌄¹

kill	[≈⌒	⊘]	
murder	[≈⌒	⊘	⌄]

destruction	≈⌒
series	◇⌢

disaster	[≈⌒	◇⌢]

Symese — Universal Symbolic Script

money	⟨money⟩		currency note	[⟨money⟩	⟨paper⟩]	
paper	⟨paper⟩		coin	[⟨money⟩	⟨metal⟩]	
metal	⟨metal⟩					

medical professional	⟨med⟩		doctor	⟨med⟩₁		
			nurse	⟨med⟩₂		
			surgeon	⟨med⟩₃		
tooth	⟨tooth⟩		dentist	[⟨med⟩	⟨tooth⟩]	
eye	⟨eye⟩		ophthalmologist	[⟨med⟩	⟨eye⟩]	
mind	⟨mind⟩		psychiatrist	[⟨med⟩	⟨mind⟩]	
customer	⟨cust⟩		patient	[⟨cust⟩	⟨med⟩₁]	

specialist	⟨spec⟩					
engine	⟨engine⟩		engineer	[⟨spec⟩	⟨engine⟩]	
history	⟨history⟩¹		historian	[⟨spec⟩	⟨history⟩¹]	
chemical	⟨chem⟩¹		chemist	[⟨spec⟩	⟨chem⟩¹]	
lifeform	⟨life⟩		biologist	[⟨spec⟩	⟨life⟩]	
eye	⟨eye⟩		optician / optometrist	[⟨spec⟩	⟨eye⟩]	
mind	⟨mind⟩		psychologist	[⟨spec⟩	⟨mind⟩]	
substance	⟨sub⟩					
healing (n)	⟨heal⟩		pharmacist	[⟨spec⟩	⟨sub⟩	⟨heal⟩]
law	⟨law⟩		lawyer / solicitor / attorney	[⟨spec⟩	⟨law⟩]₁	
			barrister	[⟨spec⟩	⟨law⟩]₂	

failure	⟨fail⟩ˣ				
expectation	⟨exp⟩		disappointment	[⟨fail⟩ˣ	⟨exp⟩]

reason	⟨reason⟩				
bad	⟨bad⟩		excuse	⟨reason⟩	⟨bad⟩

art	⟨art⟩				
fire	⟨fire⟩		fireworks	[⟨art⟩	⟨fire⟩]

Chapter 10 — Compound Syms

hole	⌴
hill	△

cave	[⌴	△]

edge	⌐
sea	⊖²
mountain	△^

beach	[⌐	⊖²]
cliff	[⌐	△^]

string (n)	⌡
fine	⊖`

thread	⌡	⊖`

group (n)	‖
tent	[△]¹

camp (n)	[‖	[△]¹]
camp (v)	[‖	[△]¹]´
camper	[‖	[△]¹]ᴵ
camping (n)	[‖	[△]¹]⁻
camping (a)	[‖	[△]¹]˅

section	⊔
book	▭

chapter	[⊔	▭]

every	⊦⋅
any	⊤
person	⊥
thing	⊢
where	⌡`

everyone / everybody	[⊥	⊦⋅]
everything	[⊢	⊦⋅]
everywhere	[⌡`	⊦⋅]
anyone / anybody	[⊥	⊤]
anything	[⊢	⊤]
anywhere	[⌡`	⊤]

how	⌐⌐
time	⊠

anyhow	[⌐⌐	⊤]
every time	[⊠	⊦⋅]
anytime	[⊠	⊤]

some	≡

sometimes	[⊠	≡]
somewhere	[⌡`	≡]
somehow	[⌐⌐	≡]
someone / somebody	[⊥	≡]
something	[⊢	≡]

Symese — Universal Symbolic Script

no	✕
person	⊥
thing	⊢
where	ↄ `

nobody	[⊥	✕]	
nothing	[⊢	✕]	
nowhere	[ↄ `	✕]	
none	[⊢	✕] ˇ	

list (n)	-│-
meaning	Σ
word	⋅
similar	╲ `

dictionary	[-│-	Σ	⋅]
thesaurus	[-│-	Σ	╲ `]

pause (n)	◁ ᵘ
talk (n)	⊗

interruption	[◁ ᵘ	⊗]
interrupt	[◁ ᵘ	⊗] ´
interrupting (n)	[◁ ᵘ	⊗] ⁻
interrupted (a)	[◁ ᵘ	⊗] ˝

go	▷ ´
in	⊏
out	⊐

enter	[▷ ´	⊏]
exit (v)	[▷ ´	⊐]

light (opp darkness)	△
fire	⊖
oil (n)	⊘
electricity	⌵⌵ ¹

candle	[△	⊖]
oil lamp	[△	⊘]
electric light	[△	⌵⌵ ¹]

mountain	△ ^
fire	⊖

volcano	[△ ^	⊖]

Chapter 10 — Compound Syms

element　　　　　ᓂ

hydrogen	ᓂ$_1$
helium	ᓂ$_2$
carbon	ᓂ$_6$
nitrogen	ᓂ$_7$
oxygen	ᓂ$_8$
aluminium	ᓂ$_{13}$
silicon	ᓂ$_{14}$
iron	ᓂ$_{26}$
copper	ᓂ$_{29}$
zinc	ᓂ$_{30}$
silver	ᓂ$_{47}$
tin (metal)	ᓂ$_{50}$
platinum	ᓂ$_{78}$
gold	ᓂ$_{79}$

iron　　　　　ᓂ$_{26}$
attraction　　-(ᶳ

magnet	ᓂ$_{26}$	-(ᶳ]

run (v)　　　人´
after　　　　)|
seek　　　　∧´

chase	[人´	)|]	
hunt	[人´	∧´	)|]

leg　　　　　人
high　　　　∧`
low　　　　∨`

upper leg	人	∧`
lower leg	人	∨`

arm　　　　　Y
high　　　　∧`
low　　　　∨`

upper arm	Y	∧`
lower arm	Y	∨`

foot	△	
back (n)	◁	
in	⊏	
out	⊐	
animal	8	
hard	⌒˙	
hand	▽	
in	⊏	
out	⊐	

heel	[△	◁]	
go in	[△ ´	⊏]	
go out	[△ ´	⊐]	
paw	[△	8]	
hoof	[△	8	⌒˙]

put / take in	▽ ´	⊏ `
put / take out	▽ ´	⊐ `

remove	⇥ ´
skin	♧

peel / skin (v)	[⇥ ´	♧]

sport(s)	▷⁻¹
ball	[o] ^{H}
foot	△
hand	▽
stick (n)	⌐
racket	⌐¹

soccer	[▷⁻¹	[o]⁻	△]₁
rugby	[▷⁻¹	[o]⁻	△]₂
basketball	[▷⁻¹	[o]⁻	▽]₁
volleyball	[▷⁻¹	[o]⁻	▽]₂
netball	[▷⁻¹	[o]⁻	▽]₃
hockey	[▷⁻¹	[o]⁻	⌐]₁
ice hockey	[▷⁻¹	[o]⁻	⌐]₂
tennis	[▷⁻¹	⌐¹	]₁
table tennis	[▷⁻¹	⌐¹	]₂
badminton	[▷⁻¹	⌐¹	]₃
cricket	[▷⁻¹	⌐¹	]₄
baseball	[▷⁻¹	⌐¹	]₅

leg	⋏
swim (v)	¥ ´
bicycle	∞

athletics	[▷⁻¹	⋏]
swimming	[▷⁻¹	¥ ´]
cycling	[▷⁻¹	∞]

measurement	×
rhythm	♭

beat (music)	[×	♂]

instrument	⌂ ˇ
musical	♂ `

musical instrument	⌂ ˇ	⌐ `

Chapter 10 — Compound Syms

game	▷ˇ
chance	⇾
card	⊓
cube	▣

card game	[▷ˇ	⇾	⊓]
roll of dice	[▷ˇ	⇾	▣]

north	↑
west	←
east	↦

northwest	[↑	←]
northeast	[↑	↦]

south	↓
west	←
east	↦

southwest	[↓	←]
southeast	[↓	↦]

part	⊔
garment (waist up)	⊓
neck	ō
arm	Y
atom	ol¹

collar	[⊔	⊓	ō]
sleeve	[⊔	⊓	Y]
proton	[⊔	ol¹	]¹
neutron	[⊔	ol¹	]²
electron	[⊔	ol¹	]³

collection	⊡
picture	⊙

photo album	[⊡	⊙]

rest (n)	⊓
work (n)	⊐

holiday / vacation	[⊓	⊐]

hat	⊓¹
hard	⌒`

helmet	⊓¹	⌒`

structure	⊟
animal	8

zoo	[⊟	8]¹
circus	[⊟	8]²

room	目				
school	◁▽	classroom	[目	◁▽]	
student	◁▽	class	[目	◁▽]	

book	⊞		
news	⌻¹	magazine	[⊞ ⌻¹]

helper	≻			
emergency	▽	police	[≻ ▽ ⌒]	
safety	⌒	firefighter	[≻ ▽ ⊖]	
fire	⊖	paramedic	[≻ ▽ ⊗]	
health	⊗	lifeguard	[≻ ▽ Ψ]	
swim (n)	Ψ			

flow (v)	⊠´		
slow (a)	⊂`	trickle / drip	[⊠´ ⊂`]
fast (a)	⊃`	torrent	[⊠´ ⊃`]

cloth	⌻¹			
floor	目	mat / rug	[⌻¹ 目]	
big	⌒`	carpet	[⌻¹ 目 ⌒`]	

price (n)	▷			
little (a – number)	▽`	cheap	[◁ ▽`]	
much	△`	expensive	[◁ △`]	
stone	⌽	gem / jewel	[⌽ ◁ △`]	

energy	⋎		
atom	◁¹	nuclear energy	[⋎ ◁¹]
		nuclear	[⋎ ◁¹]`

Chapter 10 — Compound Syms

adornment	⋈²		necklace	[⋈²	ŏ]	
neck	ŏ		hairpiece / wig	[⋈²	ô]	
hair	ô		bracelet	[⋈²	ϴ	⋎]
wrist	[ϴ					

study (n)	⟡ⁿ		mathematics	[⟡ⁿ	ξ]₁	
number (n)	ξ		arithmetic	[⟡ⁿ	ξ]₂	
			algebra	[⟡ⁿ	ξ]₃	
			calculus	[⟡ⁿ	ξ]₄	
			geometry	[⟡ⁿ	ξ]₅	
engine	⊳		engineering	[⟡ⁿ	⊳]	
place	⋈		geography	[⟡ⁿ	⋈]	
chemical	∪¹		chemistry	[⟡ⁿ	∪¹]	
lifeform	⚲		biology	[⟡ⁿ	⚲]	
healing (n)	⚕ⁱˢ		medicine (subject)	[⟡ⁿ	⚕ⁱˢ]	
mind	∝		psychology	[⟡ⁿ	∝]	
			psychiatry	[⟡ⁿ	⚕ⁱˢ	∝]

box	△		pentagon	△₅	
			hexagon	△₆	
			heptagon	△₇	
			octagon	△₈	
			nonagon	△₉	
electricity	⋁¹		battery	[△	⋁¹]

bag	⊙		wallet	[⊙	ㄴ]
pocket	ㄴ		handbag	[⊙	⋎]
hand	⋎				

joint	ϴ		ankle	[ϴ	△]
foot	△		wrist	[ϴ	⋎]
hand	⋎		knuckle	[ϴ	⋎]
finger	⋎				

Symese — Universal Symbolic Script

hit (v)	⊙¹				
hand	▽	slap	[⊙¹	△]	
knuckle	⊖	knock	[⊙¹	⊖	▽]

bicycle	⊖⊖			
electric	∿¹	electric bicycle	[⊖⊖	∿¹]

toy	⚲				
person	⊥	doll	[⚲	⊥]	
glide (n)	⅄¹				
string (n)	⌡	kite	[⚲	⅄¹	⌡]

jug	▽⌒			
boiling (a)	⊖³	kettle	▽⌒	⊖³

appreciate	⬯²			
talk (n)	෴	praise	[⬯²	෴]

picture	⊙				
series	◇ⁿ	graph	[⊙	◇ⁿ]	
moving (a)	⊃˜	video	[⊙	⊃˜]	
big	⌒`	movie	[⊙	⊃˜	⌒`]
box	▫	television	[▫	⊙	⊃˜]
building	⊟	cinema	[⊟	⊙	⊃˜]

reflection	⌒			
sound	⊙	echo	[⌒	⊙]

city	⊖⁵			
main	⋈`	capital	⊖⁵	⋈`

blow (v)	⊙¹			
music	♂	whistle	[⊙¹	♀]

Chapter 10 — Compound Syms

land	⊖					
on	⊓	island	[⊖	⊓	⊖]	
water	⊖					

storm	⊚^	thunder	[⊙	⊚^]	
sound	⊙	thunderstorm	[⊚^	⊙]	
		lightning	[w¹	⊚^]	
electricity	w¹	lightning storm	[⊚^	w¹]	
mouth	♡	cough	[⊚^	♡]	
nose	⬦	sneeze	[⊚^	⬦]	

face	♀|				
paint (n)	⟂¹⁼	clown	[♀|	⟂¹⁼	♡¹]
funny	♡¹				

talk (n)	♡			
soft	⌣`	whisper	♡	⌣`

stomach	⌒			
full	⊥`	satiated	⌒	⊥`

meal	|⌒|				
day	⊠	lunch	[|⌒|	⊠	◯]
middle (n)	◯	breakfast	[|⌒|	⊠	<`]
morning	⊠ <`	afternoon tea	[|⌒|	⊠	)|`]
afternoon	⊠)|`	dinner	[|⌒|	⊠	>`]
evening	⊠ >`				

life	⊗	birth	[⊗	▷`	⊐]
start (n)	▷	give birth	[⊗	▷`	⊐]´
out	⊐	born (v)	[⊗	▷`	⊐]″

medicine (object)	⌀¹
solid (n)	⌂
liquid (n)	⌄

pill	[⌀¹ ⌂]
lotion	[⌀¹ ⌄]

spirit	⌀
good (a)	∨`
evil (a)	×̇ˀ
imaginary	◇`

angel	⌀	∨`
demon / devil	⌀	×̇ˀ
fairy	⌀	◇`

| illness | 8 |

Diseases or disorders:

infectious or parasitic	8_1
neoplasms or cancers	8_2
blood or blood-forming organs	8_3
immune system	8_4
endocrine, nutritional, metabolic	8_5
mental, behavioural, neurodevelopmental	8_6
sleep-wake disorders	8_7
nervous system	8_8
visual system	8_9
ear or mastoid process	8_{10}
circulatory system	8_{11}
respiratory system	8_{12}
digestive system	8_{13}
skin	8_{14}
musculoskeletal, connective tissue	8_{15}
genitourinary	8_{16}

animal	8
wild	▷`
tame	◁`

wild animal	8	▷`
domesticated animal	8	◁`
pet	[8	◁`]¹

Chapter 10 — Compound Syms

bird	⚲	
Gallus gallus		
Anas platyrhynchos		
Cygnus atratus		
Accipitridae (family)		
Larus canus		

chicken	⚲	-gal
duck	⚲	-pla
swan	⚲	-cyg
eagle	⚲	-acc
seagull	⚲	-lar

mammal	♀	
Cannis familiaris		
Felis catus		
Equus caballus		
Bos taurus		
Ovis aries		
Capra hircus		
Artiodactyla suidae		
Leporidae cuniculas		
Rodentia muridae		
Panthera leo		
Panthera tigris		
Ursidae (family)		
Artiodactyl cervidae		
Proboscidea elephantidae		

dog	♀	-can
cat	♀	-cat
horse	♀	-equ
cow / bull	♀	-tau
sheep	♀	-ovi
goat	♀	-cap
pig	♀	-sui
rabbit	♀	-lep
mouse	♀	-rod
lion	♀	-leo
tiger	♀	-tig
bear	♀	-urs
deer	♀	-cer
elephant	♀	-ele

fish+	∞	
Cetacea (infraorder)		
Salmo salar		
Octopus vulgaris		
Brachyura (family)		

whale	∞	-cet
salmon	∞	-sal
octopus	∞	-oct
crab	∞	-bra

reptile	∝	
Anura ranidae		
Crocodilia niloticus		
Testudinidae (family)		
Serpentes (suborder)		

frog	∝	-anu
crocodile	∝	-cro
tortoise	∝	-tes
snake	∝	-ser

reptile	∝
ancient	⏜

dinosaur	∝	⏜

insect	∞	
Formicidae (family)		
Apocrita (suborder)		
Arachnida (class)		
Lepidoptera (order)		
baby	⚌	
Blattodea (family)		

ant	∞	-for		
bee	∞	-apo		
spider	∞	-ara		
butterfly	∞	-lep		
caterpillar	[∞	-lep	⚌	]
cockroach	∞	-bla		

bone	⚯
body	⚮

skeleton	[⚯	⚮	]

flower	⚘
Rosaceae (family)	
Helianthus annuus	
Orchidaceae (family)	
Bellis perennis	

rose	⚘	-ros
sunflower	⚘	-hel
orchid	⚘	-orc
daisy	⚘	-bel

fruit	⚶
Pyrus malus	
Citrus aurantium	
Citrus limonium	
Mangifera indica	
Musa paradisicum	
Cocos nucifera	

apple	⚶	-mal
orange (fruit)	⚶	-aur
lemon	⚶	-lim
mango	⚶	-man
banana	⚶	-mus
coconut	⚶	-coc

vegetable	⚴
Solanum tubersum	
Phaseolus vulgaris	
Lycopersican esculentum	
Cucumis sativas	
Brassica oleracea capitata	
Lactuca sativa	
Daucas carota	
Glycine max	
Theobroma cacao	
candy	◰[1]
drink (n)	⚭

potato	⚴	-tub		
bean	⚴	-pha		
tomato	⚴	-esc		
cucumber	⚴	-cuc		
cabbage	⚴	-cap		
lettuce	⚴	-lac		
carrot	⚴	-car		
soybean	⚴	-gly		
cocoa	⚴	-cac		
chocolate candy	[◰[1]	⚴	-cac	]
chocolate drink	[⚭	⚴	-cac	]

Chapter 10 — Compound Syms

grain (plant) ⚲
Triticum Aestivum
Oryza sativa
Zea mays
Hordeum vulgare

wheat	⚲	-tri
rice	⚲	-ory
corn	⚲	-zea
barley	⚲	-hor

spice ⚲
Allium cepa
Allium sativum
Piper nigrum
Zingiber officinale
Capsicum annuum

onion	⚲	-cep
garlic	⚲	-sat
pepper	⚲	-pip
ginger	⚲	-zin
chili	⚲	-cap

wheat ⚲ -tri
process food ꙮ′

bread	[⚲	-tri	ꙮ′]$_1$
pasta	[⚲	-tri	ꙮ′]$_2$
noodle / spaghetti	[⚲	-tri	ꙮ′]$_3$
pie	[⚲	-tri	ꙮ′]$_4$
pizza	[⚲	-tri	ꙮ′]$_5$

powder ⋄
wheat ⚲ -tri
rice ⚲ -ory
corn ⚲ -zea

wheat flour	[⋄	⚲	-tri]
rice flour	[⋄	⚲	-ory]
corn flour	[⋄	⚲	-zea]

CHAPTER 11
SYMESE IN PRACTICE

"There are only two feelings.
Love and fear.
There are only two languages.
Love and fear.
There are only two activities.
Love and fear.
There are only two motives,
two procedures, two frameworks, two results.
Love and fear.
Love and fear."

~ **Michael Leunig**[1]

SEMANTIC SIMPLICITY

How something appears on a page can affect how we read and what we take in, blurring the line between form and substance. Newspaper columns make for lighter reading, diagrams and shorter sentences make an instruction manual easier to understand, and speech bubbles are a natural fit for dialogue in a comic book. Using a small set of symbols to say something is a challenge that can illuminate the thought process. If nothing else, Symese offers a visual aid to supplement natural written language, akin to how emojis are used to add colour and depth to text messages.

Expressing ourselves in natural languages is often weighed down by a pedantry of syntax and semantics that hinders the flow of thought. Resilience in adversity teaches us that we don't need much to live well, that we can do without sophisticated tools. We discover that complex language can conceal muddled thought. When forced to, as when conversing with a child, we can express ourselves in ways that are simple without being simplistic. Natural languages do help us to crystallise our half-formed thoughts but when we try to convey the fullness of what we mean, it often morphs into something else.

---

[1] https://www.leunig.com.au/works/prayers

Over centuries, languages acquired layers of complexity like barnacles on a whale. Here is a short list of linguistic intricacies that English has accrued:

1. Syntactical rules around sentence construction, eg number and tense for nouns and verbs. This may or may not be necessary to avoid undue ambiguity. Some languages get by very well with numberless and tenseless verbs. In Chinese, "I sing (or sang or will sing) a (or the) song (or songs)" is 我唱歌 (I sing song), with add-ons to indicate number or tense only where the context calls for it.

2. Specific use of particles 'in', 'on', 'at', 'for', 'with' etc. For example, we say "in the event of" to indicate contingency but not "on the event of". Why not?

3. Specific use of such words as 'many' and 'much' for countable and uncountable quantities, 'I' and 'me' as first person and third person pronouns, 'each other' and 'one another' for two parties and multiple parties, 'that' and 'which' in defining and non-defining clauses.

4. Niche synonyms like 'wane', 'dim' and 'fizzle'. We say "the fire wanes", "the light dims" and "the ember fizzles out." The price for finesse (in this case, the connotation of flying sparks from a dying ember in the last expression) is unwieldy precision in shades of meaning.

5. Words with divergent meanings, eg 'about' as in 'relating to' and 'approximately', 'sterile' as in 'antiseptic' and 'barren', 'cleave' as in 'split apart' and 'cling to'.

6. Complex spelling and pronunciation, like the different pronunciations of 'ough' in the words though, through, thorough, thought, enough, cough and plough.

7. Irregular plurals, eg 'fishes' does not mean more than one fish but more than one type of fish.

Symese avoids most of these intricacies. To illustrate how this works, let us imagine two people stranded on a desert island, neither of whom speaks the other's language. How would they get along and survive or thrive together? They may use rudimentary sign language — pointing to a coconut and miming a cutting motion to suggest eating or drinking it.

Or, if they both know basic Symese, they could scribble ⊤ ∽` ? or ⊤ ⊛` ? on the sand to ask if the other was hungry or thirsty. They might improvise a writing tool to write ♀-coc for *coconut* or, more primitively, ♀ ⊙` ⌒` *(big spherical fruit)* and talk about things like family and friends. One of them may write ⊥ x^I to say "We are friends" or ᵴ △` ⊥$^+$? to ask "How many children do you have?"

Or take the scenario of a baby learning a language. He cries when he needs something – a hug or a kiss, food or a nappy change – and smiles or coos when he is happy. He slowly picks up, from listening to his parents and other people speaking to him, how to express these needs in simple words. As he learns to doodle, his mother may teach him basic syms like ♡ for *love*, ⌣ for *lip* and ⌢ for *tummy*. Later, she may teach him to write [♡ Y] *(love with arms)* for *hug* and [♡ ▷] *(love with play)* for *fun* as word-parcel synonyms for ⊖! and ⊚¹.

This introduces the twenty-fifth DP:

25. Using a combination of basic syms as a synonym for a more complex sym presents a choice between elegance of expression (and precision) and having fewer root syms to memorise. Examples include *coconut*: the more precise ♀-coc vs ♀ ⊙` ⌒` *(big spherical fruit)*, *hug*: ⊖! vs [♡ Y] *(love with arms)* and *fun*: ⊚¹ vs [♡ ▷] *(love with play)*.

Many synonyms in English convey variations of meaning closely related to the base word or something quite different in a metaphor. Here is a mind map of synonyms, metaphors, associated and augmented words for *big* – *huge, enormous, massive* (degrees of big), *great, vast, immense, substantial, extensive, considerable* (close synonyms), *big-hearted* (metaphor) and *enlarge, enlarged, enlarging* (augmentations):

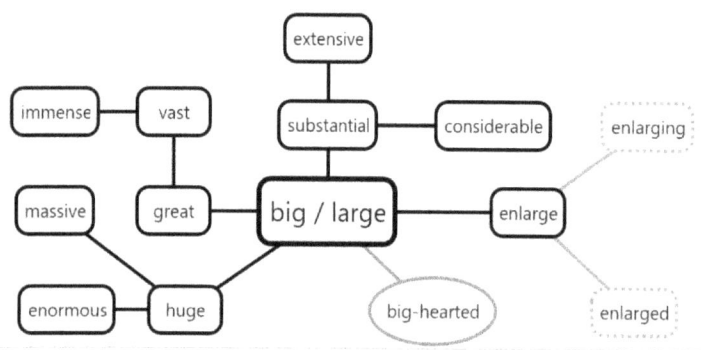

Degrees of big are denoted by compound syms – ⌒` ∧‡ *(very very big)* for *huge, enormous* or *massive*. Augmentations use qualifiers – ⌒´ , ⌒¯ and ⌒" for *enlarge, enlarging* (as noun) and *enlarged* (as adjective). Metaphors are denoted by compound syms – ♡ ⌒` for *big-hearted*. Finally, close synonyms are denoted with a fuzzy qualifier – ⌒° for *great, vast, immense, substantial, extensive* or *considerable*.

This is the twenty-sixth DP:

26. A fuzzy qualifier (FQ) indicates a close synonym of a sym.

AQ	Adjective / Adverb	`	-Q	Mini	∪	*Q	Most	≷
VQ	Verb	´	IQ	Person	I	<Q	Past tense	⟨
NQ	Noun	¯	PQ	Place	v	>Q	Future tense	⟩
OQ	Opposite	x	GQ	Group	‖	~Q	Embedded	①\
#Q	Derivative	1	SQ	Plural	+	PO	Parcel open	[
DQ	Device / substance	H	RQ	Repeat	‡	PC	Parcel close	]
EQ	Essence/nuance	ᴗ	UQ	Upper case	∧	FQ	Fuzzy	◇
=Q	Maxi	⌒	+Q	More	⟨			

Natural languages use niche synonyms for precision and finesse, with a baggage of word connotations that can trip up someone who uses a word without knowing these connotations. In ordinary communication, the price of precision and finesse can be unwieldy precision in shades of meaning.

Symese avoids this by using the same sym to denote words that mean much the same in ordinary communication, such as *big* and *large*, *small* and *little*, *many* and *much*, *simple* and *basic*, *table* and *desk*, *road* and *street*, *land* and *ground*, *try* and *attempt*, *help* and *aid*, *buy* and *purchase*, *talk* and *speech*:

Symese — Universal Symbolic Script

big / large	⌒`		path / route	⌐
small / little	⌣`		staff / cane	⌐
few / little	▽`		road / street	⌷
many / much	△`		garment / clothes	⌗
simple / basic	=`		world / earth	⊖
baby / infant	☰		land / ground	⊖
mixture / mix	⊟		country / nation	⊖³
table / desk	⊤		lid / cover	⎯
section / part	⊔		dish / plate	⌴

poison / toxin	⊠		present / now	|⊠|
pain / ache	⌴		period / term	⌛
illness / disease	8		feeling / emotion	◇
stage / phase	⋈		mystery / enigma	◈
occur / happen	∽´		happy / glad	♡`
try / attempt	∼´		calm / placid	⊚`
help / aid (v)	▷´		talk / speech	⊙
buy / purchase	△´		courage / bravery	Q̄
just / fair	⋈`		hate / hatred	⌴

Where precision or finesse is required, a field mark is used – ⌒` N° and ⌒` ⋈° to denote *substantial* and *extensive*:

big   ⌒`
quantity   N

substantial	⌒`	N°

big   ⌒`
space (physical)   ⋈

extensive	⌒`	⋈°

This is the twenty-seventh DP:

   27. A field mark (FM) qualifies a word parcel with its communication context.

Chapter 11 — Symese in Practice

AQ	Adjective / Adverb	`	-Q	Mini	∪	*Q	Most	⟨
VQ	Verb	/	IQ	Person	I	<Q	Past tense	⟨
NQ	Noun	−	PQ	Place	∨	>Q	Future tense	⟩
OQ	Opposite	x	GQ	Group	‖	~Q	Embedded	①
#Q	Derivative	1	SQ	Plural	+	PO	Parcel open	[
DQ	Device / substance	H	RQ	Repeat	±	PC	Parcel close	]
EQ	Essence/nuance	∽	UQ	Upper case	∧	FQ	Fuzzy	◇
=Q	Maxi	∩	+Q	More	⟨	FM	Field mark	□

For *basic* in the sense of something easy to learn, *just* in a legal sense, *calm* in an emotional sense and a *drop* of liquid we have ≡` |◇□ , ⋈` ⋈□ , ⊚` ◇□ and ⟨·⟩ ∪□ :

learn		◇´		
basic	≡`	basic (easy to learn)	≡`	|◇□

law	⋈			
just (fair)	⋈`	just (legal)	⋈`	⋈□

emotion	◇⁻			
calm	⊚`	calm (emotion)	⊚`	◇□

liquid (n)	∪			
dot	⟨·⟩	drop (liquid)	⟨·⟩	∪□

There are many **homographs** or **homonyms** in English – words that are spelt and/or sound the same but have divergent meanings. Examples include *about* for 'relating to' or 'approximately', *against* for 'oppose' and 'next to', *even* as an adverb (as in 'it is not even fair') or an adjective meaning 'level' or 'equal', *light* for the opposite of 'dark' or of 'heavy', *little* for 'few' or 'small', *right* as the opposite of 'left' or of 'wrong' and *short* for the opposite of 'excess' or of 'long' or of 'tall'. For the most common words, the divergent meanings are denoted by separate syms:

about (relating to)	⌒	against (oppose)	K
about (approximately)	⌒ `	against (space)	⋊

balance (harmony)	⊐	base (concept)	⌒
balance (parity)	⊏	base (place)	⌒ ˅

can (object)	▣ ³	clear (uncluttered)	⟩⟨ `
can (verb)	⟩ ´	clear (unobscured)	-¦- `

contract	⌣ ᴴ	direct (adjective)	⟩∣ `
contract (shrink)	⪤ ´	direct (verb)	⟩(´

earth (soil)	⌽	even (level)	[=] `
earth (world)	⊖	even (adverb)	⌣ `

field (object)	▷ ˅	just (adverb)	⌄∧ `
field (subject)	⊠	just (fair)	⋈ `

light (opp dark)	△ `	like (adjective)	⟍ `
light (opp heavy)	⌣ `	like (verb)	♡ ⁞

little (number)	▽ `	matter (issue)	⋀
little (size)	⌣ `	matter (object)	⊡ ᴴ

past (conjunction)	⊲	present (now)	|⊠|
past (time)	|⊠	present (opp absent)	|☾ `

right (opp left)	→ `	second (position)	2 ⁼
right (opp wrong)	↓ `	second (time)	⋈

| spring (object) | ∽ | state (noun) | ⊖⁴ |
| spring (season) | ⊕ | state (verb) | ♡ ´ |

| star | ✧ | will (noun) | ⧖ |
| star (person) | ✧ ᴵ | will (verb) | ▷ ´ |

hot (spicy smell)	/5/	short (opp excess)	≪ `
hot (spicy taste)	\5\	short (opp long)	∀ `
hot (temperature)	⌒ `	short (opp tall)	∀ `

Here are some examples of word parcels using field marks to differentiate divergent homonyms:

| place | ⋈ | | | |
| branch | ⚲ | branch (place) | ⚲ | ⋈ ▫ |

| subject | ⊟ | | | |
| point | [·] | point (subject) | [·] | ⊟ ▫ |

work (n)	⌗			
break (n)	≈	break (work)	≈	⌗ ▫
leave	▷ ´	leave (work)	▷	⌗ ▫

| talk (n) | ☺ | | | |
| blunt (a) | ⋁ ` | blunt (speech) | ⋁ ` | ☺ ▫ |

| story | ☺̄ | | | |
| account | ◁ | account (narrative) | ◁ | ☺̄ ▫ |

| culture | ♡̄ | | | |
| tasteless | ▱ ˣ | tasteless (cultural) | ▱ ˣ | ♡̄ ▫ |

A field mark is used in encapsulated metaphors like △˘ ♀▫ for *bright (clever)*, △ˣ ♀▫ for *dull (stupid)*, ∪` ♡▫ for *cold hearted* and ⌒` ♡▫ for *warm hearted*, and compound concepts:

head (n)	♀				
cool (a)	∪`	cool headed	∪`	♀▫	
close (a)	⌒`	closed minded	⌒`	♀▫	
open (a)	▽`	open minded	▽`	♀▫	
bright	△˘	bright (clever)	△˘	♀▫	
dull	△ˣ	dull (stupid)	△ˣ	♀▫	
positive	+˘	positive (mind)	+˘	♀▫	

heart	♡				
big	⌒`	big hearted	⌒`	♡▫	
cold	∪`	cold hearted	∪`	♡▫	
warm	⌒`	warm hearted	⌒`	♡▫	
heavy	⌒`	heavy hearted	⌒`	♡▫	
light	▽`	light hearted	▽`	♡▫	
touch	♡	touched (emotion)	♡˝	♡▫	

spirit	☿				
open (a)	▽`	selfless	▽`	☿▫	
close (a)	⌒`	selfish	⌒`	☿▫	
sacrifice (n)	⌡²	mercy	⌡²	☿▫	
sex (act)	☿⁻	lust	☿⁻	☿▫	
laziness	⌐˘ˣ	sloth	⌐˘ˣ	☿▫	

computer	▽				
intelligence	⊗˘	artificial intelligence	⊗˘	▽▫	
learning (n)	◁⁻	machine learning	◁⁻	▽▫	
network	⊞	computer network	⊞	▽▫	

Encapsulated metaphors also capture compound expressions and those in other languages. 'Tongue in cheek', 'chasm of a fine line' and 'funny if not tragic' are denoted by [⌒ ⊏ ♀||], [⊥ ⊂` ▽^ ] and [ ♡˙ ⊐ ✕ ✕˘ ]. *Faux pas* (in French, meaning 'social blunder'), *zeitgeist* and *schadenfreude* (in German, meaning 'spirit of an era' and 'pleasure in the misfortune of others') are denoted by [ ✕˘ ⊗`], [☿ ⊠] and [☿· →ˣ ⌐] :

Chapter 11 — Symese in Practice

tongue	⬙				
in	⊏	tongue in cheek	[⬙	⊏	⚇||]
cheek	⚇||				

line	⊐				
fine	⌒`	chasm of a fine line	[⊐	⌒`	∀^]
chasm	∀^					

funny	☺!					
if	⊐				
not	×	comic if not tragic	[☺!	⊐	×	⌣^]
tragic	⌣^					

mistake (n)	⌣"				
social	⊗`	faux pas	[⌣"	⊗`]

spirit	⌀				
era	⌛	zeitgeist	[⌀	⌛]

pleasure	⌀·				
misfortune	⇁ˣ				
other	⌐	schadenfreude	[⌀·	⇁ˣ	⌐]

Natural languages grow increasingly complex, finessing definitions to the point where Mark Twain's "difference between the right word and the almost right word is the difference between lightning and a lightning bug" is offset by the need for a vast vocabulary to read and write correctly. Symese reverses this with a small vocabulary set. A fuzzy qualifier can be used alongside a word in a natural language to denote an augmentation of a root sym. "A pictogram bridges the tangible and the intangible" can be written as:

⌣ ⊙° (pictogram) ⊢´ ⌒ ☺° (tangible) ＼ ⌒ ☺ˣ (intangible).

93

Which can be more precisely expressed as:

⌣ [╅ ⊚] ʜ´ ⌒ ☺ ⟨` \ ⌒ ☺ ⟨`

Words have meanings on different levels – literal or metaphorical, objective or emotive, formal or casual. Simple words like *big* and *small*, *hot* and *cold*, *warm* and *cool* mean different things at different times or in different contexts. Words in a manual, news item or essay carry shades of meaning that the same words in other contexts may not convey. In both natural language and Symese, context clarifies meaning.

SAMPLE SENTENCES

Like emojis and doodles, Symese offers a visual gateway to transient thought with back-to-basics semantics that cuts through layers of complexity embedded in natural languages. On its journey to maturity as a living language, it may serve as an auxiliary tool for cross-cultural communication. Here are some examples of sentences expressed in Symese:

1. More than a meeting of minds, real communication is a meeting of hearts.

    ⩓` ᓂ [≻ ⋈], ⎡♡⎤ˇ ✓` ⟩´ [≻ ♡].

    - More than mind-convergence, real communication is heart-convergence.

2. A difference of opinion led to a clash of emotions.

    ⌣ [✵ ☻] ᔄ ⌣ [✕ ⇔].

    - An opinion difference resulted in an emotion fight.

3. The thunder and the lightning combined to create a stormy mood.

    ⌒ [⊙ w¹ ☉³] \ ⌒ [w¹ ☉³] ⫽` ≋⟩ ⌣ [⇔ ☉³].

    - The storm electricity sound and the storm electricity together made a stormy feeling.

4. We are not happy from being rich but rich from being happy.

- We are not happy from being rich but rich from being happy.

5. The currency exchange rate is steady but will not be for long.

- The money trade-price is static but will not be for much time.

6. Tomorrow's cities are being designed like clusters of villages.

- Future cities are being design like village groups.

7. He who knows not and knows he knows not, teach him.

- He who knows not and knows he knows not, teach him.

8. Write down the thoughts of the moment. Those that come unsought are commonly the most valuable. [Francis Bacon]

- Write the thoughts of the moment. Those which come seek-not are often the value-most.

9. The young do not know enough to be prudent, and therefore they attempt the impossible – and achieve it, generation after generation. [Pearl S Buck]

- The young people know not enough to be prudent, and so they attempt the impossible and achieve it, generation after generation.

10. If you would not be forgotten as soon as you are dead and rotten, either write something worth reading or do things worth the writing. [Benjamin Franklin]

- If you want not be forgotten as soon as you are dead and rotten, write something worth reading about or do things worth writing about.

11. An intellectual is a man who says a simple thing in a difficult way; an artist is a man who says a difficult thing in a simple way. [C Bukowski]

- An intellectual is a man who says a simple thing in a difficult way; an artist is a man who says a difficult thing in a simple way.

12. Computers are incredibly fast, accurate and stupid; humans are incredibly slow, inaccurate and brilliant; together they are powerful beyond imagination. [Einstein]

- Computers are incredibly fast, accurate and stupid; humans are incredibly slow, inaccurate and brilliant; together they are powerful beyond imagination.

13. The shadows in the cave are being mistaken for the world outside the entranceway. [Plato]

- The shadows in the hill-hole are mistaken for the world outside the entrance.

As it matures into a viable language, Symese can be used in hybrid mode, denoting key concepts with syms while retaining native words for less significant concepts as well as gaps in the Symese lexicon. There will be more such gaps for someone just starting to learn the language. To illustrate how this might work, here are some quotes expressed in hybrid Symese/English:

14. Be afraid not of going too slowly but of standing still. Every moment you are happy is a gift to the rest of the world. [Harry Palmer]

15. The most beautiful thing we can experiene is the mysterious. It is the source of all true art and science. [Albert Einstein]

    ... mysterious.
    ... source ...

    or

    ... source ...

Appendices

Appendix A – Complete Set of Root Syms

or	╱	the	⌒
and	╲	a / an	⌣

on	⊓	with	⊓_
off	⊔	without	⊔‾
in	⊏	of	_⊓_
out	⊐	if	‾⊔‾

this	⌐	around	_⌐_
that	¬	amid	‾⌐‾
how	⌐⌐	common (shared)	⌐`
so that	⌐	common (frequent)	¬`

between	▽	within	⌒
among	△	beyond	⌣
beside	▷	since	⟨
past (conjunction)	◁	until	⟩

during	⌢	what	⌠
while (conjunction)	⌣	who / which	⌡
at	⌢	when	⟨
so	⌣	where	⟩

also	⌢`	why	⟨`
only	⌣`	because	⟩`
just (adv)	⌢`	but	⟨`
almost	⌣`	though	⟩`

Appendix A — Complete Set of Root Syms

across	∧		there	∧`
through	∨		here	∨`
ago	<`		near	<`
along	>		far	>`

do (v)	∼´		has / have	∩´
be	∪´		own / possess	∪´
take (v)	⊂´		need (v)	⊂´
give	⊃´		want (v)	⊃´

big / large	∩`		solid (n)	⌒
small / little	∪`		liquid (n)	⌒
slow (a)	⊂`		be still	⊂´
fast (a)	⊃`		move (v)	⊃´

strong	A`		wide	A`
weak	∀`		narrow (a)	∀`
oppose	⊄´		contract (shrink)	⊄´
propose	⊅´		expand	⊅´

hard	⌒`		heavy	⌒`
soft	⌣`		light (opp heavy)	⌣`
fine	⊂`		tight	⊂`
rough	⊃`		loose	⊃`

firm (a)	A`		thick	A`
flexible	∀`		thin	∀`
control (v)	⊄´		truncate	⊄´
manage	⊅´		extend	⊅´

hot (temperature)	⌒`		warm (a)	⌒·`
cold (a)	∪`		cool (a)	∪·`
against (space)	⊂`		present (opp absent)	⎮⊂`
against (oppose)	⊃`		absent	⊃⎮`

old (of person)	⌒·`		female (a)	(·`
young	∪·`		male (a)	)·`
old (of thing)	⌒·̄`		previous	⎮(`
new	∪·̲`		next	)⎮`

close (a)	⌒`		top	⌒̄`
open (a)	∪`		bottom	∪̲`
back (opp front)	(`		before	⎮(`
front (a)	)`		after	)⎮`

high	∧`		very	A`
low	∨`		not very	V`
seldom	<`		early	<`
often	>`		late	>`

many / much	△`		more	⩓`
few / little	▽`		less	⩔`
stop (v)	◁´		short (opp excess)	≪`
start (v)	▷´		excess / too	≫`

above	△̲`		tall	A`
below	▽̄`		short (opp tall)	∀`
behind	◁⎮`		arrive	◁´
ahead / in front	▷⎮`		leave	▷´

Appendix A — Complete Set of Root Syms

long	Aˋ
short (opp long)	∀ˋ
return (v)	◁ʹ
travel (v)	▷ʹ

over	⊼
under	⊻
towards	⊬
away from	⊢

rise (v)	Aʹ
fall / drop (v)	∀ʹ
come	◁ʹ
go	▷ʹ

light (opp darkness)	△
darkness	▽
opp of change	◁
change (n)	▷

shape (n)	△
material	▽
static	◁ˋ
dynamic	▷ˋ

surface (n)	△
core (n)	▽
focus (n)	◁
dispersal	▷

up	↑ˋ
down	↓ˋ

left (opp right)	←ˋ
right (opp left)	→ˋ

flip (v)	↕ʹ
turn (v)	↔ʹ

about (relating to)	⌢
about (approx)	⌣ˋ
number (n)	ξ

than	ഗ
then	ഗˋ
as	℮
such	ഗ

ready	℮ˋ
available	∂ˋ

sight	○	appear	⊘ ´	
eye	⊙	seem	⊘ ´	
picture	⊙	image	⌀	
view (v)	⊖ ´	reflection	⊘	
read (v)	⌽ ´			

hearing	( )	phone (n)	θ
ear	(·)	tablet (electrical)	⫶
record (v)	(⊙) ´	noise	∅
		lull	⦶

essence	□	sound	⊙
substance	⊡	silence	⊙
form (n)	▫		

love (agape)	♡	heart	♡	joy	♡
eros	⌒	cry (v)	⌒´	sorrow	⌒
philia	♡	laugh (v)	♡ ´	excited	♡ `
storge	♡	smile (v)	♡ ´	calm / placid	♡ `

happy / glad	♡ `	elated	♡ `	mother	⌒
sad	♡ `	depressed	♡ `	father	⌒
care (n)	♡	kind	♡ `	daughter	⌒
concern (n)	♡	gentle	♡ `	son	⌒

time (n)	⊠	past (time)	|⊠
period / term	⊠	future	⊠|
duration	⊠	day	⋈
		night	⋈

moment	⋈	space (physical)	⋈
hour	⋈	place	⋈
second (time)	⋈	era	⊠
minute	⋈		

Appendix A — Complete Set of Root Syms

today	x̄	present / now	⊠
tonight	⩟	last night	⋈
yesterday	⋈	tomorrow night	⋈
tomorrow	⋈		

delay (n)	⋈	noon	x̄
immediate	⋈	midnight	⩟
not soon	x̄		
soon	x̄		

group (n)	∥	all	∥∥	yes	+
every	¦·¦	some	≡	no / not	×
any	⸫				

full	⌢	interest (topic)	⌢	enough	⌢
empty (a)	⌣	curiosity	⌣	not enough	⌣
pull (v)	⊣(	opportunity	←	choose	←
push (v)	)⊢	chance	→	randomise	→

include	⌒	difficult	⌢	indirect	((
exclude	⌣	easy	⌣	direct (a)	))

base	⌒	enclosure	⌒
lid / cover	⌐	receptacle	⌄
hide	⌒	secret (n)	⌒
reveal	⌣	exposure	⌄

pressure	△	reaction	(⊢
release (n)	▽	response	⊣)
safety	⇧	sudden	⊃⋅
risk (n)	⇩	gradual	⊲

recent	⑴`	area	⌒	
current (time)	‖⟩`	zone	⌒ǀ	
former	ǀ⟨`			
latter	⟩ǀ`			

wait	⟨´	follow	⟨ǀ´
proceed	⟩´	lead	ǀ⟩´

use (v)	∿´	accept	⟩´	do not	∾´
try / attempt	∾´	apply	⟩´	be not	∽´
occur / happen	∽´	provide	⟨´	take not	⟨´
result (v)	∿´	supply	⟨´	give not	⟨´

make	∾´	strategy	⁀⁀
keep	∽´	tactic	‿‿
receive	∽∽´	source (v)	⁀⁀´
send	∾∾´	produce (v)	‿‿´

has / have not	⋏´	break (v)	∾´
own not	⋎´	discard (v)	∽´
need not	⋞´		
want not	⋟´		

I / me	⊥	person	⊥
you	⊤	thing	⊢
he / she / him / her	⊢	item	⊥
it	⊣	list (n)	-ǀ-

you all	⊤	general	⌐`
we / us	⊥	particular	¬`
they / them	⊩	other	⌐
it all	⊣	self	¬

Appendix A — Complete Set of Root Syms

question (n)	↱	to	→
answer (n)	↰	by	←
valid	↳	for	⇁
right (opp wrong)	↲	invalid	⇂
from	⌐	wrong (a)	⇂

precise		reason	◊
accurate		except	◊
imprecise		to and fro	-◊
inaccurate		up and down	◊-

seek	∧	may / maybe	⟨
find (v)	∧	can (able to)	⟩
possible	⟨	true	∨
is / are	⟩	good (a)	∨

impossible	⟨	false	⤬
is / are not	⟩	bad	⤬
may / maybe not	⤫		
cannot	⤬		

expect	∧	option	⟨
relate	∧	will / shall (v)	⟩
probable / likely	⟨	real	✓
should	⟩	virtue	∨

improbable / unlikely	⟨	unreal	⤬
should not	⟩	vice	⤬
will / shall not	⤬		

quest	△	even (adv)	◁
research (n)	△	agree	◡
certain	◁	moral (a)	▽
must	▷		

uncertain	⚹`	disagree	⚹´
must not	⚹´	immoral	⚹`
not even (adv)	⚹`		

centre	()	success	⊖
middle (n)	○	achievement	⊖
role	)(	harmony	⊕
function	⋈	accord	⊕

job	⋉	topic	⋊
career	⋇	theme	⋊
duty	⋉	sub	⋊`
loyalty	⋇	main	⋊`

freedom	⊔	direction	⋋
restriction	⊓	distance	⋈
scope	⊰		
range (n)	⊱		

clear (unobscured)	⋅¦⋅`	grain (texture)	⟨⊙⟩
clear (uncluttered)	⟩⟨`	magic	✳
matrix	⟨⟩	swap (v)	⊓´
powder	⟨∴⟩	replace	⊔´

quality	И	blunt (a)	∨`
quantity	N	sharp	∧`
serious	∑`		
important	Z`		

method	M	north	↑
rule (n)	W	south	↓
check (n)	∑	west	←
proof	⋺	east	→

Appendix A — Complete Set of Root Syms

table / desk	⊓		sibling	⊓
limit (n)	⊥		ladder	⊢
shelf	⊢		peer	⊥⊢
cupboard	⊐		step (n)	⊥

wife	⊂		bridge	⊢
husband	⊃		tunnel	⊣
marriage	⊗		station	⊠
friendship	⊗		stage / phase	⋈

facet	F		path / route	⊥
layer (n)	⊢		way	⊤
key (n)	⊔		line	⊐
lock (n)	⊓		row	⊔

chair	⊢		work (v)	⊡′
column	⊣		earn	⊡′
beam (object)	⊢			

corner	⌈		edge	⌉
tip	⌉		hammer	⌈
hole	⌊		screwdriver	⌋
gap	⌋		tape (n)	⌊

tap (object)	⌈·		vent	⌉·
pipe / tube	⌉·		nail	⌈·
pocket	⌊·		screw	⌋·
drain	⌋·		net	⌊·

staff / cane	⌠		board (n)	⊂
stick (n)	⌠		tray	⊂
pin (n)	⌡		handle (n)	⊃
string (n)	⌡		band (object)	⊃

pole	⌒	platform	⊏	
bat (object)	⌐	drawer	⊑	
hook	ᴸ	brush (n)	⊐	
knot	˩	belt	⊒	

leg	⋀	foot	△	
arm	⋎	hand	▽	
support (v)	≺′	train (v)	◁′	
help / aid (v)	≻′	play (v)	▷′	

sole (of foot)	△̲	toe	△̇	
palm (of hand)	▽̅	finger	▽̇	
knee	⋀̇	toenail	△̲̇	
elbow	⋎̇	fingernail	▽̇̅	

walk (v)	·⋀′	catch (v)	·⋎′	
run (v)	⋀·′	throw (v)	⋎·′	
jump (v)	·⋀·′	hold (v)	·⋎·′	
kick	⋀̇′	carry	⋎̇′	

wing	⋀	fly (v)	⋀′	
fin	⋁	swim (v)	⋎′	
tradition	≪	order	⋠	
trend	≫	chaos	⋡	

peak (n)	△	hill	△	sequence (n)	◇
trough	▽	valley	▽	arrangement	◇
moderate	◁`	condition / status	◁	measurement	⋋
extreme	▷`	position	▷	set	⋋⋌

Appendix A — Complete Set of Root Syms

tool	⇧		pencil	⍐
device	⇩		pen	⍗
utensil	⇦		insert	⍇
cutlery	⇨		remove	⍈

machine	⇧		spring (object)	∽
computer	⇩		wire	ω
mechanism	⇦		tail	ε
engine	⇨			

shallow	⊢˙		concept	⊦
deep	⊢˙		factor	⊣
ancestor	⊥˙		adult	⊤
descendant	⊤˙		child	⊥

old person	≡		entity	⊩
baby / infant	≣		family	⫞
human	⊨		context	⫢
couple	⩵		situation	⫤

garment (waist up)	⊐		covering (head)	⊓
garment (waist dn)	⊏		covering (foot)	⊔
inner garment	⊐−		background	⊣
outer garment	−⊏		foreground	⊢

sleep (v)	⊓ ′		stand (v)	⊓ ′
rest (v)	⊔ ′		reach (v)	⊐ ′
kneel	⊔ ′		sit	⊔ ′
bow (v)	⊓ ′		reside	⊔ ′

Symese — Universal Symbolic Script

building	⊟	ceiling	⊟	window	⊟
room	⊟	floor	⊟	door	⊟
structure	⊟	frame	⊟	wall	⊟

attic	⊟	roof	⊟
basement	⊟	foundation	⊟
shutter	⊟	home	⊟
gate	⊟	house	⊟

book	⊟	catalog (n)	⊟
data	⊟	furniture	⊟
card	⊟	paper	⊟
index	⊟		

bench	⊟	vehicle	⊠
bed	⊟	transport	⊠
cart	⊟	car	⊠
carriage	⊟	bus	⊠

flow (n)	⊠	truck	⊠
road / street	⊠	train (n)	⊠
aircraft	⊠	garment / clothes	⊟
boat	⊠		

operate	⊠′	network	⊞
maintain	⊠′	field (subject)	⊠
factory	⊠	internet	⊞
depot	⊠	industry	⊠

world / earth	⊖	team (n)	⊘	nature	⊕
planet	⊖	company (n)	⊘	season	⊕
environment	⊖	community (n)	⊘	society	⊗
space (astronomy)	⊖	business (n)	⊘	government	⊗

Appendix A — Complete Set of Root Syms

fire	⊖	wood	⊖
water	⊖	metal	⊖
air	⊕	earth (soil)	⊕
wind	⊕	stone	⊕

sky	⊖	summer	⊖
land / ground	⊖	winter	⊖
private	⊕`	autumn	⊕
public	⊕`	spring (season)	⊕

office (n)	⊘	climate	⊖
administration	⊘	weather (n)	⊖
politics	⊘	vapour	⊕
political party	⊘	gas	⊕

rain (n)	⊖	plastic	⊘
cloud (n)	⊖	oil (n)	⊘
mist / fog	⊕	sand	⊘
smog	⊕	glass (material)	⊘

head (n)	♀	bubble	○─
torso	⊥○	bulb	─○

brain	⊙	forehead	♀̄	chin	♀
organ	⊙	groin	○	neck	○̄

scalp	○̄	hair	♀̂
buttock	○	beard	♀
jaw	♀	fur	○̂
shoulder	○		

back of head	♀|	face	♀|	cheek	♀||
back of body	|○	chest	○|	breast	○||

horizon		link (n)	
perspective		joint	
sun		bond	
moon		hinge	

aim (n)		bicycle	
spiral (n)		lens	
body		roll (n)	
corpse		either	
toy		neither	

tree		fruit	
branch		nut	
root		seed	
leaf		vegetable	

fungus		flower	
grain (plant)		herb	
grass		spice	
moss		bud	

flesh		blood	
fat (bio)		white blood cell	
muscle		red blood cell	
tissue		cell (bio)	
bone		organism	

sense (n)		conscious	
instinct		subconscious	
skin			
touch (n)			

Appendix A — Complete Set of Root Syms

spirit	⊘	desire (n)	·⊘	
life	⊚	pleasure	⊘·	
health	⊖	courage / bravery	⊖	
gender	⊙	character	⊘	
sex (gender)	⊖			

inspiration	l⊘	distress (n)	ll⋈
aspiration	⊘l	pain / ache	⋈ll
ego	⋈	hate / hatred	·⋈
death	⊙⋈	anger	⋈·
fear (n)	⋈		

animal	8	lifeform	8	mammal	♀
illness / disease	8	plant	⚭	bird	♂
micro-organism	∞	giant	8	reptile	∝
insect	∞	beast	8	fish+	∝

same / alike	∕∕ `	complex	≡ `
similar / like	∖ `	simple / basic	≡ `
different	⨯ `	together	‖ `
unlike	⨯ `	apart	‖ `

word	⌊·	standard (a – norm)	⌐·⌐ `
letter (character)	·⌋	standard (a – class)	⌊·⌋ `
regular (even)	⌐· `	indication	⌊·
regular (norm)	·⌐ `	sign	·⌋

description	·⊥	literature	⊢
name (n)	⊥·	poetry	⊢·
science	·⊤	craft	⊣
technology	⊤·	art	⊣·

subject	⊟	preparation	⊞	
object (n)	⊟	execution (task)	⊬	
project (n)	⟦	process (n)	⟬	
delivery	⟧	program (n)	⟭	

balance (parity)	⊓	collection	⊓	
balance (harmony)	⊔	unit	⊔	
match (v)	⟦ ′	develop	⟦· ′	
compare	⟧ ′	build	·⟧ ′	

model (n)	⊓	category	⊓·	
example	⊔	type	⊔·	
code	⊣	compound	⊣·	
symbol	⊢	mixture / mix	⊢·	

whole	⊓	complete (a)	⊓ `	
section / part	⊔	incomplete	⊔ `	
template	E	design (n)	∈	
pattern	∃	system	∃	

major	⌒ `	automatic	⟨ `	
minor	⌣ `	manual (a)	⟩ `	

claim (v)	◅ ′	please	q ′	
refer	◁ ′	thank	p ′	
review (v)	▽ ′	sorry	d `	
recap (v)	▽ ′	again	b `	

win (v)	⟊ ′	digital	⏳	
lose	⟋ ′	analog	⋈	
adapt	⋈ ′	will (n)	⟊	
access (v)	⋈ ′	mind	∝	

Appendix A — Complete Set of Root Syms

buy / purchase	△´	cost (n)	◁	shop (n)	△△
sell	▽´	price (n)	▷	trade (n)	▽▽
hire in	▽	account	◁	economy	◁
hire out	▽	transaction	▷	market (n)	▷

funnel (n)	⋏	issue / matter	∧	secure (a)	A´
filter (n)	⋎	detail (n)	∨	insecure	∀´
divergence	≺	visit (n)	<	tame	⊲´
convergence	≻	escape (n)	>	wild	⊳´

specific	๑´	practice	∾
various	๏´	plan (n)	∽
serve	ᵬ´	value (n)	$
share (v)	ᵭ´	money	₿

special	∞´	clean (a)	○´
ordinary / usual	∞´	dirty	○´
subtle	8´	element	◌
obvious	β´	feature (n)	▯

justice	⊢⊣	master	⊢⊣
law	⊣⊢	slave	⊣⊢
meaning	Ξ	discern	Ξ´
purpose	⊼	consider	⊼´

force (n)	⋀	permission	⋊⋉
energy	⋁	decision	⋉
potential	⋚		
power	⋛		

purity	⨯	problem	⨯
beauty	⨯	solution	⨯
principle	⨯	cooperate	⨯´
theory	⨯	compete	⨯´

blade	✀	scissors	✀	
fight (n)	✄	weapon	✄	
defence	✕	peace	✕	
attack (n)	✕	war	✕	

grow	⌒´	advantage	⌒	
revert	⌣´	disadvantage	⌣	
regress	⊂´	discontinue	⊂´	
progress (v)	⊃´	continue	⊃´	

perception	◇	feel (v)	◇´	
impression	◈	think	◈´	
cognition	◉	understand	◇´	
		imagine	◇´	

empathy	◇	experience	◇	
insight	◇	knowledge	◇	
idea	◇	wise	◇`	
analysis	◇	clever	◇`	

advice	◇	mystery / enigma	◈	
doubt (n)	◇	trust (n)	◇	
guess (n)	◇	belief	◇	
wonder (n)	◇	resource	◇	
consult	◈´	hope (n)	◇	

assume	◇´	confident	◇|`	
deduce	◇´	remember	◇´	
pride	◇	forget	◇´	
humility	◇	learn	|◇´	
diffident	|◇`	teach	◇|´	

Appendix A — Complete Set of Root Syms

smell (n)	▱	taste (n)	▱	
nose	▱	tongue	▱	
breath	▱	saliva	▱	
perfume	▱	antidote	▱	
stench	▱	poison / toxin	▱	

music		pitch (sound)	
melody		tone (sound)	
tempo		volume (sound)	
rhythm		timbre	

voice		statement	
mouth		comment (n)	
talk / speech		report (n)	
culture		call (v)	
language		tell (v)	

message		explanation	
story		information	
opinion		instruction	
conversation		lip	
		tooth	

appetite		food	
stomach		defecation	
thirst		consumption	

meal		refreshment	
drink (n)		small intestines	
urination		large intestines	

bucket / basin	⌣	glass / tumbler	⏃	dish / plate	|⌒|
cup	⌣	bell	⏃	bowl	|⌣|
pot	⌣				

royalty	✿	palace	⊟
king	✿	castle / fortress	⊟
queen	✿	kingdom	⊞

rich (a)	⌢`	process food	ℰ´
poor (a)	⌣`	cook (v)	β´

block (n)	▫	parcel	△
box	△	package	△
bag	⊙	content	△

star	✧	transcendence	⊨
universe	◇	eternity	⊨
infinity	✧	god	❂

Appendix B – Complete Set of Augmented Syms

size	∩	smallness	∪
enlarge	∩′	shrink	∪′
enlarging (n)	∩⁻	shrinking (n)	∪⁻
enlarged (a)	∩˝	shrinking (a)	∪˜

slowness	⊂	speed (n)	⊃
slow (v)	⊂′	speed (v)	⊃′
slowing (n)	⊂⁻	speeding (n)	⊃⁻
slowing (a)	⊂˜	speeding (a)	⊃˜

hardness	⌒·	hardening (a)	⌒·˜	soften	⌣·′
harden	⌒·′	hardened (a)	⌒·˝	softening (n)	⌣·⁻
hardening (n)	⌒·⁻	softness	⌣·	softening (a)	⌣·˜

width	A	narrowness	∀
widen	A′	narrow (v)	∀′
widening (n)	A⁻	narrowing (n)	∀⁻
widening (a)	A˜	narrowing (a)	∀˜

thickness	A	fatness	A¹	thinness	∀
thickening (n)	A⁻	fat (a)	A¹˜	thinning (n)	∀⁻
thickening (a)	A˜	fattening (n)	A¹⁻	thinning (a)	∀˜
		fattening (a)	A¹˜		

solid (a)	⌂`	liquid (a)	⌒`	chemical	⌒¹
solidify	⌂′	liquify	⌒′		

strength	A	weakness	∀	frailty	∀˝
strengthen	A′	weaken	∀′	frail	∀˜
strengthening (n)	A⁻	weakening (n)	∀⁻		
strengthening (a)	A˜	weakening (a)	∀˜		

Symese — Universal Symbolic Script

heaviness	⌒̇	lightness	⌣̇		
weight	⌒̇⁻	lighten	⌣̇′		
gram	⌒̇¹	lightening (n)	⌣̇⁻		
ounce	⌒̇²	lightening (a)	⌣̇˜		
pound (weight)	⌒̇³				

firmness	⌒	flexibility	⌣
firm (v)	⌒′	flex (v)	⌣′
firming (n)	⌒⁻	flexing (n)	⌣⁻

heat (n)	⌒̄	heating (a)	⌒̄˜	temperature	⌒̄ˇ
heat (v)	⌒̄′	heated (a)	⌒̄˝	centigrade	⌒̄ˇ₁
heating (n)	⌒̄⁻	heater	⌒̄ᴴ	fahrenheit	⌒̄ˇ₂

cold (n)	⌣	freezing (a)	⌣˜		
coldness	⌣⁻	frozen	⌣˝		
freeze	⌣′	freezer	⌣ᴴ		
freezing (n)	⌣̄⁻	refrigerator	⌣ᴴ₁		

warmth	⌒̇̄	warming (a)	⌒̇̄˜	cooling (n)	⌣̇⁻
warm (v)	⌒̇̄′	coolness	⌣̇	cooling (a)	⌣̇˜
warming (n)	⌒̇̄⁻	cool (v)	⌣̇′	cooler (object)	⌣̇ᴴ

presence	⊂̇	attending (n)	⊂̇¹	attention	⊂̇²
attendance	⊂̇¹	attending (a)	⊂̇¹˜	absence	⊃̇∣
attend	⊂̇¹				

close (v)	⌒′	open (v)	⌣′
closing (n)	⌒⁻	opening (n)	⌣⁻
closing (a)	⌒˜	opening (a)	⌣˜
closed (a)	⌒˝		

120

Appendix B — Complete Set of Augmented Syms

back (n)	◖	backing (a)	◖ ˜	retreat (v)	◖ ˒
back (v)	◖ ʹ	backward	◖ ˆ	retreating (n)	◖ ⸗
backing (n)	◖ ⁻	retreat (n)	◖ ¹	retreating (a)	◖ ⸗˜

front (n)	◗	forward (a)	◗ ˆ	advancing (n)	◗ ⸗
front (v)	◗ ʹ	advance (n)	◗ ¹	advancing (a)	◗ ⸗˜
fronting (a)	◗ ˜	advance (v)	◗ ˒	advanced (a)	◗ ⸗ʺ

stillness	◖	movement	◗ ⸗
still (a)	◖ ˋ	motion	◗ ˢ
move (n)	◗	moved (a)	◗ ʺ
moving (n)	◗ ⁻	moveable	◗ ‴
moving (a)	◗ ˜	mover	◗ ᴵ

drive (n)	◗ ¹	driving (a)	◗ ⸗˜
drive (v)	◗ ˒	driver	◗ ⸗ᴵ
driving (n)	◗ ⸗	passenger	◗ ⸗ᴵ

proposition	◖	proposed (a)	◖ ʺ
proposing (n)	◖ ⁻	proposer	◖ ᴵ
proposing (a)	◖ ˜	proponent	◖ ᴵ

opposition	◗	opposite	◗ ˋ
opposing (n)	◗ ⁻	opposer	◗ ᴵ
opposing (a)	◗ ˜	opponent	◗ ᴵ

fineness	◖	niceness	◖ ¹
finesse	◖ ˢ	nice	◖ ˒
		roughness	◗

tightness	◖	tightening (a)	◖ ˜
tighten / fasten	◖ ʹ	tightened (a)	◖ ʺ
tightening (n)	◖ ⁻	fastener	◖ ᴴ

peg (n)	◁¹	zip (n)	◁²
peg (v)	◁¹′	zip (v)	◁²′
pegging (n)	◁¹⁻	zipping (n)	◁²⁻
pegged (a)	◁¹″	zipped (a)	◁²″

looseness	▷	loosening (a)	▷˜
loosen	▷′	loosened (a)	▷″
loosening (n)	▷⁻		

control (n)	𝔻	management	ℂ
controlling (n)	𝔻⁻	managing (n)	ℂ⁻
controlling (a)	𝔻˜	managing (a)	ℂ˜
controlled (a)	𝔻″	managed (a)	ℂ″
controller	𝔻ᴵ	manager	ℂᴵ

expansion	⊃	contraction	⊂
expanding (n)	⊃⁻	contracting (a)	⊂˜
expanding (a)	⊃˜	contracted (a)	⊂″
expanded (a)	⊃″		

extension	⊃	extent	⊃⁼
extending (n)	⊃⁻	truncation	⊂
extending (a)	⊃˜	truncating (n)	⊂⁻
extended (a)	⊃″	truncated (a)	⊂″

fullness	⊥	filling (a)	⊥˜
fill (v)	⊥′	fill (n)	⊥⁼
filling (n)	⊥⁻		

pack (n)	⊥¹	packed (a)	⊥¹″
pack (v)	⊥¹′	unpack	⊥¹ˣ′
packing (n)	⊥¹⁻	unpacking (n)	⊥¹ˣ⁻

Appendix B — Complete Set of Augmented Syms

emptiness		vacancy		
empty (v)		vacant		
emptying (n)		vacate		
emptying (a)		vacating (n)		

hollowness	
hollow	
vacuum	

pull (n)		attract	
pulling (n)		attractive	
attraction		attracting (n)	

stretch (n)		stretching (n)	
stretch (v)		stretched (a)	

push (n)		repel	
pushing (n)		repelling (n)	
pushy		repellant (a)	

interest (v)		interested	
interesting		curious (a)	

take a chance		gambling (n)		gamble (n)	
luck		gambling (a)		gamble (v)	
lucky		gambler		unlucky	
misfortune					

choice		chosen (person)		voting (a)	
choosing (n)		vote (n)		voter	
choosy		vote (v)		randomness	
chosen (a)		voting (n)		random	

123

Symese — Universal Symbolic Script

age	⌒	aging (a)	⌒ ̃	youthfulness	‿ ̄
age (v)	⌒ ´	old age	⌒ ̄	young person	‿ ᴵ
aging (n)	⌒ ̄	youth	‿		

female (n)	(·	male (n)	·)		
woman	(· ᴵ	man	·) ᴵ		
lady	(· ᴵ/s	gentleman	·) ᴵ/s		

ancient	≖ ̂
another	)‖ ̌

free (a)	⌣ `	restrict	⌐ ´
free (v)	⌣ ´	restricting (n)	⌐ ̄
freeing (n)	⌣ ̄	restrictive	⌐ `
freed (a)	⌣ ˝	restricted (a)	⌐ ˝

range (v)	⊢ ´
ranging (n)	⊢ ̄
ranging (a)	⊢ ̃

direct (v)	)(´	separation	⋈ ˢ	separating (n)	⋈ ᴵˢ
directing (n)	)(̄	separate (a)	⋈ ˢ̃	separated (a)	⋈ ˢ̋
director	)(ᴵ	separate (v)	⋈ ˢ́		

do (n)	∼	acting (n)	∼ ˢ	passive	∼ ˢˣ̃
doing (n)	∼ ̄	acting (a)	∼ ˢ̃	passivity	∼ ˢˣ
act / action	∼ ˢ	activity	∼ ˢ̿	inaction	∼ ˣ
act (v)	∼ ˢ́	actor	∼ ˢᴵ	inactive	∼ ˣ̃
active (a)	∼ ˢ̃	stage (place)	∼ ˢᵥ		

effort	∼ ¹
busyness	∼ ²
busy	∼ ²̃

Appendix B — Complete Set of Augmented Syms

being (n)	ʃ ⁻
become	ʃ ″
being (person)	ʃ ᴵ

take (n)	ʂ	taker	ʂ ᴵ
taking (n)	ʂ ⁻	get	ʂ ˞
taken	ʂ ˵	getting (n)	ʂ ˭

borrow	ʂ¹	borrower	ʂ¹ᴵ	stolen (a)	ʂ²˵
borrowing (n)	ʂ¹⁻	steal	ʂ²˞	theft	ʂ²
borrowed (a)	ʂ¹˵	stealing (n)	ʂ²⁻	thief	ʂ²ᴵ

gift	ʓ	offer (n)	ʓ ˵
giving (n)	ʓ ⁻	offer (v)	ʓ ˞
giver	ʓ ᴵ	offering (n)	ʓ ˭
given (n)	ʓ ⁼		

lend	ʓ¹˞	sacrifice (n)	ʓ²
lending (n)	ʓ¹⁻	sacrifice (v)	ʓ²˞
lender	ʓ¹ᴵ	sacrificial	ʓ²˂
		sacrificing (n)	ʓ²⁻

number (v)	ƹ ´	count (n)	ƹ ˵
numbering (n)	ƹ ⁻	count (v)	ƹ ˞
numbering (a)	ƹ ˋ	counting (n)	ƹ ˭
numbered (a)	ƹ ˵	counted	ƹ ˵

springy	ᴖ `
wiry	ω `

ownership / possession	ᴗ	own (a)	ᴗ `
owning / possessing (n)	ᴗ ⁻	owner	ᴗ ᴵ

want (n)	⟂	wanting (a)	⟂ ̄
wanting (n)	⟂ ⁻	wanted	⟂ ˮ

need (n)	⟂	needed	⟂ ˮ	require	⟂ ´
needing (n)	⟂ ⁻	necessary	⟂ ‴	requiring (n)	⟂ ⁼
needy	⟂ `	requirement	⟂ ˇ	required (a)	⟂ ˮ

unwanted	⟂ `	wasted (a)	⟂ ˮ
waste (n)	⟂ ˇ	wastage	⟂ H
wasting	⟂ ⁼	unneeded	⟂ ˮ
waste (v)	⟂ ´	unnecessary	⟂ ‴

including (prep)	⌒	included	⌒ ˮ	exclusion (n)	⌣ ⁼
including (n)	⌒ ⁻	excluding (n)	⌣ ⁻	exclusion (a)	⌣ ⁼
inclusion	⌒ ⁼	excluding (prep)	⌣	excluded	⌣ ˮ

ease	⌣	easing (a)	⌣ ̄
easing (n)	⌣ ⁻	difficulty	⌒

ready (v)	℮ ´	availability	∂
readying (n)	℮ ⁻	unavailable	∂ ˣ
readiness	℮		

enclosing (n)	⌓ ⁻	trap (n)	⌓ ¹
enclose	⌓ ´	trapped (a)	⌓ ¹ˮ
enclosed (a)	⌓ ˮ	trap (v)	⌓ ¹´
		trapping (n)	⌓ ¹⁻

secret (a)	⌓ `	expose	⊤ ´
secrecy	⌓ ⁻	exposing (n)	⊤ ⁻
		exposed (a)	⊤ ˮ

Appendix B — Complete Set of Augmented Syms

base (v)	basis		
basing (n)	base (place)		
based (a)			

cover (v)		covered (a)		uncover	
covering (n)		shell		uncovering (n)	
covering (a)				uncovered (a)	

hiding (n)		disguise (n)		disguising (n)	
hiding (a)		disguise (v)		disguised (a)	
hidden					

revelation		discovery		exploration	
revealing (n)		discovering (n)		explore	
revealing (a)		discover		exploring (n)	
revealed (a)		discovered		explored	
				unexplored	

wait (n)		waiting (a)	
waiting (n)		waiter	

following (n)		obedience		leading (n)	
following (a)		obey		leading (a)	
follower		obeying (n)		leader	
		obedient			

press (v)		urgency	
pressing (n)		urgent	
pressing (a)			

release (v)		relief (a)		relieving (n)	
releasing (n)		relieve		relieved (a)	
relief (n)					

Symese — Universal Symbolic Script

risk (v)	▽´	dangerous	▽⌒	
risking (n)	▽⁻	emergency	▽⌒͜	
risky	▽`	hazard	▽¹	
danger	▽⌒	hazardous	▽¹͜	

safe (a)	⌒)`	save	⌒)´
safe (object)	⌒)ᴴ	saver	⌒)ᴵ
saving (n)	⌒)⁻	saviour	⌒)ᴵ͇
saving (a)	⌒)͜	umbrella	⌒)¹

respond	⊃)´	responsive	⊃)`	responsible	⊃)͡
responding (n)	⊃)⁻	unresponsive	⊃)ˣ	irresponsible	⊃)ˣ͡
responding (a)	⊃)͜	responsibility	⊃)ᵛ		

react	(⊢´	reactive	(⊢`
reacting (n)	(⊢⁻	proactive	(⊢ˣ
reacting (a)	(⊢͜		

use (n)	∿	used (a)	∿"
using / usage	∿⁻	user	∿ᴵ

trial	∿	testing (n)	∿¹	examination	∿²
trialling (n)	∿⁻	testing (a)	∿¹͜	examine	∿²´
test (n)	∿¹	tester	∿¹ᴵ	examining (n)	∿²⁻
test (v)	∿¹´			examiner	∿²ᴵ

occurrence	∽	event	∽¹	result (n)	∽
occurring (n)	∽⁻	eventful	∽¹͜	resulting (a)	∽͜

Appendix B — Complete Set of Augmented Syms

acceptance		invitation		rejection	
accepting (n)		invite		rejecting (n)	
accepting (a)		inviting (n)		reject (v)	
accepted (a)		inviting (a)		reject (n)	
		invited (a)			

application	
applying (n)	
applied (a)	

provision		provider		supply (n)	
providing (n)		supplied (a)		supplying (n)	
providence		supplier		supplying (a)	

make (n)		creative		invention	
making (n)		creating (n)		invent	
maker		creator		inventing (n)	
creation		creature		invented	
create				inventor	

store (n)		storage	
store (v)		stored (a)	
storing (n)			

receipt		received (a)		sending (n)	
receiving (n)		receiver		sent (a)	
receiving (a)		recipient		sender	

strategise		strategising (n)		tactical	
strategic		strategist		tactician	

Symese — Universal Symbolic Script

source (n)	⧠	produce (n)	⧠	production	⧠
sourcing (n)	⧠	producing (n)	⧠	producer	⧠
sourcing (a)	⧠	producing (a)	⧠	product	⧠

break (n)	⧠	damaged (a)	⧠	destroying (n)	⧠
breaking (n)	⧠	decay / rot (n)	⧠	destructive	⧠
breaking (a)	⧠	decay / rot (v)	⧠	destroyer	⧠
broken	⧠	decaying / rotting (n)	⧠	crack (n)	⧠
damage (n)	⧠	decaying / rotting (a)	⧠	crack (v)	⧠
damage (v)	⧠	decayed / rotten	⧠	cracking (n)	⧠
damaging (n)	⧠	destruction	⧠	cracked	⧠
damaging (a)	⧠	destroy	⧠		

discard (n)	⧠
discarded (a)	⧠

my / mine	⊥	his / her(s)	⊢
your(s)	⊤	its	⊣

our(s)	⊥

personal	⊥	personality	⊥
impersonal	⊥	crowd	⊥

describe	⊥
describing (n)	⊥

name (v)	⊥	named (a)	⊥	labelling (n)	⊥
naming (n)	⊥	label (n)	⊥	reputation	⊥
naming (a)	⊥	label (v)	⊥	fame	⊥

Appendix B — Complete Set of Augmented Syms

scientific	·⊤ `	technological	⊤· `	technical	⊤· ˢ
scientist	·⊤ ᴵ	technique	⊤· ˢ	technician	⊤· ˢᵢ
unscientific	·⊤ ˣ				

literary	⊢· `	artistic	·⊣ `
poetic	⊢· `	artist	·⊣ ᴵ
poet	⊢· ᴵ		

adulthood	⊤ ˢ	childishness	⊥ ²
childhood	⊥ ˢ	childish	⊥ ²
child-like	⊥ ¹		

conception	⊩ ⁻	conceived (a)	⊩ ˎ	factor (v)	⊩ ′
conceptual	⊩ `	conceivable	⊩ ‴	factoring (n)	⊩ ⁻
conceive	⊩ ′	inconceivable	⊩ ˣ	factored (a)	⊩ ˎ
conceiving (n)	⊩ ⁻				

shallowness	⊢·
depth	⊢·
generation	⊥· ″

itemise	÷ ′	list (v)	-|- ′
itemising (n)	÷ ⁻	listing (n)	-|- ⁻
itemised (a)	÷ ˎ	listed (a)	-|- ˎ

generalisation	⌊ ⁻	selfish	⌐ `
generalising (n)	⌊ ⁻	unselfish	⌈ `
generalise	⌊ ′	altruism	⌈ ¹
		altruistic	⌈ ¹

phrase / clause	⌊· ″	text	⌊· ″₂
sentence	⌊· ″₁	string of letters	·⌋ ″

regulate (even)	⌐·⌐ ′	regulating (norm)	¬⌐ ⁻	regulation	¬⌐
regulating (even)	⌐· ⁻	regulated (norm)	¬⌐ \\	regulator (person)	¬⌐ ᴵ
regulate (norm)	¬⌐ ′	unregulated	¬⌐ ˣ	regulatory	¬⌐ ᴵ

standard (n - norm)	⌐·⌐	standardising (a)	⌐·⌐ ˢ
standardise	⌐·⌐ ′	standardised (a)	⌐·⌐ \\
standardising (n)	⌐·⌐ ⁻		

indicate	⌐·⌐ ′	indicative	⌐·⌐ `
indicating (n)	⌐·⌐ ⁻	indicated (a)	⌐·⌐ \\
indicator	⌐·⌐ ᴴ		

switching on (n)	⌐⌐ ¹	switching off (n)	⌐⌐ ¹
switch on	⌐⌐ ¹ʹ	switch off	⌐⌐ ¹ʹ

internal (n)	⌐ ˢ	intrinsic / inherent	⌐ ²	externalised (a)	⌐ ˢ\\
internal / inside	⌐ ˢ`	entrance	⌐ ᴴ	outer	⌐ ¹`
internalising (n)	⌐ ˢ⁻	external (n)	⌐ ˢ	extrinsic	⌐ ²
internalised (a)	⌐ ˢ\\	external / outside	⌐ ˢ`	exit (n)	⌐ ᴴ
inner	⌐ ¹`	externalising (n)	⌐ ˢ⁻		

clarity	-¦-	clear (declutter)	⟩⟨ ′
clarify	-¦- ′	cleared (a)	⟩⟨ \\

granular	⟨○⟩ `
button	⟨○⟩ ¹

magical	⋇ `	miracle	⋇ ˢ
magician	⋇ ᴵ	miraculous	⋇ ˢ`

Appendix B — Complete Set of Augmented Syms

these	┗ +
those	┓ +

manner	ᴄ̆ ᵛ	effective	┗ ᵛ	
effect (n)	┗ ᵛ	affect	┗ ´	
effect (v)	┗ ʸ	affecting (n)	┗ ¹	
effecting (n)	┗ ᵥ	affected (a)	┗ ˎ	

swap (n)	⊓ ⁻	replacement	⊔ ⁻
swapping (n)	⊓ ⁻	replacing (n)	⊔ ⁻

individual (a)	ᑌ ˣ
uncommon / rare	ᑎ ˣ

cause (n)	⟩ ᵛ	causing (n)	⟩ ᵥ	despite / in spite of	⟩ ˇ
cause (v)	⟩ ʸ	causal	⟩ ˇ		

location	⟩ ᵛ	local (a)	⟩ ˇ	map	⟩ ²
locate	⟩ ʸ	located (a)	⟩ ˎ	mapping (n)	⟩ ²
locating (n)	⟩ ᵥ	locality	⟩ ᵥ	mapped (a)	⟩ ²
locating (a)	⟩ ᵥ	address	⟩ ¹		

majority	⌢
minority	⌣

pin (v)	ᑌ ´	string (v)	ᑎ ´	
pining (n)	ᑌ ⁻	stringing (n)	ᑎ ⁻	
pinned (a)	ᑌ ˎ	strung (a)	ᑎ ˎ	
needle	ᑌ ¹			

handle (v)	⊐ ´
handling (n)	⊐ ⁻

flag (n)	⌒ ¹		flagged (a)	⌒ ⸝⸝	
flag (v)	⌒ ´		racket	⌒ ¹	
flagging (n)	⌒ ⁻				

hook (v)	ι ´		hanging (a)	ι ¹	
hooking (n)	ι ⁻		knotted (a)	ل ⸝⸝	
hooked (a)	ι ⸝⸝		tie (v)	ل ´	
hang	ι ´		tying (n)	ل ⁻	
hanging (n)	ι ⁻		tied (a)	ل ⸝⸝	

brush (v)	⌐ ´		brushed (a)	⌐ ⸝⸝	
brushing (n)	⌐ ⁻		broom	⌐ ¹	

grouping (n)	‖ ⁻		pile	‖ ¹	
group (v)	‖ ´		grouped	‖ ⸝⸝	

case	≡ ¹

positivity	+ ¹		negativity	× ¹	
positive	+ ´		negative	× ´	

height / altitude	∧		raised (a)	∧ ⸝⸝		lowering (a)	∨ ⁻
raise (v)	∧ ´		lowness	∨		lowered	∨ ⸝⸝
raising (n)	∧ ⁻		lowering (n)	∨ ⁻		frequency	>

height (tall)	A
shortness (height)	∀

many (n)	△
few / little (n)	▽
bit	▽ ⸝⸝

Appendix B — Complete Set of Augmented Syms

stop (n)	◁	ending (a)	◁ ⱽ	pause (n)	◁ ᵁ
end (n)	◁ ˢ	ended (a)	◁ ˵	pause (v)	◁ ᵁ′
end (v)	◁ ˢ′	final (a)	◁ ¹	pausing (n)	◁ ᵁ⁻
ending (n)	◁ ˢ⁻	finalise	◁ ¹′	paused (a)	◁ ᵁ˵

start (n)	▷	started (a)	▷ ˵	beginner	▷ ᴴ
starting (n)	▷ ⁻	beginning (n)	▷ ˢ⁻	initial (a)	▷ ¹
starting (a)	▷ ˜	begin	▷ ˢ′	initialise	▷ ¹′
starter	▷ ᴴ				

increase (n)	⩓	increasing (a)	⩓ ˜	increment (v)	⩓ ′
increase (v)	⩓ ′	increased (a)	⩓ ˵	incremental	⩓ ˜
increasing (n)	⩓ ⁻	increment (n)	⩓ ˢ	most	⩓ ᶜ

reduction / decrease	⩔	reducing / decreasing (a)	⩔ ˜	
reduce / decrease	⩔ ′	reduced / decreased (a)	⩔ ˵	
reducing / decreasing (n)	⩔ ⁻	least	⩔ ᶜ	

excess (n)	≫	excessive	≫ ˵	surplus	≫ ˢ
exceeding (n)	≫ ⁻	extra (n)	≫ ˢ	shortness (quantity)	≪
exceed	≫ ′	extra (a)	≫ ᴴ	shortage	≪ ˢ

arrival	◁	departure	▷ ˢ
arriving (n)	◁ ⁻	depart	▷ ˢ′
arriving (a)	◁ ˜	departing (n)	▷ ˢ⁻
leaving (n)	▷ ⁻	departing (a)	▷ ˢ˜
leaving (a)	▷ ˜	departed (a)	▷ ˢ˵

length	A	metre	A¹
lengthen	A′	inch	A²
lengthening (n)	A⁻	foot (measure)	A³
lengthening (a)	A˜	yard (measure)	A⁴
lengthened (a)	A˵	mile	A⁵

Symese — Universal Symbolic Script

shortening (n)	∀ ⁻
shortening (a)	∀ ˇ
shortened (a)	∀ ʺ

bring forward	< ˒	deferring (n)	> ⁼
defer	> ˒	deferred (a)	> ˇ
deferral	> ˢ		

return (n)	⋖	returned (a)	⋖ ʺ	travelling (a)	⋗ ˇ
returning (n)	⋖ ⁻	travel (n)	⋗	traveller	⋗ ᴵ
returning (a)	⋖ ˇ	travelling (n)	⋗ ⁻	journey	⋗ ˢ

rise (n)	△	float (v)	△ ¹
rising (n)	△ ⁻	floating (n)	△ ⁼
rising (a)	△ ˇ	floating (a)	△ ¹ˇ
risen (a)	△ ʺ		

fall / drop (n)	∀	sink (v)	∀ ¹
falling / dropping (n)	∀ ⁻	sinking (n)	∀ ⁼
falling (a)	∀ ˇ	sinking (a)	∀ ¹ˇ
fallen (a)	∀ ʺ		

coming	⊲ ⁻
going	⊳ ⁻

light (v)	△ ˊ	shine	△ ¹
lighting (n)	△ ⁻	shining (n)	△ ⁼
lighted (a)	△ ʺ	shining (a)	△ ¹ˇ
bright	△ ˢ	flash	△ ᵘ
brighten	△ ˒	dull	△ ˣ

darken	▽ ˊ	darkening (a)	▽ ˇ
darkening (n)	▽ ⁻	shadow	▽ ¹

Appendix B — Complete Set of Augmented Syms

unchanged	◁ "	changing (n)	▷ ⁻
unchanging (a)	◁ ˜	changing (a)	▷ ˜
change (v)	▷ ´	changed	▷ "

shape (v)	△ ´
shaping (n)	△ ⁻
shaped	△ "

surface (a)	△ `
superficial	△ ˢ
core (a)	▽ `

focus (v)	◁ ´	disperse	▷ ´
focussing (n)	◁ ⁻	dispersing (n)	▷ ⁻
focussing (a)	◁ ˜	dispersing (a)	▷ ˜
focussed (a)	◁ "	dispersed (a)	▷ "

hilly	△ `	mountainous	△ ⌒
mountain	△ ⌒	chasm	▽ ⌒

peak (a)	⚠ `	moderation	◁	extremism	▷
trough (a)	▽ `	moderator	◁ ᴵ	extremist	▷ ᴵ

sequence (v)	◇ ´	sorted (a)	◇ ˢ
sequencing (n)	◇ ⁻	arrange	⟨⟩ ´
series	◇ ˢ	arranging (n)	⟨⟩ ⁻
sort (v)	◇ ˢ	arranged (a)	⟨⟩ "
sorting (n)	◇ ˢ		

measure	⋎ ´	gauging (n)	⋎ ᴴ		
measuring (n)	⋎ ⁻	gauge (v)	⋎ ᴴ,		
measuring (a)	⋎ ˇ	level (measure)	⋎ ¹		
measured	⋎ ʽʽ	superset	⋊⋉ ⌒		
gauge (n)	⋎ ᴴ	subset	⋊⋉ ⌣		

question / ask	↑ ´	unquestionable (a)	↑ ˣ	pleading (n)	↑ ¹
questionable	↑ `	unquestioning (a)	↑ ˣ	prayer	↑ ²
questioning (n)	↑ ⁻	unquestioned (a)	↑ ˣʽʽ	pray	↑ ²
questioning (a)	↑ ˇ	plea	↑ ¹	praying (n)	↑ ²
questioned	↑ ʽʽ	plead	↑ ¹,		

answer (v)	↾ ´	answered	↾ ʽʽ	
answering (n)	↾ ⁻	answerable	↾ ʽʽʽ	
answering (a)	↾ ˇ			

validate	↓ ´	right (v)	↲ ´	rectification / correction	↲ ˢ
validating (n)	↓ ⁻	righting (n)	↲ ⁻	rectify / correct	↲ ˢ,
validation	↓ ⁼	rightful	↲ ʽʽ	rectifying / correcting (n)	↲ ˢ
validated (a)	↓ ʽʽ			rectified / corrected (a)	↲ ˢʽʽ

invalidate	↧ ´
wrong (v)	↧ ´
wrongful	↧ ʽʽ

precision	↰	imprecision	↉
accuracy	↱	inaccuracy	↉

flip (n)	↕	turn (n)	↔
flipping (n)	↕ ⁻	turning (n)	↔ ⁻
flipped (a)	↕ ʽʽ	turning (a)	↔ ˇ

Appendix B — Complete Set of Augmented Syms

reasoning (n)	♀ ⁻	unreasonable	♀ ˣ
reasonable	♀ ˋ	exception	◊ ⁻
reasoned	♀ ˵	exceptional	◊ ˋ

seeking (n)	∧ ⁻	ability	⟩ ⁻	enabling (a)	⟩ ˢ⁼
find (n)	∧	able	⟩ ˋ	skill	⟩ ¹
finding (n)	∧ ⁻	enable	⟩ ˢ	skilled	⟩ ¹˵
possibility	⟨	enabling (n)	⟩ ˢ⁼	unskilled	⟩ ¹ˣ

impossibility	⟨	disability	⟩ ¹	disable	⟩ ¹
inability	⟩	disabling (n)	⟩ ¹⁼	disabled	⟩ ¹˵

truth	✓	honest	✓ ¹ˋ
truthful	✓ ˋ	dishonesty	✓ ¹ˣ
fact	✓ ˢ	dishonest	✓ ¹ˣ
factual	✓ ˢˋ	good (n)	∨
honesty	✓ ¹	goodness	∨ ⁻

falsehood	✗	mistaken	✗ ˢ˵	pretending (n)	✗ ²
falsify	✗ ˊ	nonsense	✗ ¹	pretentious	✗ ²ˋ
falsifying (n)	✗ ⁻	nonsensical	✗ ¹ˋ	badness	✗
error / mistake	✗ ˢ	pretence	✗ ²	tragedy	✗ ∩
erroneous	✗ ˢˋ	pretend	✗ ²ˊ	tragic	✗ ∩ˋ
mistake (v)	✗ ˢˊ				

expectation	⌒	unexpected	⌒ ˣ˵	related (a)	⌒ ˵
expecting (n)	⌒ ⁻	relationship	⌒	relative (a)	⌒ ˢ
expecting (a)	⌒ ⁻ˋ	relevant	⌒ ˋ	relative (person)	⌒ ˢᴴ
expected	⌒ ˵	relating (n)	⌒ ⁻		

probability / likelihood	⟨
optional	⟨ ˋ

Symese — Universal Symbolic Script

reality	✓	realise	✓ˢ	realised (a)	✓ˢˢ
realisation	✓ˢ	realising (n)	✓⁼ˢ	virtuous	↘`

improbability / unlikelihood	✗	malicious	✗¹	naughtiness	✗ᵘ
viciousness	✗⁻	wickedness	✗²	naughty	✗ᵛᵘ
vicious	✗˜	wicked	✗²ˇ	evil (n)	✗∩
malice	✗¹	iniquity	✗³	evil (a)	✗∩ˇ

research (v)	△´
researching (n)	△⁻
researcher	△ᴵ

certainty	⊲⁻	ascertaining (n)	⊲⁻
ascertain	⊲´	indeed	⊲¹

agreement	⌄	contractual	⌄ᴴ	ethics	⌄ˢ
agreed	⌄``	contractor	⌄ᴴᵢ	ethical	⌄ˢˇ
contract (deal)	⌄ᴴ	morality	⌄	unethical	⌄ˣˢˇ

uncertainty	⊲⁻
immorality	⋋

central	( )`	decentralise	( )ˣ´
centralise	( )´	decentralising (n)	( )ˣ⁻
centralising (n)	( )⁻	decentralisation	( )ˣ⁼
centralisation	( )⁼	decentralised (a)	( )ˣ``
centralised (a)	( )``	middle (a)	⌒`

succeed	⊖´	failure	⊖ˣ	failing (a)	⊖ˣˇ
successful	⊖`	fail	⊖ˣ´	failed (a)	⊖ˣ``
succeeding (n)	⊖⁻	failing (n)	⊖ˣ⁻	harmonious	⌽`

Appendix B — Complete Set of Augmented Syms

achieve	⊖´	achieving (a)	⊖˜
achieving (n)	⊖⁻	achiever	⊖ᴵ

loyal	⋆`
disloyalty	⋆ˣ
disloyal	⋆ˣ

claim (n)	⌒	staking (n)	⌒⁻ˢ
claiming (n)	⌒⁻	stakeholder	⌒ᴵˢ
claimant	⌒ᴵ	reference	⌓
stake (claim)	⌒ˢ	referring (n)	⌓⁻

recap (n)	◡	review (n)	◠
recapping (n)	◡⁻	reviewer	◠ᴵ
referral	◡⁼		

gratitude	ρ
thankful / grateful	ρ`

apology	d ˢ	apologise	d ˢ́	forgiving (n)	d ¹⁻
apologising (n)	d ⁼ˢ	forgiveness	d ¹	forgiving (a)	d ¹˜
apologetic	d ˢ̃	forgive	d ¹́	forgiven (a)	d ¹ˣ

repetition	b ˢ	repetitive	b ˢ̃
repeating (n)	b ⁼ˢ	repeat	b ˢ́
repeating (a)	b ˢ̃	repeated	b ˢˣ

fence	◠¹
fencing	◠¹⁻
fenced	◠¹ˣ

Symese — Universal Symbolic Script

win (n)	⟋⟍	reward (v)	⟋⟍ ᴴ⸱	loss	⟋⟍		
winning (n)	⟋⟍ ⁻	rewarding (n)	⟋⟍ ᴴ⁻	punishment	⟋⟍ ¹		
winning (a)	⟋⟍ ˜	rewarding (a)	⟋⟍ ᴴ˜	punish	⟋⟍ ¹⸱		
reward / prize	⟋⟍ ᴴ						

adaptation	∝	access (n)	⋊⋉
adaptable	∝ `	accessible	⋊⋉ `
adapting (n)	∝ ⁻	accessing (n)	⋊⋉ ⁻
adapted (a)	∝ ˮ	inaccessible	⋊⋉ ˣ

digitise	⟋⟍ ′
digitising (n)	⟋⟍ ⁻
digitised (a)	⟋⟍ ˮ

variance	∽	varied (a)	∽ ˮ
vary	∽ ′	variable (n)	∽ ⁼
varying (n)	∽ ⁻	variable (a)	∽ ˜⁼
varying (a)	∽ ˜	variety	∽ ¹

specify	∾ ′	unspecified	∾ ˣˮ
specifying (n)	∾ ⁻	vague / fuzzy	∾ ˣ¹
specified	∾ ˮ		

service	§	server	§ ᴴ	sharing (n)	⨇ ⁻
serving (n)	§ ⁻	servant	§ ᴵ	sharing (a)	⨇ ˜
serving (a)	§ ˜	share (n)	⨇	shared (a)	⨇ ˮ

practise	∿ ′	practical	∿ `
practising (n)	∿ ⁻	practised (a)	∿ ˮ
practising (a)	∿ ˜	impractical	∿ ˣ

Appendix B — Complete Set of Augmented Syms

plan (v)		planned (a)	
planning (n)		planner	
planning (a)			

value (v)		valuation		currency	
valuing (n)		valuer		cash	
valuable		worth (n)		bank	
valued (a)		worth (v)			

specialisation		specialty	
specialise		specialised (a)	
specialising (n)		specialist	

plain (ordinary)		strange / weird	
unusual / odd		extraordinary	

cleanliness		cleaner		cleansed	
clean (v)		cleanse		cleanser	
cleaning (n)		cleansing (n)		sterile	
cleaning (a)		cleansing (a)			

dirt		dust	
dirtiness		dusty	
		dustiness	

elemental		molecular	
atom		feature (v)	
atomic		featuring (n)	
molecule		featured (a)	

Symese — Universal Symbolic Script

qualification	⋁⋀ ˢ	quantification	⋂ ˢ
qualify	⋁⋀ ˢ′	quantify	⋂ ˢ′
qualifying (n)	⋁⋀ ˢ⁻	quantifying (n)	⋂ ˢ⁻
qualifying (a)	⋁⋀ ˢ˜	quantified (a)	⋂ ˢ˜
qualified (a)	⋁⋀ ˢ″		

importance	Z	seriousness	⅀
critical	Z ᶜ	casual	⅀ ˣ
unimportant	Z ˣ		

bluntness	⋁⋀	sharpen	⋀ ′
blunt (v)	⋁⋀ ′	sharpening (n)	⋀ ⁻
blunting (n)	⋁⋀ ⁻	sharpening (a)	⋀ ˜
sharpness	⋀	sharpened (a)	⋀ ″

methodical	M `	ruling (a)	⋁⋀ ˜
rule (v)	⋁⋀ ′	ruler (person)	⋁⋀ ᴵ
ruling (n)	⋁⋀ ⁻	ruled (person)	⋁⋀ ᴵ̠

check (v)	⅀ ′	prove	⋝ ′
checking (n)	⅀ ⁻	proving (n)	⋝ ⁻
checked (a)	⅀ ″	proven	⋝ ″

northern	↑ `	western	← `
southern	↓ `	eastern	→ `

integrity	⊓ ˢ	integrated (a)	⊓ ˢ″	honoured (a)	⊓ ¹″
integrating (n)	⊓ ˢ⁻	honour (n)	⊓ ¹	dishonour (n)	⊓ ¹ˣ
integrating (a)	⊓ ˢ˜	honour (v)	⊓ ¹′	dishonour (v)	⊓ ¹ˣ′
integration	⊓ ˢ=	honourable	⊓ ¹`	dishonourable	⊓ ¹ˣ`
integral	⊓ ˢ	honouring (n)	⊓ ¹⁻	dishonouring (n)	⊓ ¹ˣ⁻

Appendix B — Complete Set of Augmented Syms

modelling (n)	⊢¯	modelled (a)	⊢˝
modelling (a)	⊢ˋ	model (person)	⊢ᴵ
model (v)	⊢ˊ		

exemplify	⊔ˊ	sample	⊔ᴴ	sample (v)	⊔ᴴˊ
exemplifying (n)	⊔¯	sampling (n)	⊔ᴴ¯	sampled (a)	⊔ᴴ˝
exemplary	⊔ˋ				

code (v)	⊏ˊ	coded	⊏˝
coding (n)	⊏¯	coder	⊏ᴵ
coding (a)	⊏ˋ		

symbolise	⊦ˊ	alphabet	⊦¹
symbolising (n)	⊦¯	icon / logo	⊦²
symbolic	⊦ˋ	mark	⊦³

categorise	⊢ˊ	mix (v)	⊦ˊ
categorising (n)	⊢¯	mixing (n)	⊦¯
		mixed (a)	⊦˝

completeness	⊢	finish (n)	⊢ˢ	finished (a)	⊢ˢ˝
complete (v)	⊢ˊ	finish (v)	⊢ˢˊ	fix / repair (n)	⊢¹
completing (n)	⊢¯	finishing (n)	⊢ˢ¯	fix / repair (v)	⊢¹ˊ
completion	⊢⁼	finishing (a)	⊢ˢˋ	fixing / repairing (n)	⊢¹¯
completed (a)	⊢˝				

design (v)	⋿ˊ	designer	⋿ᴵ
designing (n)	⋿¯	systematic	⊦ˋ
designed	⋿˝		

deliver	⊐ˊ	deliverer	⊐ᴵ
delivering (n)	⊐¯	deliverable	⊐ᴴ
delivered	⊐˝		

Symese — Universal Symbolic Script

prepare	日 ´	preparedness	日 ˝	executive (n)	廿 ᴵ
preparing (n)	日 ¯	execute (task)	廿 ´	executive (a)	廿 ᴵ
prepared	日 ˝	executing (n)	廿 ¯	executor	廿 ᴵ

process (v)	╪ ´	processor	╪ ᴴ		
processing (n)	╪ ¯	processed (a)	╪ ˝		
processing (a)	╪ ˜	unprocessed	╪ ˟		

program (v)	廾 ´	programming (a)	廾 ˜	programmer	廾 ᴵ
programmable	廾 `	programmed (a)	廾 ˝	app	廾 ᴴ
programming (n)	廾 ¯				

balance (v)	🏳 ´	balancing (a)	🏳 ˜	imbalance	🏳 ˟
balancing (n)	🏳 ¯	balanced	🏳 ˝	unbalanced	🏳 ˟

match (n)	〖	fit (n - suit)	〖 ˇ	suitability	〖 ¹
matching (n)	〖 ¯	fit (v - suit)	〖 ´	suitable	〖 ¹
matching (a)	〖 ˜	fitted (a)	〖 ˝	suited (a)	〖 ¹
matched	〖 ˝				

comparison	〗	comparative	〗 ˝		
comparing (n)	〗 ¯	incomparable	〗 ˟		
comparable	〗 `				

collect	🏴 ´	collective	🏴 `	collected (a)	🏴 ˝
collecting (n)	🏴 ¯	collectible	🏴 ᴴ	collector	🏴 ᴵ
collecting (a)	🏴 ˜				

development	〖·	developed (a)	〖· ˝		
developing (n)	〖· ¯	developer	〖· ᴵ		
developing (a)	〖· ˜				

Appendix B — Complete Set of Augmented Syms

sleep (n)	⌑	sleepless	⌑ˣ	dreamer	⌑¹ᴵ
sleeping (n)	⌑⁻	dream (n)	⌑¹	awake	⌑ˣ
sleeping (a)	⌑˜	dream (v)	⌑¹	awakening (n)	⌑ˣ⁻
sleepy	⌑ˋ	dreaming (n)	⌑¹⁻	awakened (a)	⌑ˣ
asleep	⌑				

rest (n)	⌐	rested (a)	⌐
resting (n)	⌐⁻	restless	⌐ˣ
resting (a)	⌐˜		

kneeling (n)	⊓⁻	bowing (n)	⊐⁻
kneeling (a)	⊓˜	bowing (a)	⊐˜
bow (action)	⊓	bowed (a)	⊐

stand (n)	⊐	reach (n)	⊐	reachable	⊐ˋ
standing (n)	⊐⁻	reaching (n)	⊐⁻	unreachable	⊐ˣ
standing (a)	⊐˜				

seat	⊔	seated	⊔	residing (n)	⊓⁻
sitting (n)	⊔⁻	recline / lie down	⊔¹	residential	⊓ˋ
sitting (a)	⊔˜	reclining (n)	⊔¹⁻	resident (n)	⊓ᴵ
seating	⊔ᴴ	reclining (a)	⊔¹˜	resident (a)	⊓ᴵ

shirt	⊓¹	coat	⊓⁴	trousers	⊔¹
blouse	⊓²	jacket	⊓⁵	skirt	⊔²
vest	⊓³	jumper	⊓⁶	shorts	⊔³

underpants	⊐¹	singlet	⊐³
bra	⊐²	dress	⊣¹

Symese — Universal Symbolic Script

hat	⌐¹	shoe	⊤¹	sneaker	⊤³
cap	⌐²	boot	⊤²	sandal	⊤⁴
				sock	⊤⁵

work (n)	⌗	diligent	⌗ˢ	laziness	⌗ˣˢ
working (n)	⌗⁻	idleness	⌗ˣ	lazy	⌗ˣˢ
working (a)	⌗ˢ	idle (a)	⌗ˣ	earning (n)	⌐⁻
worker	⌗ᴵ	idle (v)	⌗ˣ	earned (a)	⌐"
diligence	⌗ˢ				

daily	✕`	week	✕¹	
calendar	✕"	month	✕²	
date (n)	✕ˢ	year	✕³	
date (v)	✕ˢ	decade	✕⁴	
dated (a)	✕"	century	✕⁵	
		millennium	✕⁶	

weekly	✕¹	fortnight	✕¹₊	
monthly	✕²	two months	✕²₊	
yearly / annual	✕³	two years	✕³₊	

January	✕² ₁	May	✕² ₅	September	✕² ₉
February	✕² ₂	June	✕² ₆	October	✕² ₁₀
March	✕² ₃	July	✕² ₇	November	✕² ₁₁
April	✕² ₄	August	✕² ₈	December	✕² ₁₂

nightly	✕`
momentary	⋉`
hourly	⋊`

delay (v)	‖✕´	delaying (a)	‖✕ˢ
delaying (n)	‖✕⁻	delayed (a)	‖✕"

Appendix B — Complete Set of Augmented Syms

time (v)	⌛ ´	timer	⌛ ᴴ
timely	⌛ `	clock	⌛ ᴴ₁
timing (n)	⌛ ¯	watch (device)	⌛ ᴴ₂
timed	⌛ ˵	hourglass	⌛ ᴴ₃
temporal	⌛ ˶		

periodic	⌛ ˇ	historical	|⌛ ¹
history	|⌛ ¹	historic	|⌛ ²

thumb	▽ ¹	ring finger	▽ ⁴
index finger	▽ ²	little finger	▽ ⁵
middle finger	▽ ³		

lounge	目 ¹	bedroom	目 ⁴
kitchen	目 ²	bathroom	目 ⁵
dining room	目 ³	toilet	目 ⁶

continent	⊖ ¹	city / town	⊖ ⁵
region	⊖ ²	suburb / district	⊖ ⁶
country / nation	⊖ ³	village	⊖ ⁷
state (n)	⊖ ⁴	national	⊖ ³̌

ocean	⊖ ¹	river	⊖ ⁵
sea	⊖ ²	stream	⊖ ⁶
lake	⊖ ³	creek	⊖ ⁷
pond	⊖ ⁴	marine	⊖ ²̌

white	⊙	spectrum	⊕
black	⊖	rainbow	⊕ ˵
colour	⊘	colourless	⊗
grey	⊘		

Symese — Universal Symbolic Script

red	②	brown	⑧	light green	|⑤
orange (colour)	③	cyan	㊺	dark green	⑤|
yellow	④	maroon	㊾	light blue	|⑥
green	⑤	pink	|②	dark blue	⑥|
blue	⑥	dark red	②|	violet	⑦|
purple	⑦				

table (v)	π ′	tabulate	π ⸝
tabling (n)	π ⁻	tabulating (n)	π ⸗
tabulation	π ⸜	tabulated (a)	π ⸜⸜

limit (v)	⊥ ′	unlimited	⊥ ˣ⸜
limiting (n)	⊥ ⁻	boundary	⊥ ¹
limiting (a)	⊥ ˇ	border	⊥ ²
limited	⊥ ⸜⸜	shelve	⊣ ′
limitless	⊥ ˣ	shelving (n)	⊣ ⁻

step (v)	╪ ′	stepping (a)	╪ ˇ
stepping (n)	╪ ⁻	stepped (a)	╪ ⸜⸜

bridge (v)	н ′
bridging (n)	н ⁻
bridging (a)	н ˇ

marry	⊻ ′	marital (a)	⊻ ˋ
marrying (n)	⊻ ⁻	married	⊻ ⸜⸜
marrying (a)	⊻ ˇ		

friend	X ᴵ	unfriendly	X ˣ	partner (n)	X ¹ᵢ
befriend	X ′	enemy	X ˣᵢ	partner (v)	X ¹′
befriending (n)	X ⁻	enmity	X ˣ⸗	companionship	X ²
friendly	X ˋ	partnership	X ¹	companion	X ²ᵢ
friendliness	X ⸗				

Appendix B — Complete Set of Augmented Syms

word	sym	word	sym
layer (v)	ヒ ´	folding (n)	ヒ ¹⁻
layered (a)	ヒ ˝	folding (a)	ヒ ¹˜
fold (n)	ヒ ¹	folded	ヒ ¹˝
fold (v)	ヒ ¹´		

word	sym	word	sym
key (a)	ㄦ ´	keying (a)	ㄦ ˜
keying (n)	ㄦ ⁻	keyed (a)	ㄦ ˝

word	sym	word	sym
locked (a)	ㄱ ˝	locker	ㄱ ᴴ
lock (v)	ㄱ ´	unlock (v)	ㄱ ˣ´
locking (n)	ㄱ ⁻	unlocking (n)	ㄱ ˣ⁻
locking (a)	ㄱ ˜	unlocked (a)	ㄱ ˣ˝

word	sym	word	sym
route (v)	ᄃ ´	router	ᄃ ᴴ
routing (n)	ᄃ ⁻	lane	ᄃ ¹
routing (a)	ᄃ ˜	avenue	ᄃ ²

word	sym	word	sym
guidance	ᄃ ˢ	guiding (n)	ᄃ ˢ⁻
guide (v)	ᄃ ˢ´	guiding (a)	ᄃ ˢ˜
guide (object)	ᄃ ˢᴴ	guided (a)	ᄃ ˢ˝
guide (person)	ᄃ ˢᴴ		

word	sym
queue (n)	ユ ¹
queue (v)	ユ ¹´
queueing (n)	ユ ¹⁻

word	sym	word	sym
pierce	ㄴ ´	dig	ㄴ ¹´
piercing (n)	ㄴ ⁻	digging (n)	ㄴ ¹⁻
piercing (a)	ㄴ ˜	digger	ㄴ ¹ᴴ

word	sym	word	sym
tape (v)	ㄷ ´	hammer (v)	ㄷ ´
taping (n)	ㄷ ⁻	hammering (n)	ㄷ ⁻
taped (a)	ㄷ ˝		

piping (n)	ꓩ ⁻	basket	ᒪ ¹
piped (a)	ꓩ ⸌⸌	cage	ᒪ ²
		caged (a)	ᒪ ²⸌⸌

essential	□ ˋ
non-essential	□ ˣ

substantial	⊡ ˋ
substantive	⊡ ⸌⸌
matter (object)	⊡ ᴴ

form (v)	⊙ ˊ	forming (n)	⊙ ⁻
formed	⊙ ⸌⸌	formation	⊙ ⸗

building (n)	⊟ ⁻	establish	⊟ ˢ
building (a)	⊟ ˋ	establishing (n)	⊟ ⁻ˢ
built (a)	⊟ ⸌⸌	establishment	⊟ ⹀ˢ
builder	⊟ ᴵ	established	⊟ ˢ⸌⸌

structuring (n)	⯂ ⁻
structural	⯂ ˋ
structured	⯂ ⸌⸌

frame (v)	目 ˊ
framing (n)	目 ⁻
doorway	目| ⁻

homely	⟨⊟ ˋ	hut / cabin	⊟⟩ ᵛ
housing (n)	⊟⟩ ⁻	villa	⊟⟩ ¹
housing (a)	⊟⟩ ˋ	townouse	⊟⟩ ²
mansion	⊟⟩ ^	apartment	⊟⟩ ³

Appendix B — Complete Set of Augmented Syms

founding (n)	🗍⁻	founded (a)	🗍ˋˋ
founding (a)	🗍ˇ	founder	🗍ᴴ

book collection	▱ ⁰⁰
library	▱ ᵁ

cardboard	▱ ¹	cataloging (n)	▱ ⁻
catalog (v)	▱ ′	cataloged (a)	▱ ˋˋ

page	▱ ¹

pillow	▱ ¹
blanket	▱ ²
quilt	▱ ³

flow (v)	▱ ′	wave (n)	▱ ᴴ
flowing (n)	▱ ⁻	wave (v)	▱ ᴴ′
flowing (a)	▱ ˇ	wavy (a)	▱ ᴴˇ
		waving (n)	▱ ᴴ⁻

cloth	▱ ¹
towel	▱ ²

traffic	▱ ⁰⁰
garage	▱ ⱽ
bus depot	▱ ⱽ

jetplane	▱ ¹	ferry	▱ ¹	port / harbour	▱ ⁰
rocket / missile	▱ ²	marina	▱ ⱽ	truck depot	▱ ⱽ
airport	▱ ⱽ	ship	▱ ^	train station	▱ ⱽ

operation	⌷		operated (a)	⌷ ⸜
operational	⌷ ˋ		operator	⌷ ᴵ
operating (n)	⌷ ˉ		maintenance	⌺
operating (a)	⌷ ˜		maintaining (n)	⌺ ˉ

network (v)	⊞ ˊ		networking (a)	⊞ ˜
networking (n)	⊞ ˉ		networked	⊞ ⸜

industrial	⊠ ˋ		industrialisation	⊠ ⁼
industrialise	⊠ ˊ		industrialised (a)	⊠ ⸜
industrialising (n)	⊠ ˉ		industrialist	⊠ ᴵ
industrialising (a)	⊠ ˜			

catch (n)	·Y ˊ		throw (n)	Y·
catcher	·Y ᴵ		throwing (n)	Y· ˉ
catching (n)	·Y ˉ			

hold (n)	·Y·		holding (n)	·Y· ˉ
holder (object)	·Y· ᴴ		carrying (n)	¥ ˉ
holder (person)	·Y· ᴵ			

walk (n)	火	crawling / creeping (n)	火 ¹	rush / hurry (n)	火 ⌒
walking (n)	火 ˉ	run (n)	火 ·	rush / hurry (v)	火 ⌒·
walking (a)	火 ˜	running (n)	火 ˉ	rushing / hurrying (n)	火 ⌒⁼
walker	火 ᴵ	running (a)	火 ˜	rushed / hurried (a)	火 ⌒⸜
crawl / creep	火 ¹·	runner	火 ᴵ		

jump (n)	火	hop (v)	火 ¹·	dancing (n)	火 ²
jumping (n)	火 ˉ	hopping (n)	火 ¹	dancing (a)	火 ²˜
jumping (a)	火 ˜	dance (n)	火 ²	dancer	火 ²ᴵ
hop (n)	火 ¹	dance (v)	火 ²·	kicking (n)	大 ˉ

Appendix B — Complete Set of Augmented Syms

support (n)	≺	supported	≺"	helping (a)	≻˜
supporting (n)	≺⁻	supporter	≺ᴵ	helpful	≻ˋ
supporting (a)	≺˜	help / aid (n)	≻	helper	≻ᴵ
supportive	≺ˋ	helping / aiding (n)	≻⁻	unhelpful	≻ˣ

training (n)	◁⁻	trainer	◁ᴵ
training (a)	◁˜	trainee	◁ᴵ̳
trained	◁"	training course	◁ˢ

play (n)	▷	playground	▷ᵛ	sporting (a)	▷-¹˜
playing (n)	▷⁻	game	▷ˢ	sports person	▷-¹ᴵ
playing (a)	▷˜	sport(s)	▷-¹	court / arena / field	▷-ᵛ
player	▷ᴵ	sporting (n)	▷-¹⁻		

traditional	≼ˋ	trending (n)	≽⁻
trendy	≽ˋ	trending (a)	≽˜

orderly	≼ˋ	tidy (v)	≼ˢ˒	make a mess	≼ˣ˒
neatness / tidiness	≼ˢ	disorder / mess	≼ˣ	chaotic	≽ˋ
neat / tidy	≼ˢ˜	disorderly / messy	≼ˣ˜		

flight	人	glide (n)	人¹
flying (n)	人⁻	glide (v)	人¹˒
flying (a)	人˜	gliding (n)	人¹⁻
flyer	人ᴵ	gliding (a)	人¹˜

swim (n)	Ψ	drown	Ψˣ˒
swimming (n)	Ψ⁻	drowning (n)	Ψˣ⁻
swimming (a)	Ψ˜	drowning (a)	Ψˣ˜
swimmer	Ψᴵ		

instrument	⇧ ˇ	kitchen knife	⇦¹	spoon	⇨¹
equipment	⇩ ʺ	ladle	⇦²	fork	⇨²
				chopsticks	⇨³

draw	⇧ ′	painting	⇧¹
drawing (n)	⇧ ‾	paint (n)	⇧¹₌
drawing (a)	⇧ ˜	paint (v)	⇧¹,
drawn (a)	⇧ ʺ	painted (a)	⇧¹ ʺ
drawer (person)	⇧ ᴵ	painter	⇧¹ᴵ

write	⇩ ′	written	⇩ ʺ
writing (n)	⇩ ‾	writer	⇩ ᴵ
writing (a)	⇩ ˜		

print (n)	⇩¹	printed (a)	⇩¹ʺ	authorised (a)	⇩²ʺ
print (v)	⇩¹,	authority	⇩²	author	⇩²ᴵ
printing (n)	⇩¹‾	authorise	⇩²,	mandate	⇩³
printing (a)	⇩¹˜	authorising (n)	⇩²‾	mandatory	⇩³˜

insertion	⇤	removal	⇥	erasure	⇥¹
inserting (n)	⇤ ‾	removing (n)	⇥ ‾	erase	⇥¹,
				erasing (n)	⇥¹‾

machinery	⇧ ʺ
mechanical	⇦ `
mechanic	⇦ ᴵ

see / look	○ ′	visible	○ ʺ	blind (a)	○ˣ
seeing / looking (n)	○ ‾	visibility	○ ″	blind (v)	○ˣ,
seeing (a)	○ ˜	invisible	○ˣ‾	blinding (n)	○ˣ‾
visual	○ `	unseen (a)	○ˣʺ	blinding (a)	○ˣ˜

Appendix B — Complete Set of Augmented Syms

notice (n)	⌒¹	appreciate	⌒²′
notice (v)	⌒¹′	appreciating (n)	⌒²⁻
noticing (n)	⌒¹⁻	appreciative	⌒²ˇ
appreciation	⌒²	unappreciative	⌒²ˣ

picturesque	⊙ˋ	camera	⊙¹ₕ
photograph	⊙¹	diagram	⊙²

view (n)	⊖	viewing (a)	⊖˜
viewing (n)	⊖⁻	viewer	⊖ᴵ

read (n)	⊕	reading (a)	⊕˜
reading (n)	⊕⁻	reader	⊕ᴵ

appearance	⊘	disappearance	⊘ˣ
appearing (n)	⊘⁻	disappear	⊘ˣ′
apparition	⊘⁼	disappearing (n)	⊘ˣ⁻
apparent	⊘ˋ	disappearing (a)	⊘ˣˇ

imaging (n)	⊘⁻	reflecting (n)	⊘⁻	mirror	⊘ᴴ₁
imaging (a)	⊘˜	reflective	⊘ˋ	mirroring (n)	⊘ᴴ₁
reflect	⊘′	reflector	⊘ᴴ	mirrored	⊘ᴴ₁

hear	◯′	listener	◯ˢᴵ	deaf	◯ˣ
listen	◯ˢ	aural	◯ˋ	deafen	◯ˣ′
listening (n)	◯ˢ⁻	audio	◯ˋˋ	deafening (a)	◯ˣˇ
listening (a)	◯ˢˇ	audience	◯ᴵ		

recording (n)	⊙⁻	recorded	⊙ˋˋ
recording (a)	⊙˜	recording studio	⊙ᵛ
recorder	⊙ᴴ		

phone (v)	θ ´		phoning (n)	θ ⁻
phone (a)	θ `		noisy	∅ `

silent	⊙ `

worldly / earthly	⊖ `		ecology	⊕ ˢ
environmental	⊕ `		ecological	⊕ ˢ

communal	⊘ `
team (a)	⊘ `
crew	⊘ ¹

planetary	⊖ `

business (a)	⊘ `
company (a)	⊘ `

natural	⊕ `		unnatural	⊕ ˣ
raw (natural)	⊕ ¹		artificial	⊕ ˣ
naked / nude	⊕ ²			

seasonal	⊕ `

social	⊗ `
societal	⊗ ``

govern	⊠ ´		governor	⊠ ᴵ
governing (n)	⊠ ⁻		governance	⊠ ˢ
governing (a)	⊠ `			

Appendix B — Complete Set of Augmented Syms

fiery	⊖	burning (a)	⊖	spark	⊖
burn (n)	⊖	burnt (a)	⊖	sparking (n)	⊖
burn (v)	⊖	flame	⊖	sparked	⊖
burning (n)	⊖	furnace	⊖		

smoke (n)	⊖¹	smoking (n)	⊖¹
smoke (v)	⊖¹	smoking (a)	⊖¹
smoky	⊖¹	ash	⊖²

watery	⊖	wetting (n)	⊖	dry	⊖ˣ
water (v)	⊖	wetting (a)	⊖	drying (n)	⊖ˣ
watering (n)	⊖	flood	⊖	drying (a)	⊖ˣ
watering (a)	⊖	damp (a)	⊖	dryer	⊖ˣ
wet (a)	⊖	dampen	⊖	dried (a)	⊖ˣ
wet (v)	⊖	dampening (n)	⊖	desert	⊖ˣ

ice	⊖¹	steamy	⊖²	boiling (n)	⊖³
icy	⊖¹	steaming (n)	⊖²	boiling (a)	⊖³
iced	⊖¹	steaming (a)	⊖²	boiled (a)	⊖³
steam	⊖²	steamed (a)	⊖²	boil (v)	⊖³

airy	⊘	gale	⊘
airing (n)	⊘	breeze	⊘
atmosphere	⊘¹	breezy	⊘
atmospheric	⊘¹	blow (v)	⊘
windy	⊘	blowing (n)	⊘¹

wooden	⊖	rock	⊘
metallic	⊖	pebble	⊘

Symese — Universal Symbolic Script

privacy	⊕	privatised (a)	⊕ `
privatisation	⊕ ¹	publicity	⊙ ¹
privatise	⊕ ?	publicise	⊙ ?
privatising (n)	⊕ ⁻	publicising (n)	⊙ ⁻
privatising (a)	⊕ `	publicised (a)	⊙ `

office (a)	⊘ `	administer	⊘ ´	administerial	⊘ "
official (a)	⊘ ¹	administered	⊘ "	administrator	⊘ ᴵ
official (person)	⊘ ᴵ	administering (n)	⊘ ⁻	political	⊘ `
unofficial	⊘ ˣ	administrative	⊘ `	politician	⊘ ᴵ

climatic	☺	weathered	☺ "
weather (v)	☺ ´	gaseous	⊕ `
weathering (n)	☺ ⁻		

oil (v)	⊙ ´	wax (n)	⊙ ¹	sandy	⊙ `
oiling (n)	⊙ ⁻	wax (v)	⊙ ?	mud	⊙ ¹
oily	⊙ `	waxy	⊙ `	muddy	⊙ `
oiled (a)	⊙ "	waxed (a)	⊙ `	clay	⊙ ²
				glassy	⊗ `

solar	☼ `	lunar	☾ `
sunlight	☼ ˢ	moonlight	☾ ˢ
sunny	☼ `		

cloud (v)	☁ ´	clouding (n)	☁ ⁻
cloudy	☁ `	misty / foggy	⊙ `

rain (v)	☂ ´	snow (v)	☂ ?	frosty	☂ ²
rainy	☂ `	snowy	☂ `	frosted (a)	☂ ²
raining (n)	☂ ⁻	snowing (n)	☂ ⁻	storm	☂ ⌒
snow (n)	☂ ¹	frost	☂ ²	stormy	☂ ⌒

Appendix B — Complete Set of Augmented Syms

head (v)	♀´	face (v)	♀|
head (a)	♀`	facing (n)	♀|⁻
heading (n)	♀⁻	facing (a)	♀|˷
head (person)	♀ᴵ	face (person)	♀|ᴵ

balloon	○⁻¹

mind (n)	☉ᔍ	mindful	☉ᔍ
mind (v)	☉ᔍ	minder	☉ᴵ
minding (n)	☉ᔍ		

link (v)	⊙⊙´	chain	⊙⊙ᴴ
linking (n)	⊙⊙⁻	chained	⊙⊙ᴴ˷
linked (a)	⊙⊙˷		

join (v)	ϴ´	attach	ϴ¹	split (v)	ϴˣ
joining (n)	ϴ⁻	attaching (n)	ϴ¹	splitting (n)	ϴˣ
joining (a)	ϴ˷	attached (a)	ϴ¹˷	splitting (a)	ϴˣ˷
jointed (a)	ϴ˷	split (n)	ϴˣ	split (a)	ϴˣ˷

bond (v)	⊚´	bind (v)	⊚ᔍ
bonding (n)	⊚⁻	binding (n)	⊚ᔍ
bonding (a)	⊚˷	binding (a)	⊚ᔍ
bonded (a)	⊚˷	bound (a)	⊚ᔍ˷
bondage	⊚¹	hinge (v)	⊛´

aim (v)	⊙´	miss (n)	⊙ˣ	missing (a)	⊙ˣ
aiming (n)	⊙⁻	miss (v)	⊙ˣ	missed (a)	⊙ˣ˷
target / goal	⊙ᴴ	missing (n)	⊙ˣ		

Symese — Universal Symbolic Script

hit (n)	◉ ¹	beat (v)	◉ ²	crash (n)	◉ ³
hit (v)	◉ ¹́	beating (n)	◉ ²́	crash (v)	◉ ³́
hitting (n)	◉ ¹̄	beating (a)	◉ ²̄	crashing (n)	◉ ³̄
hit (a)	◉ ¹̌	beaten (a)	◉ ²̌	crashing (a)	◉ ³̌

spiral (a)	◎ `	coil (n)	◎ ᴴ
spiral (v)	◎ ´	coil (v)	◎ ᴴ́
spiralling (n)	◎ ¯	coiling (n)	◎ ᴴ̄
spiralling (a)	◎ ̌	coiled (a)	◎ ᴴ̌

cycle (v)	⊖⊖ ´	cyclist	⊖⊖ ᴵ
cycling (n)	⊖⊖ ¯	motorcycle	⊖⊖ ¹
cycling (a)	⊖⊖ ̌	motorcyclist	⊖⊖ ¹ᴵ

spectacles	⌒⌒ ¹	microscopic	⌒⌒ ³̌
bespectacled	⌒⌒ ¹̌	roll (v)	⌒⌒ ´
telescope	⌒⌒ ²	rolling (n)	⌒⌒ ¯
telescopic	⌒⌒ ²̌	rolling (a)	⌒⌒ ̌
microscope	⌒⌒ ³	rolled (a)	⌒⌒ ̀̀

forest	♀ ″	branch (v)	♀ ´
jungle	♀ ″∩	branching (n)	♀ ¯
grove	♀ ″∪		

fruity	♀ `	fruit orchard	♀ ˇ
fruiting (n)	♀ ¯	nursery	♀ ˇ
fruiting (a)	♀ ̌		

vegetarian (person)	♀ ᴵ	mushroom	♀ ¹
vegetarian (a)	♀ ᴵ̌	lawn	♀ ˇ

garden / park	♀ ˇ	gardening (a)	♀ ˇ̌
gardening (n)	♀ ˇ̄	gardener	♀ ˇᴵ

Appendix B — Complete Set of Augmented Syms

| fleshy | 8ˋ | bloody | ∞ˋ |
| meat | 8ᵛ | | |

fatty	8ˋ
lean (a)	8ˣ
muscular	8ˋ

| bony | 8ˋ |

sense (v)	⌃ˊ	sensor	⌃ᴴ	insensitive	⌃ˣ
sensitive	⌃ˋ	sensuous	⌃ʷ	senseless	⌃ˣˣ
sensing (n)	⌃⁻	sensible	⌃¹	instinctive	♡ˋ
sensing (a)	⌃˜	sensibility	⌃¹	intuition	♡ᵛ

skinny	⌃ˋ	click (n)	♡¹
touch (v)	♡ˊ	click (v)	♡¹
touching (n)	♡⁻	clicking (n)	♡¹
touching (a)	♡˜	nerve	♡ᴴ

| consciousness | ⊛ | unconscious | ⊛ˣ |
| unconsciousness | ⊛ˣ | subconscious (n) | ♡ |

spiritual	ⵀˋ
soul	ⵀ¹
ghost	ⵀ²

live (v)	ⵀˊ	living (a)	ⵀ˜	lively	ⵀᵛ
alive	ⵀˋ	lived (a)	ⵀˋˋ	lifetime	ⵀ^
living (n)	ⵀ⁻	liveliness	ⵀᵛ	living (person)	ⵀᴵ

Symese — Universal Symbolic Script

die (v)	⊙ ´	dead	⊙ `	deadly	⊙ ˇ
dying (n)	⊙ ¯	dying (person)	⊙ ᴵ	deadening (n)	⊙ ˇ
dying (a)	⊙ ˇ	deaden	⊙ ˊ	deadened (a)	⊙ ˇ

sex (act)	☿ ¯	copulate	☿ ´		
sexual	☿ `	sexuality	☿ =		

desire (v)	·☿ ´	desired (a)	·☿ ˝		
desiring (n)	·☿ ¯	undesirable	·☿ ˟		
desirable	·☿ `	pleasurable	☿· `		

hate (v)	·⊙ ´	hater	·⊙ ᴵ	disgust	·⊙ ²
hateful	·⊙ `	despise (n)	·⊙ ¹	disgusting (a)	·⊙ ²
hating (n)	·⊙ ¯	despise (v)	·⊙ ¹	disgusted (a)	·⊙ ²
hated (a)	·⊙ ˝	despicable (a)	·⊙ ¹		

angry	⊙· `	fury / wrath	⊙· ⌒		
fierce	⊙· ¹	furious	⊙· ⌒		

healthy	☿ `	unhealthy	☿ ˟	medicine (object)	☿ ¹
healing (n)	☿ ˇ	pharmacy	☿ ᵛ₁	medical	☿ `
healing (a)	☿ ˇ	clinic	☿ ᵛ₂	medical professional	☿ ¹
heal	☿ ˊ	hospital	☿ ᵛ₃		

fear (v)	⋈ ´	fright / scare (n)	⋈ ˇ	terror	⋈ ⌒
fearful / afraid	⋈ `	frighten / scare	⋈ ˊ	terrify	⋈ ⌒
fearing (n)	⋈ ¯	scary	⋈ ˇ	terrifying (n)	⋈ ⌒
feared (a)	⋈ ˝	frightening	⋈ ˇ	terrifying (a)	⋈ ⌒
fearlessness	⋈ ˟	frightened / scared	⋈ ˝	terrified (a)	⋈ ⌒
fearless	⋈ ˟				

Appendix B — Complete Set of Augmented Syms

dread (n)		dreadful	
dread (v)		dreaded	
dreading (n)			

courageous / brave		encouragement		discouraging (n)	
encourage		fortitude		discouraging (a)	
encouraging (n)		discouragement		discouraged (a)	
encouraging (a)		discourage			

inspire		inspiring (a)		aspirational	
inspirational		inspired (a)		aspiring (n)	
inspiring (n)		aspire		aspiring (a)	

distress (v)		distressing (a)	
distressing (n)		distressed (a)	

painful		hurt / injured (a)	
painfulness		wound (n)	
hurt / injury		wound (v)	
hurt / injure (v)		wounding (n)	
hurting / injuring (n)		wounded (a)	

bacteria		virus		virulent	
bacterial		viral		ill / sick	

farm		farmer		agricultural	
farming (n)		agriculture		crop	
farming (a)					

sameness		copied (a)		analogy	
copy (n)		literal		analogous	
copy (v)		liken		metaphor	
copying (n)		likening (n)		metaphorical	

165

difference	⨰	differentiation	⨰¹		
differ (v)	⨰′	differentiating (n)	⨰⁻¹		
differing (n)	⨰⁻	differentiated (a)	⨰˵		
differing (a)	⨰˵				

complexity	≡
simplicity	≡

togetherness	‖	uniting (n)	‖⁻	disunity	‖ˣ
unity	‖″	uniting (a)	‖˵	disunited	‖ˣ
unite	‖′	united	‖˵		

gather / assemble	‖′	bundle (n)	‖²	bundling (n)	‖²
gathering / assembly	‖⁻	bundle (v)	‖²	bundled (a)	‖²

solitude	‖¹	loneliness	‖²
solitary / alone	‖˵	lonely	‖²

ascent	△¹	climb (n)	△²	climber	△²ᵢ
ascend	△′	climb (v)	△²	descent	▽¹
ascending (n)	△⁻	climbing (n)	△²	descend	▽′
ascendant (a)	△˵	climbing (a)	△˵	descending (n)	▽⁻

force (v)	⋀′	energetic	⋁`	energised (a)	⋁″
forcing (n)	⋀⁻	energise	⋁′	electricity	⋁¹
forceful	⋀`	energising (n)	⋁⁻	electric	⋁¹
forced (a)	⋀˵	energising (a)	⋁˵	electrical	⋁˵

potential (a)	≲`	powered	≳″	empowered (a)	≳ˢ
power (v)	≳′	empower	≳ˢ	powerless	≳ˣ
powerful	≳`	empowering (n)	≳ˢ	unpowered (a)	≳ˣ
powering (n)	≳⁻	empowering (a)	≳ˢ		

Appendix B — Complete Set of Augmented Syms

just / fair	⊨`	judge (v)	⊨⁵	unlawful	⊭ˣ⁵
unjust / unfair	⊨ˣ	judging (n)	⊨⁵⁻	lawless	⊭ˣ
judgement	⊨⁵	lawful	⊭⁵	criminal (n)	⊭ˣ⁼
judge (person)	⊨⁵⁼	lawfulness	⊭⁵⁻	criminal (a)	⊭ˣ⁼ˣ

justification	⊨¹	justified	⊨¹`
justify	⊨¹ʼ	unjustified	⊨¹ˣ`
justifying (n)	⊨¹⁻		

mean (v)	Σ´	meaningless	Σˣ`
meaningful	Σ`	accident	ℝˣ
meant (a)	Σ"	accidental	ℝˣ`

discernment	Σ̄	consideration	ℤ̄	assessment / evaluation	ℤ̄¹
discerning (n)	Σ̄⁻	considering (n)	ℤ̄⁻	assess / evaluate	ℤ̄¹ʼ
discerning (a)	Σ̄ˉ	considered (a)	ℤ̄"	assessing / evaluating (n)	ℤ̄¹⁻

permit / allow	⋈´	permit (n)	⋈ᴴ	permissive (a)	⋈¹`
permitting / allowing (n)	⋈⁻	permissiveness	⋈¹	forbidden	⋈ˣ"
permitted / allowed (a)	⋈"				

decide	X´	deciding (n)	X⁻	indecision	Xˣ⁻
decisive	X`	deciding (a)	Xˉ	indecisive	Xˣ`
decisiveness	X⁻	decided	X"	indecisiveness	Xˣ⁻
		decider	X⁼	undecided	Xˣ"

pure	⋈`	purified	⋈"
purify	⋈´	purifier	⋈ᴴ
purifying (n)	⋈⁻	impurity	⋈ˣ
purifying (a)	⋈ˉ	impure	⋈ˣ`

beautiful	⋈`	ugliness	⋈ˣ	decorating (n)	⋈¹⁻
beautify	⋈´	ugly	⋈ˣ̧	decorated	⋈¹‟
beautifying (n)	⋈⁻	decoration	⋈¹	adornment	⋈²
beautified (a)	⋈‟	decorate	⋈¹´	adorn	⋈²´

principled	⟫‟		
principal	⟫ᴵ		
theoretical	⟪`		

problematic	⟨⟩`	solved (a)	⟨⟩‟
solve	⟨⟩´	solver	⟨⟩ᴵ
solving (n)	⟨⟩⁻		

cooperation	⋈	competitive	⋈`
cooperative	⋈`	competing (n)	⋈⁻
cooperating (n)	⋈⁻	competing (a)	⋈˜
competition	⋈	competitor	⋈ᴵ

cut (v)	⋈´	chopper	⋈¹
cutting (n)	⋈⁻	sword	⋈²
cutting (a)	⋈˜	axe	⋈³
knife	⋈¹		

fight (v)	⋈´	fighter	⋈ᴵ
fighting (n)	⋈⁻	battle	⋈"
fighting (a)	⋈˜	battlefield	⋈"ᵥ

defend	⋈´	defender	⋈ᴵ	guarding (n)	⋈¹⁻
defensive	⋈`	guard (n)	⋈¹	guarded (a)	⋈¹‟
defending (n)	⋈⁻	guard (v)	⋈¹´	guardian	⋈¹ᴵ
defended (a)	⋈‟				

Appendix B — Complete Set of Augmented Syms

attack (v)	⚔︎ ′
attacking (n)	⚔︎ ⁻

attacking (a)	⚔︎ ˜
attacker	⚔︎ ᴵ

peaceful	⚔︎ `
warring	⚔︎ ˜

purchase (n)	△ ⁻
purchasing (n)	△ ⁻
purchasing (a)	△ ˜
purchased (a)	△ ″
purchaser	△ ᴵ

sale	△
selling (n)	△ ⁻
selling (a)	△ ˜
sold (a)	△ ″
seller	△ ᴵ

cost (v)	◁ ′
costing (n)	◁ ⁻
price (v)	▷ ′
pricing (n)	▷ ⁻
priceless	▷ ˣ

transact	▷ ′
transacting (n)	▷ ⁻
transacting (a)	▷ ˜
transacted (a)	▷ ″

shop (v)	△△ ′	shopping mall	△△ ″	traded (a)	▽▽ ″
shopping (n)	△△ ⁻	trade (v)	▽▽ ′	trader	▽▽ ᴵ
shopping (a)	△△ ˜	trading (n)	▽▽ ⁻	customer	▽▽ ᴵ
shopper	△△ ᴵ	trading (a)	▽▽ ˜		

economical	◁ `
economise	◁ ′
economising (n)	◁ ⁻

market (v)	▷ ′
marketing (n)	▷ ⁻
marketing (a)	▷ ˜

funnel (v)	∧ ′
funnelling (n)	∧ ⁻

filter (v)	∨ ′
filtering (n)	∨ ⁻
filtered (a)	∨ ″

diverge	⋞′	converge	⋟′	
divergent	⋞`	convergent	⋟`	
diverging (n)	⋞⁻	converging (n)	⋟⁻	
diverging (a)	⋞˜	converging (a)	⋟˜	

matter (v)	∧′	detailing (n)	∨⁻
detail (v)	∨′	detailed	∨"

visit (v)	<′	visitor	<ᴵ	escaping (a)	>˜
visiting (n)	<⁻	escape (v)	>′	escaped (a)	>"
visiting (a)	<˜	escaping (n)	>⁻	escapee	>ᴵ

security	⩚	securing (n)	⩚⁻	insecurity	⩛
secure (v)	⩚′	secured	⩚"	unsecured	⩛"

growth	⌂	grower	⌂ᴵ	barren	⌂ˣ
growing (n)	⌂⁻	fertility	⌂¹	stunted	⌂ˣˣ
growing (a)	⌂˜	fertile	⌂¹	reversion	⌄
grown (a)	⌂"	barrenness	⌂ˣ	reverting (n)	⌄⁻

regression	⊂	progress (n)	⊃
regressive	⊂`	progressive	⊃`
regressing (n)	⊂⁻	progressing (n)	⊃⁻
		progression	⊃⁼

advantageous	⊓`
disadvantageous	⊔`

continuation	Σ	discontinuation	⊂
continuing (n)	Σ⁻	discontinuing (n)	⊂⁻
continuing (a)	Σ˜		

Appendix B — Complete Set of Augmented Syms

perceptive	◇`	perceiving (n)	◇⁻
perceptiveness	◇⁼	perceived (a)	◇"
perceive	◇′		

impress	⬦′	impressing (n)	⬦⁻
impressive	⬦`	impressed (a)	⬦"

cognitive	⊚`	recognising (n)	⊚⁼ˢ
recognition	⊚ˢ	recognised (a)	⊚"ˢ
recognise	⊚′ˢ		

feel (n)	⇔	emotional	⇔`
feeling / emotion (n)	⇔⁻	felt (a)	⇔"

thought	◇	thoughtfulness	◇ˢ	thoughtlessness	◇ˢₓ
thinking (n)	◇⁻	thoughtful	◇ˢ	thoughtless	◇ˢₓ
thinking (a)	◇⁼	thinker	◇ᴵ	unthinking (a)	◇ˣ⁼

trust (v)	⬦′	trustworthiness	⬦⁼	faithful (person)	⬦ˢᴵ
trusting (n)	⬦⁻	trusted (a)	⬦"	faithfulness	⬦ˢ⁼
trusting (a)	⬦⁼	faith	⬦ˢ	unfaithful	⬦ˢₓ
trustworthy	⬦`	faithful (a)	⬦ˢ`	unfaithfulness	⬦ˢₓ⁼

believe	◇′	disbelieve	◇ˣ′	credible	◇ˢ`
believing (n)	◇⁻	unbelievable	◇ˣ`	incredibility	◇ˢₓ
believer	◇ᴵ	unbeliever	◇ˣᴵ	incredible	◇ˢₓ`
disbelief	◇ˣ	credibility	◇ˢ		

understanding (n)	◇	misunderstanding	◇ˣ	imaginary	◇
understanding (a)	◇	misunderstand	◇	imagining (n)	◇
understandable	◇	misunderstood	◇ˣ	imagined	◇
understood (a)	◇	imagination	◇	imaginative	◇

empathise	◇	confusion	◇ˣ	confusing (a)	◇ˣ
empathic	◇	confuse	◇	confused	◇ˣ
empathising (n)	◇	confusing (n)	◇ˣ		

| analyse | ◈ | analytical | ◈ |
| analysing (n) | ◈ | analyst | ◈ |

| experiencing (n) | ◇ |
| experienced (a) | ◇ |

know	◈	expertise	◈
knowing (n)	◈	expert	◈
knowing (a)	◈	unknown (n)	◈ˣ
knowledgeable	◈	unknown (a)	◈ˣ
known (a)	◈	unknowing (a)	◈ˣ

advise	◇	advised (a)	◇
advisable	◇	advisor	◇
advising (n)	◇	advisory	◇

doubt (v)	◇	doubting (a)	◇
doubtful	◇	undoubted (a)	◇ˣ
doubting (n)	◇		

guess (v)	◇	hint (n)	◇¹
guessing (n)	◇	hint (v)	◇¹
guessing (a)	◇		

Appendix B — Complete Set of Augmented Syms

wonder (v)	⟡ ´
wonderful	⟡ `
wondering (n)	⟡ ⁻

consultation	⟡	consulting (a)	⟡ ˇ
consulting (n)	⟡ ⁻	consultant	⟡ ᴵ

mysterious / enigmatic	⟡ `	puzzled (a)	⟡ ¹˽
puzzle	⟡ ¹	riddle	⟡ ²
puzzling (n)	⟡ ¹⁻	myth	⟡ ³
puzzling (a)	⟡ ¹ˇ	mythical	⟡ ³ˇ

resourceful	⟐ `	hoping (n)	⟐ ⁻
resourcing (n)	⟐ ⁻	hopeful	⟐ `
resourcing (a)	⟐ ˇ	hopefulness	⟐ ᐟ
resourcefulness	⟐ ᐟ	hopeless	⟐ ˣ
hope (v)	⟐ ´	hopelessness	⟐ ˣᐟ

assumption	⟐	unassuming (a)	⟐ ˣˇ
assuming (n)	⟐ ⁻	deduction	⟐
assumed (a)	⟐ ˵	deducing (n)	⟐ ⁻

proud (a)	⟐̄ `	arrogant (person)	⟐̄ ⌒ᴵ	humiliate	⟐̲ ¹
proud (person)	⟐̄ ᴵ	humble (a)	⟐̲ `	humiliating (n)	⟐̲ ¹⁻
arrogance	⟐̄ ⌒	humble (person)	⟐̲ ᴵ	humiliating (a)	⟐̲ ¹ˇ
arrogant (a)	⟐̄ ⌒ˇ	humiliation	⟐̲ ¹	humiliated	⟐̲ ¹˽

diffidence	⟨⟩	confiding (n)	⟩∣ ¹⁻
confidence	⟩∣	confidential	⟩∣ ¹ˇ
confide	⟩∣ ¹		

Symese — Universal Symbolic Script

memory	⌀	reminder	⌀¹	forgetting (n)	⌀ ⁻
remembering (n)	⌀ ⁻	remind	⌀ ¹	forgetfulness	⌀ ⁻
memento	⌀ ᴴ	reminding (n)	⌀ ¹	forgotten (a)	⌀ ˵

learning (n)	⟨⌀ ⁻	school	⟨⌀ ᵛ	studious	⟨⌀ ˬ
learning (a)	⟨⌀ ˬ	study (n)	⟨⌀ ˬ	studied (a)	⟨⌀ ˬ
learned	⟨⌀ ˵	study (v)	⟨⌀ ˬ	student	⟨⌀ ˬᵢ
learner	⟨⌀ ᴵ	studying (n)	⟨⌀ ˬ		

teaching (n)	⌀⏐⁻	teacher	⌀⏐ᴵ
teaching (a)	⌀⏐ˬ	teachable	⌀⏐`
taught	⌀⏐˵	unteachable	⌀⏐ˣ

wisdom	⊕	foolishness	⊕ ˣ
prudence	⊕ ¹	fooling (n)	⊕ ˣ
prudent	⊕ ¹	foolish	⊕ ˣ
imprudent	⊕ ¹ˣ		

cleverness	⊗	intellect	⊗ ᴴ
brilliance	⊗ ⌒	intellectual (a)	⊗ ᴴ
brilliant	⊗ ⌒	intellectual (person)	⊗ ᴴᵢ
intelligence	⊗ ˬ	stupidity	⊗ ˣ
intelligent	⊗ ˬ	stupid	⊗ ˣ

smell (v)	▱ ´	smelling (a)	▱ ˬ
smelly	▱ `	odourless	▱ ˣ
smelling (n)	▱ ⁻		

taste (v)	▱ ´	tastefulness	▱ ¹	flavoured (a)	▱ ²
tasty / delicious	▱ `	tasteful	▱ ¹	tasteless / insipid	▱ ˣ
tasting (n)	▱ ⁻	flavour	▱ ²	yucky	▱ ˣ
tasting (a)	▱ ˬ	flavouring (n)	▱ ²		

Appendix B — Complete Set of Augmented Syms

breathe		breathlessness		
breathing (n)		breathless		
breathing (a)				

sweet smell	1	hot (spicy) smell	5	
salty smell	2	pungent smell	6	
sour smell	3	savoury smell	7	
bitter smell	4			

sweet taste	1	sweet	1	sugar	1	
salty taste	2	salty	2	candy	1¹	
sour taste	3	sour	3	honey	1²	
bitter taste	4	bitter	4	salt	2	
hot (spicy) taste	5	hot (spicy)	5	vinegar	3	
pungent taste	6	pungent	6	poisonous / toxic	x	
savoury taste	7	savoury	7			

musical		singing (a)	
musician		sung (a)	
song		singer	
sing		rhythmic	
singing (n)		melodious	

love (v)		loving (a)		loved / beloved (a)	
lovely		loveable		charity	
loving (n)		loved / beloved (person)		charitable	

heartfelt		tear (n)	
cry (n)		tearing (n)	
crying (n)		tearful	
crying (a)			

laugh / laughter		laughing (a)	
laughing (n)		joke	

smile (n)	☺	frown (n)	☺ˣ
smiling (n)	☺ ⁻	frown (v)	☺ ˣ′
smiling (a)	☺ ⁻̌	frowning (n)	☺ ˣ⁻
		frowning (a)	☺ ˣ̌

joyful / joyous	☺ `	enjoyment	☺ ˢ	fun	☺ ¹
rejoice	☺ ′	enjoy	☺ ˢ′	funny	☺ ¹̌
rejoicing (n)	☺ ⁻	enjoying (n)	☺ ˢ⁻	humour	☺ ²
		enjoyable	☺ ˢ̌	humourous	☺ ²̌

sorrowful	☹ `	grievous	☹ ˢ	blame (n)	☹ ³
grief	☹ ˢ	guilt	☹ ¹	blame (v)	☹ ³′
grieve	☹ ˢ′	guilty	☹ ¹̌	blaming (n)	☹ ³⁻
grieving (n)	☹ ˢ⁻	shame	☹ ²	blamed (a)	☹ ³\\
grieving (a)	☹ ˢ̌	shameful	☹ ²̌		

excitement	⊙	boredom (n)	⊙ ˣ
excite	⊙ ′	bore (v)	⊙ ˣ′
exciting (n)	⊙ ⁻	boring (n)	⊙ ˣ⁻
exciting (a)	⊙ ̌	boring (a)	⊙ ˣ̌
		bored (a)	⊙ ˣ\\

surprise	⊙ ¹	amazement	⊙ ²
surprising (n)	⊙ ¹⁻	amazed (a)	⊙ ²\\
surprising (a)	⊙ ¹̌	amazing (a)	⊙ ²̌
surprised (a)	⊙ ¹\\	eagerness / keeness	⊙ ³
amaze	⊙ ²′	eager / keen	⊙ ³̌

calmness	⊚	calming (a)	⊚ ̌
calm (v)	⊚ ′	nervousness	⊚ ˣ
calming (n)	⊚ ⁻	nervous	⊚ ˣ̌

Appendix B — Complete Set of Augmented Syms

comfort (n)	☺¹	comforting (a)	☺¹	worried	☺ˣ
comfort (v)	☺	anxiety / worry	☺ˣ	worrying (n)	☺ˣ
comfortable	☺	anxious	☺ˣ	worrying (a)	☺ˣ
comforting (n)	☺¹	worry (v)	☺ˣ		

happiness	♡	favour (v)	♡²
like (v)	♡	favourite	♡²
liking (n)	♡¹	favoured (a)	♡²
liked (a)	♡	dislike (v)	♡ˣ
favour (n)	♡²	sadness	♡

care (v)	⊖	hug (n)	⊖¹	cuddling (n)	⊖²
careful	⊖	hug (v)	⊖¹	carelessness	⊖ˣ
caring (n)	⊖	hugging (n)	⊖¹	careless	⊖ˣ
caring (a)	⊖	cuddle (n)	⊖²	concern (v)	⊖
uncaring (a)	⊖ˣ	cuddle (v)	⊖²	concerned (a)	⊖

elation	♡	depressing (n)	◠
elating (a)	♡	depressing (a)	◠
depression	◠		

kindness	ᗪ	callous	ᗪˣ
unkindness	ᗪˣ	cruelty	ᗪˣ²
unkind	ᗪˣ	cruel	ᗪˣ²
callousness	ᗪˣ		

mothering (n)	ෆ	fathering (n)	ෆ
motherly (a)	ෆ	fatherly (a)	ෆ
motherhood	ෆ	fatherhood	ෆ

state (v)	♡	comment (v)	♡
stating (n)	♡	commenting (n)	♡
stated (a)	♡	commenting (a)	♡
		commenter	♡

report (v)	�'	reporter	� ᴵ
reporting (n)	� ⁻	news	� ¹
reporting (a)	� ˋ	newspaper	� ¹ₕ

call (n)	|♡	tell (n)	♡|
calling (n)	|♡ ⁻	telling (n)	♡| ⁻
caller	|♡ ᴵ		

message (v)	|♡|'	mail / letter	|♡|¹
messaging (n)	|♡| ⁻	email (n)	|♡|²
messaging (a)	|♡| ˋ	email (v)	|♡|²'
messenger	|♡| ᴵ		

communication	|♡|ˢ	communicative	|♡|ˢ
communicate	|♡|ˢ'	cultural	♡ˋ

talk / speak / say	♡'	expression	♡ˢ
talking / speaking (n)	♡ ⁻	express (v)	♡ˢ'
talking / speaking (a)	♡ ˋ	expressing (n)	♡ˢ⁻
talkative	♡ ˋ	expressive	♡ˢˋ

explain	|♡'	informed	♡|ˋˋ
explaining (n)	|♡ ⁻	misinformation	♡|ˣ
inform	♡|'	misinform	♡|ˣ'
informing (n)	♡| ⁻	misinforming (n)	♡|ˣ⁻
informative	♡| ˋ	misinformed (a)	♡|ˣˋ

instruct	|♡|'	demand (n)	|♡|¹	command (v)	|♡|²'
instructing (n)	|♡| ⁻	demand (v)	|♡|¹'	command (n)	|♡|²
instructive	|♡| ˋ	demanding (n)	|♡|¹⁻	commanding (n)	|♡|²⁻
		demanding (a)	|♡|¹ˋ	commanding (a)	|♡|²ˋ

Appendix B — Complete Set of Augmented Syms

converse (v)	☺ ′	discussion	☺ ¹	meet (v)	☺ ²
conversing (n)	☺ ⁻	discuss	☺ ⸴	meeting (n)	☺ ²
		discussing (n)	☺ ⁻¹	meeting (a)	☺ ²

kiss (n)	↔ ¹
kiss (v)	↔ ⸴
kissing (n)	↔ ⁻¹

bite (n)	⌣ ¹	chew	⌣ ²
bite (v)	⌣ ⸴	chewing (n)	⌣ ⁻²
biting (n)	⌣ ⁻¹		

hungry	⌢ `	fast (hunger)	⌢ ˣ
hunger	⌢ ⁻	fast (v)	⌢ ˣ
greed	⌢ ¹	fasting (n)	⌢ ⁻ˣ
greedy	⌢ ⸴		

eat	⌒ ′	feeding (a)	⌒ ⁻¹
eating (n)	⌒ ⁻	defecate	⌣ ′
feed (v)	⌒ ⸴	defecating (n)	⌣ ⁻
feeding (n)	⌒ ⁻¹		

consume	⌒ ′	feast (n)	\⌒\ ⁿ
consuming (n)	⌒ ⁻	feast (v)	\⌒\ ⸴
consuming (a)	⌒ ˇ	feasting (n)	\⌒\ ⁻
consumed (a)	⌒ ″		

thirsty	☻ `	alcohol / drink	☻ ¹	drink (v - alcohol)	☻ ⸴
drink (v)	☻ ′	alcoholic (a)	☻ ⸴	drunk / drunken	☻ ⸴⸴
drinking (n)	☻ ⁻	alcoholism	☻ ⁻¹	urinate	☻ ′
drinking (a)	☻ ˇ	drunkard	☻ ⁻¹	urinating (n)	☻ ⁻

refresh	⊚ ′
refreshing (n)	⊚ ⁻
refreshing (a)	⊚ ˋ

cooking (n)	B ⁻	cooktop / stove	B ᴴ
cooking (a)	B ˋ	raw (uncooked)	B ˣ
cooked (a)	B ˵	uncooked	B ˣ˵
cook (person)	B ᴵ		

bake	B ¹́	fry	B ²́	grilling (a)	B ³ˋ
baking (n)	B ¹⁻	frying (n)	B ²⁻	grilled (a)	B ³˵
baking (a)	B ¹ˋ	frying (a)	B ²ˋ	grill (n)	B ³ᴴ
baked (a)	B ¹˵	fried (a)	B ²˵	stew (n)	B ⁴
baker	B ¹ᴵ	fryer	B ²ᴴ	stew (v)	B ⁴́
bakery	B ¹ᵥ	grill (v)	B ³́	stewing (n)	B ⁴⁻
oven	B ¹ᴴ	grilling (n)	B ³⁻	stewed (a)	B ⁴˵

rich (person)	⌒ ᴵ	destitution	⌒ ⁀
richness / wealth	⌒	destitute	⌒ ⁀ˋ
poverty	⌣	destitute (person)	⌣ ⁀ᴵ
poor (person)	⌣ ᴵ		

royal	⌒ ˋ

fisherman	∞ ᴵ

block (v)	▫ ′	box (v)	△ ′
blocking (n)	▫ ⁻	boxing (n)	△ ⁻
blocked (a)	▫ ˵	boxed (a)	△ ˵

bag (v)	⊙ ′	contain	△ ′
bagging (n)	⊙ ⁻	containing (n)	△ ⁻
bagged (a)	⊙ ˵	container	△ ⁻

Appendix B — Complete Set of Augmented Syms

star (person)	✧ᴵ		starring (a)	✧ ̃
starry	✧`		galaxy	✧"
starring (n)	✧⁻			

transcend	⊐´		philosophy	⊐¹
transcendent	⊐`		philosopher	⊐¹ᵢ
transcending (n)	⊐⁻		religion	⊐²

universal	◇`		eternal	⊐`
infinite	✧`		divine	⌬`
finite	✧ˣ		divinity	⌬⁻

jug	⌣ⁿ		coffee	⌣³
milk	⌣¹		butter	⌣¹⁻
tea	⌣²		cheese	⌣¹₌

fragile	⎈`		wine	⎈²
juice	⎈¹		beer	⎈³

pointed	[·]"
point	[·]
spotted	[:]"

horizontal	[–]`
vertical	[ı]`

even	[=]`		flattened (a)	[=]˜
uneven	[=]ˣ		steadiness / stability	[=]¹
flat / level	[=]˜		steady / stable	[=]¹˜
flatten	[=]˜		unsteadiness / instability	[=]¹ˣ
flattening (n)	[=]˜		unsteady / unstable	[=]¹ˣ

alignment	[ı]	aligned	[ı]⟍	
align	[ı]´	parallel	[ı]⸜	
aligning (n)	[ı]⁻			

slant / slope (n)	[╱]
slant / slope (v)	[╱]´
slanted / sloped	[╱]⟍

stripe	[⫽]
striped	[⫽]⟍

angle	[∠]
angular	[∠]`
angled	[∠]⟍

bend (n)	[∧]	bending (n)	[∧]⁻
bend (v)	[∧]´	bent	[∧]⟍

curve (n)	[∼]	curved	[∼]⟍	curling (n)	[∼]ᴴ⁻
curve (v)	[∼]´	curl (n)	[∼]ᴴ	curled	[∼]ᴴ⟍
curving (n)	[∼]⁻	curl (v)	[∼]ᴴ´		

crooked	[∿]⟍

arc	(‿)	dip	(‿)	
arch	(‿)ᴴ	dipping (n)	(‿)⁻	
arching (n)	(‿)ᴴ⁻	pit	(‿)ᴴ	
arched (a)	(‿)ᴴ⟍			

cross (shape)	[✕]
cross-shaped	[✕]`

Appendix B — Complete Set of Augmented Syms

circle	[○]	cycle (n)	[○]⁽⁾
circling (n)	[○]⁻	cyclical	[○]⁽⁾
circled (a)	[○]``	wheel	[○]ᴴ
circular	[○]`	wheeling (n)	[○]H̲

square (n)	[□]	squaring (n)	[□]⁻
square (a)	[□]`	squared (a)	[□]``

rectangle	[▭]
rectangular	[▭]`

triangle	[△]	triangulate	[△]′
triangular	[△]`	triangulating (n)	[△]⁻

diamond shape	[◇]
diamond-shaped	[◇]`
diamond	[◇]⁻

oval	[⬭]
egg	[⬭]¹
egg-shaped	[⬭]⸜

sphere	[⊙]
spherical	[⊙]`
ball	[⊙]ᴴ

cube	[▣]
cubic	[▣]`

cylinder	[◉]	tin / can	[◉] ³
cylindrical	[◉] `	bin	[◉] ⁴
jar	[◉] ¹	barrel	[◉] ⁵
bottle	[◉] ²		

cone	[△]	pyramid	[△] ²
conical	[△] `	pyramid-shaped	[△] ²`
tent	[△] ¹		

addition	⟨+⟩	adding (n)	⟨+⟩ ⁻
add	⟨+⟩ ′	added	⟨+⟩ ⟍

subtraction	⟨−⟩
subtract	⟨−⟩ ′
subtracting (n)	⟨−⟩ ⁻

multiplication	⟨×⟩
multiply	⟨×⟩ ′
multiplying (n)	⟨×⟩ ⁻

division	⟨÷⟩	divided	⟨÷⟩ ⟍
divide	⟨÷⟩ ′	dividing (n)	⟨÷⟩ ⁻

straight	⟨│⟩ `	straightening (n)	⟨│⟩ ⁻
straighten	⟨│⟩ ′	straightened (a)	⟨│⟩ ⟍

dot	⟨·⟩	average (n)	⟨··⟩
ratio	⟨:⟩	average (a)	⟨··⟩ `
fraction	⟨:⟩ ⁿ	average (v)	⟨··⟩ ′
		averaging (n)	⟨··⟩ ⁻

Appendix B — Complete Set of Augmented Syms

ten times	⟨10⟩
one-tenth	⟨1/10⟩

letter A	⟨A⟩
letter B	⟨B⟩
letter C	⟨C⟩

equality	⟨=⟩	equalise	⟨=⟩ ''	inequitable	⟨=⟩ $\overset{s}{x}$
equal (a)	⟨=⟩ `	equity	⟨=⟩ ^{s}	inequality	⟨=⟩ ^{x}
equal (v)	⟨=⟩ '	equitable	⟨=⟩ $\overset{s}{`}$	unequal	⟨=⟩ $\overset{x}{`}$
equalling (n)	⟨=⟩ ⁻	inequity	⟨=⟩ $\overset{s}{x}$		

ring (shape)	⟨O⟩
ringed (a)	⟨O⟩ ``
ring (object)	⟨O⟩ ^{H}

half	⟨½⟩
one-third	⟨⅓⟩
quarter	⟨¼⟩

once	⟨1⟩
twice	⟨2⟩
thrice	⟨3⟩

single (n)	1 ⁻	double (n)	2 ⁻	triple (n)	3 ⁻
single (a)	1 `	double (a)	2 `	triple (a)	3 `
singling (n)	1 ⁼	doubling (n)	2 ⁼	tripling (n)	3 ⁼

pair	2 $^{||}$
twin	2 ^{H}
triplet (n)	3 ^{H}

first (n)	1 ^{s}	second (position)	2 ^{s}	third (n)	3 ^{s}
first (a)	1 $\overset{s}{`}$	second (a)	2 $\overset{s}{`}$	third (a)	3 $\overset{s}{`}$

ages	⌒ ⁺	retrying (n)	∿ ‡	
people	⊥ ⁺	Earth	⊖ ^	
retry (n)	∿ ‡	God	✺ ^	
retry (v)	∿ ⸵			

better	⌄ ς	closed (v)	⌒ (	
best	⌄ ⸵	will close	⌒)	
worse	⤫ ς	opened	⌣ (	
worst	⤫ ⸵	will open	⌣)	

Appendix C – Index of Root and Augmented Syms

word	word	word	word
a	active (a)	advising (n)	
ability	activity	advisor	
able	actor	advisory	
about (approx)	adapt	affect	
about (relating to)	adaptable	affected (a)	
above	adaptation	affecting (n)	
absence	adapted (a)	afraid	
absent	adapting (n)	after	
accept	add	again	
acceptance	added	against (oppose)	
accepted (a)	adding (n)	against (space)	
accepting (a)	addition	age	
accepting (n)	address	age (v)	
access (n)	administer	ages	
access (v)	administered	aging (a)	
accessible	administerial	aging (n)	
accessing (n)	administering (n)	ago	
accident	administration	agree	
accidental	administrative	agreed	
accord	administrator	agreement	
account	adorn	agricultural	
accuracy	adornment	agriculture	
accurate	adult	ahead	
ache	adulthood	aid (n)	
achieve	advance (n)	aid (v)	
achievement	advance (v)	aiding (n)	
achiever	advanced (a)	aim (n)	
achieving (a)	advancing (a)	aim (v)	
achieving (n)	advancing (n)	aiming (n)	
across	advantage	air	
act	advantageous	aircraft	
act (v)	advice	airing (n)	
acting (a)	advisable	airport	
acting (n)	advise	airy	
action	advised (a)	alcohol	

Symese — Universal Symbolic Script

word	symbol	word	symbol	word	symbol
alcoholic (a)		anger		appreciative	
alcoholism		angle		April	
align		angled		arc	
aligned		angry		arch	
aligning (n)		angular		arched (a)	
alignment		animal		arching (n)	
alike		annual		are	
alive		another		are not	
all		answer (n)		area	
allow		answer (v)		arena	
allowed (a)		answerable		arm	
allowing (n)		answered		around	
almost		answering (a)		arrange	
alone		answering (n)		arranged (a)	
along		antidote		arrangement	
alphabet		anxiety		arranging (n)	
also		anxious		arrival	
altitude		any		arrive	
altruism		apart		arriving (a)	
altruistic		apartment		arriving (n)	
amaze		apologetic		arrogance	
amazed (a)		apologise		arrogant (a)	
amazement		apologising (n)		arrogant (person)	
amazing (a)		apology		art	
amid		app		artificial	
among		apparent		artist	
an		apparition		artistic	
analog		appear		as	
analogous		appearance		ascend	
analogy		appearing (n)		ascendant (a)	
analyse		appetite		ascending (n)	
analysing (n)		application		ascent	
analysis		applied (a)		ascertain	
analyst		apply		ascertaining (n)	
analytical		applying (n)		ash	
ancestor		appreciate		ask	
ancient		appreciating (n)		asleep	
and		appreciation		aspiration	

188

Appendix C — Index of Root and Augmented Syms

word	sym	word	sym	word	sym	word	sym
aspirational		audio		bag (v)		bagged (a)	
aspire		August		bagging (n)		bake	
aspiring (a)		aural		baked (a)		baker	
aspiring (n)		author		bakery		baking (a)	
assemble		authorise		baking (n)		balance (harmony)	
assembly		authorised (a)		balance (parity)		balance (v)	
assess		authorising (n)		balanced		balancing (a)	
assessing (n)		authority		balancing (n)		ball	
assessment		automatic		balloon		band (object)	
assume		autumn		bank		barrel	
assumed (a)		availability		barren		barrenness	
assuming (n)		available		base		base (place)	
assumption		avenue		base (v)		based (a)	
at		average (a)		basement		basic	
atmosphere		average (n)		basin		basing (n)	
atmospheric		average (v)		basis		basket	
atom		averaging (n)		bat (object)		bathroom	
atomic		awake		battle		battlefield	
attach		awakened (a)		be		be not	
attached (a)		awakening (n)					
attaching (n)		away from					
attack (n)		axe					
attack (v)							
attacker		baby					
attacking (a)		back (n)					
attacking (n)		back (opp front)					
attempt (v)		back (v)					
attend		back of body					
attendance		back of head					
attending (a)		background					
attending (n)		backing (a)					
attention		backing (n)					
attic		backward					
attract		bacteria					
attracting (n)		bacterial					
attraction		bad					
attractive		badness					
audience		bag					

be still	◁´	bend (v)	[∧]´	blood	∞
beam (object)	⊤	bending (n)	[∧]⁻	bloody	∞`
beard	♀	bent	[∧]``	blouse	⊡²
beast	⚭	beside	▷	blow (v)	◐¹
beat (v)	◎²	bespectacled	∞¹	blowing (n)	◐¹⁻
beaten (a)	◎²``	best	∨?	blue	⑥
beating (a)	◎²⁼	better	∨?	blunt (a)	⋁`
beating (n)	◎²⁻	between	▽	blunt (v)	⋁´
beautified (a)	⋈``	beyond	⌣	blunting (n)	⋁⁻
beautiful	⋈`	bicycle	∞	bluntness	⋁
beautify	⋈´	big	⌒`	board (n)	⌐
beautifying (n)	⋈⁻	bin	[⊡]⁴	boat	⊠
beauty	⋈	bind (v)	⊚´	body	8
because	⁀	binding (a)	⊚⁼	boil (v)	⊖³
become	∽⁻	binding (n)	⊚⁻	boiled (a)	⊖³``
bed	⊟	bird	♂	boiling (a)	⊖³⁼
bedroom	⊟⁴	bit	▽⁻	boiling (n)	⊖³⁻
beer	⊻³	bite (n)	◌¹	bond	⊚
before		⟨	bite (v)	◌¹´	bond (v)	⊚´
befriend	x´	biting (n)	◌¹⁻	bondage	⊚¹
befriending (n)	x⁻	bitter	⊿`	bonded (a)	⊚``
begin	▷⁵	bitter smell	⊿⁷	bonding (a)	⊚⁼
beginner	▷ᴵ	bitter taste	⊿	bonding (n)	⊚⁻
beginning (n)	▷⁻	black	⊖	bone	8
behind	◁		blade	✂	bony	8`
being (n)	∽⁻	blame (n)	ⓐ³	book	⊓
being (person)	∽ᴵ	blame (v)	ⓐ³´	book collection	⊓"
belief	◇	blamed (a)	ⓐ³``	boot	⊤²
believe	◇´	blaming (n)	ⓐ³⁻	border	⊥²
believer	◇ᴵ	blanket	⊟²	bore (v)	⊚´
believing (n)	◇⁻	blind (a)	◯ˣ	bored (a)	⊚ˣ``
bell	⊼	blind (v)	◯ˣ´	boredom (n)	⊚ˣ
beloved (a)	♡ᴵ⁼	blinding (a)	◯ˣ⁼	boring (a)	⊚ˣ⁼
beloved (person)	♡ᴵ	blinding (n)	◯ˣ⁻	boring (n)	⊚ˣ⁻
below	▽	block (n)	▫	borrow	⌒?
belt	⌒	block (v)	▫´	borrowed (a)	⌒``
bench	⊟	blocked (a)	▫``	borrower	⌒ᴵ
bend (n)	[∧]	blocking (n)	▫⁻	borrowing (n)	⌒⁻

Appendix C — Index of Root and Augmented Syms

bottle		bright		butter	
bottom		brighten		buttock	
bound (a)		brilliance		button	
boundary		brilliant		buy	
bow (action)		bring forward		by	
bow (v)		broken			
bowed (a)		broom		cabin	
bowing (a)		brown		cage	
bowing (n)		brush (n)		caged (a)	
bowl		brush (v)		calendar	
box		brushed (a)		call (n)	
box (v)		brushing (n)		call (v)	
boxed (a)		bubble		caller	
boxing (n)		bucket		calling (n)	
bra		bud		callous	
brain		build		callousness	
branch		builder		calm	
branch (v)		building		calm (v)	
branching (n)		building (a)		calming (a)	
brave		building (n)		calming (n)	
bravery		built (a)		calmness	
break (n)		bulb		camera	
break (v)		bundle (n)		can (able to)	
breaking (a)		bundle (v)		can (object)	
breaking (n)		bundled (a)		candy	
breast		bundling		cane	
breath		burn (n)		cannot	
breathe		burn (v)		cap	
breathing (a)		burning (a)		car	
breathing (n)		burning (n)		card	
breathless		burnt (a)		cardboard	
breathlessness		bus		care (n)	
breeze		bus depot		care (v)	
breezy		business (a)		career	
bridge		business (n)		careful	
bridge (v)		busy		careless	
bridging (a)		busyness		carelessness	
bridging (n)		but		caring (a)	

word	symbol	word	symbol	word	symbol	word	symbol
caring (n)		chair		circled (a)			
carriage		chance		circling (n)			
carry		change (n)		circular			
carrying (n)		change (v)		city			
cart		changed		claim (n)			
case		changing (a)		claim (v)			
cash		changing (n)		claimant			
castle		chaos		claiming (n)			
casual		chaotic		clarify			
catalog (n)		character		clarity			
catalog (v)		charitable		clause			
cataloged (a)		charity		clay			
cataloging (n)		chasm		clean (a)			
catch (n)		check (n)		clean (v)			
catch (v)		check (v)		cleaner			
catcher		checked (a)		cleaning (a)			
catching (n)		checking (n)		cleaning (n)			
categorise		cheek		cleanliness			
categorising (n)		cheese		cleanse			
category		chemical		cleansed			
causal		chest		cleanser			
cause (n)		chew		cleansing (a)			
cause (v)		chewing (n)		cleansing (n)			
causing (n)		child		clear (declutter)			
ceiling		childhood		clear (uncluttered)			
cell (bio)		childish		clear (unobscured)			
centigrade		childishness		cleared (a)			
central		child-like		clever			
centralisation		chin		cleverness			
centralise		choice		click (n)			
centralised (a)		choose		click (v)			
centralising (n)		choosing (n)		clicking (n)			
centre		choosy		climate			
century		chopper		climatic			
certain		chopsticks		climb (n)			
certainty		chosen (a)		climb (v)			
chain		chosen (person)		climber			
chained		circle		climbing (a)			

Appendix C — Index of Root and Augmented Syms

word	sym	word	sym	word	sym	word	sym
climbing (n)		collective		competing (a)			
clinic		collector		competing (n)			
clock		colour		competition			
close (a)		colourless		competitive			
close (v)		column		competitor			
closed (a)		come		complete (a)			
closed (v)		comfort (n)		complete (v)			
closing (a)		comfort (v)		completed (a)			
closing (n)		comfortable		completeness			
cloth		comforting (a)		completing (n)			
clothes		comforting (n)		completion			
cloud (n)		coming		complex			
cloud (v)		command (n)		complexity			
clouding (n)		command (v)		compound			
cloudy		commanding (a)		computer			
coat		commanding (n)		conceivable			
code		comment (n)		conceive			
code (v)		comment (v)		conceived (a)			
coded		commenter		conceiving (n)			
coder		commenting (a)		concept			
coding (a)		commenting (n)		conception			
coding (n)		common (frequent)		conceptual			
coffee		common (shared)		concern (n)			
cognition		communal		concern (v)			
cognitive		communicate		concerned (a)			
coil (n)		communication		condition			
coil (v)		communicative		cone			
coiled (a)		community (n)		confide			
coiling (n)		companion		confidence			
cold (a)		companionship		confident			
cold (n)		company (a)		confidential			
coldness		company (n)		confiding (n)			
collect		comparable		confuse			
collected (a)		comparative		confused			
collectible		compare		confusing (a)			
collecting (a)		comparing (n)		confusing (n)			
collecting (n)		comparison		confusion			
collection		compete		conical			

conscious	⊛`	controlling (n)	𝔻¯	cost (v)	◁´	
consciousness	⊛	converge	≻´	costing (n)	◁¯	
consider	⊉´	convergence	≻	count (n)	ξ "	
consideration	⊉	convergent	≻`	count (v)	ξ´	
considered (a)	⊉"	converging (a)	≻˜	counted	ξ"	
considering (n)	⊉¯	converging (n)	≻¯	counting (n)	ξ¯	
consult	⊗´	conversation	⊚	country	⊖³	
consultant	⊗ᴵ	converse (v)	⊚´	couple	⏊	
consultation	⊗	conversing (n)	⊚¯	courage	Ⓧ	
consulting (a)	⊗˜	cook (person)	Bᴵ	courageous	Ⓧ`	
consulting (n)	⊗¯	cook (v)	B´	court	▷ᵛ	
consume	⍹	cooked (a)	B"	cover (n)	⊖	
consumed (a)	⍹"	cooking (a)	B˜	cover (v)	⊖´	
consuming (a)	⍹˜	cooking (n)	B¯	covered (a)	⊖"	
consuming (n)	⍹¯	cooktop	Bᴴ	covering (a)	⊖˜	
consumption	⍹	cool (a)	ᴗ´	covering (foot)	⊤	
contain	△´	cool (v)	ᴗ´	covering (head)	⊓	
container	△¯	cooler (object)	ᴗᴴ	covering (n)	⊖¯	
containing (n)	△¯	cooling (a)	ᴗ˜	crack (n)	≋ᵛ	
content	△	cooling (n)	ᴗ¯	crack (v)	≋´	
context	⫲	coolness	ᴗ	cracked	≋"	
continent	⊖¹	cooperate	⋈´	cracking (n)	≋˜	
continuation	Σ	cooperating (n)	⋈¯	craft	⊣	
continue	Σ´	cooperation	⋈	crash (n)	⊚³	
continuing (a)	Σ˜	cooperative	⋈`	crash (v)	⊚³´	
continuing (n)	Σ¯	copied (a)	⫽"	crashing (a)	⊚³˜	
contract (deal)	⌣ᴴ	copulate	⚲´	crashing (n)	⊚³¯	
contract (shrink)	⊄´	copy (n)	⫽¹	crawl	人¹	
contracted (a)	⊄"	copy (v)	⫽¹´	crawling (n)	人¹¯	
contracting (a)	⊄˜	copying (n)	⫽¹¯	create	≈˜	
contraction	⊄	core (a)	▽`	creating (n)	≈˜¯	
contractor	⌣ᴴᴵ	core (n)	▽	creation	≈˜	
contractual	⌣ᴴ`	corner	⌐	creative	≈˜`	
control (n)	𝔻	corpse	∞	creator	≈˜ᴴ	
control (v)	𝔻´	correct (v)	↓´	creature	≈˜ᴴ"	
controlled (a)	𝔻"	corrected (a)	↓"	credibility	◇"	
controller	𝔻ᴵ	correcting (n)	↓¯	credible	◇`	
controlling (a)	𝔻˜	cost (n)	◁	creek	⊖⁷	

Appendix C — Index of Root and Augmented Syms

word	sym	word	sym	word	sym
creep		customer		data	
creeping (n)		cut (v)		date (n)	
crew		cutlery		date (v)	
criminal (a)		cutting (a)		dated (a)	
criminal (n)		cutting (n)		daughter	
critical		cyan		day	
crooked		cycle (n)		dead	
crop		cycle (v)		deaden	
cross (shape)		cyclical		deadened (a)	
cross-shaped		cycling (a)		deadening (n)	
crowd		cycling (n)		deadly	
cruel		cyclist		deaf	
cruelty		cylinder		deafen	
cry (n)		cylindrical		deafening (a)	
cry (v)				death	
crying (a)		daily		decade	
crying (n)		damage (n)		decay (n)	
cube		damage (v)		decay (v)	
cubic		damaged (a)		decayed	
cuddle (n)		damaging (a)		decaying (a)	
cuddle (v)		damaging (n)		decaying (n)	
cuddling (n)		damp (a)		December	
cultural		dampen		decentralisation	
culture		dampening (n)		decentralise	
cup		dance (n)		decentralised (a)	
cupboard		dance (v)		decentralising (n)	
curiosity		dancer		decide	
curious (a)		dancing (a)		decided	
curl (n)		dancing (n)		decider	
curl (v)		danger		deciding (a)	
curled		dangerous		deciding (n)	
curling (n)		dark blue		decision	
currency		dark green		decisive	
current (time)		dark red		decisiveness	
curve (n)		darken		decorate	
curve (v)		darkening (a)		decorated	
curved		darkening (n)		decorating (n)	
curving (n)		darkness		decoration	

195

word	symbol	word	symbol	word	symbol	word	symbol
decrease (n)	∨	depart	>˘	destroyer	≈⚲		
decrease (v)	∨´	departed (a)	>˝	destroying (n)	≈⌒		
decreased (a)	∨˝	departing (a)	>˜	destruction	≈⌒		
decreasing (a)	∨˜	departing (n)	>˘	destructive	≈⌒		
decreasing (n)	∨¯	departure	>˘	detail (n)	∨		
deduce	◇´	depot	⌑	detail (v)	∨´		
deducing (n)	◇¯	depressed	⌒ˋ	detailed	∨˝		
deduction	◇	depressing (a)	⌒˜	detailing (n)	∨¯		
deep	⊢ˋ	depressing (n)	⌒¯	develop	[·´		
defecate	⌒´	depression	⌒	developed (a)	[·˝		
defecating (n)	⌒¯	depth	⊢	developer	[·ᴵ		
defecation	⌒	descend	∀˘	developing (a)	[·˜		
defence	⚔	descendant	⊥	developing (n)	[·¯		
defend	⚔´	descending (n)	∀¹	development	[·		
defended (a)	⚔˝	descent	∀¹	device	↧		
defender	⚔ᴵ	describe	⊥´	diagram	⊙²		
defending (n)	⚔¯	describing (n)	⊥¯	diamond	[◇]¯		
defensive	⚔ˋ	description	⊥	diamond shape	[◇]		
defer	>˘	desert	⊖˘	diamond-shaped	[◇]ˋ		
deferral	>˘	design (n)	⊨	die (v)	⊠´		
deferred (a)	>˝	design (v)	⊨´	differ (v)	⚹´		
deferring (n)	>˘	designed	⊨˝	difference	⚹		
delay (n)	‖⚹	designer	⊨ᴵ	different	⚹ˋ		
delay (v)	‖⚹´	designing (n)	⊨¯	differentiated (a)	⚹˞		
delayed (a)	‖⚹˝	desirable	·Ǫˋ	differentiating (n)	⚹¹		
delaying (a)	‖⚹˜	desire (n)	·Ǫ	differentiation	⚹¹		
delaying (n)	‖⚹¯	desire (v)	·Ǫ´	differing (a)	⚹˜		
delicious	⌒ˋ	desired (a)	·Ǫ˝	differing (n)	⚹¯		
deliver	⊐´	desiring (n)	·Ǫ¯	difficult	⌢ˋ		
deliverable	⊐ᴴ	desk	π	difficulty	⌢		
delivered	⊐˝	despicable (a)	·⋊˞	diffidence	|↔		
deliverer	⊐ᴵ	despise (n)	·⋊¹	diffident	|↔ˋ		
delivering (n)	⊐¯	despise (v)	·⋊˘	dig	∟¹		
delivery	⊐	despite	>˘	digger	∟ᴵ		
demand (n)	|◯|¹	destitute	⊡⌒	digging (n)	∟¹		
demand (v)	|◯|˘	destitute (person)	⊡⚲	digital	⌶		
demanding (a)	|◯|¹	destitution	⊡⌒	digitise	⌶´		
demanding (n)	|◯|¹	destroy	≈˘	digitised (a)	⌶˝		

Appendix C — Index of Root and Augmented Syms

word		word		word		word	
digitising (n)		discouraged (a)		distress (v)			
diligence		discouragement		distressed (a)			
diligent		discouraging (a)		distressing (a)			
dining room		discouraging (n)		distressing (n)			
dip		discover		district			
dipping (n)		discovered		disunited			
direct (a)		discovering (n)		disunity			
direct (v)		discovery		diverge			
directing (n)		discuss		divergence			
direction		discussing (n)		divergent			
director		discussion		diverging (a)			
dirt		disease		diverging (n)			
dirtiness		disguise (n)		divide			
dirty		disguise (v)		divided			
disability		disguised (a)		dividing (n)			
disable		disguising (n)		divine			
disabled		disgust		divinity			
disabling (n)		disgusted (a)		division			
disadvantage		disgusting (a)		do (n)			
disadvantageous		dish		do (v)			
disagree		dishonest		do not			
disappear		dishonesty		doing (n)			
disappearance		dishonour (n)		door			
disappearing (a)		dishonour (v)		doorway			
disappearing (n)		dishonourable		dot			
disbelief		dishonouring (n)		double (a)			
disbelieve		dislike (v)		double (n)			
discard (n)		disloyal		doubling (n)			
discard (v)		disloyalty		doubt (n)			
discarded (a)		disorder		doubt (v)			
discern		disorderly		doubtful			
discerning (a)		dispersal		doubting (a)			
discerning (n)		disperse		doubting (n)			
discernment		dispersed (a)		down			
discontinuation		dispersing (a)		drain			
discontinue		dispersing (n)		draw			
discontinuing (n)		distance		drawer			
discourage		distress (n)		drawer (person)			

word	symbol	word	symbol	word	symbol	word	symbol
drawing (a)		dull		effect (n)			
drawing (n)		duration		effect (v)			
drawn (a)		during		effecting (n)			
dread (n)		dust		effective			
dread (v)		dustiness		effort			
dreaded		dusty		egg			
dreadful		duty		egg-shaped			
dreading (n)		dying (a)		ego			
dream (n)		dying (n)		either			
dream (v)		dying (person)		elated			
dreamer		dynamic		elating (a)			
dreaming (n)				elation			
dress		eager		elbow			
dried (a)		eagerness		electric			
drink (n - alcohol)		ear		electrical			
drink (n)		early		electricity			
drink (v - alcohol)		earn		element			
drink (v)		earned (a)		elemental			
drinking (a)		earning (n)		email (n)			
drinking (n)		Earth		email (v)			
drive (n)		earth (soil)		emergency			
drive (v)		earth (world)		emotion			
driver		earthly		emotional			
driving (a)		ease		empathic			
driving (n)		easing (a)		empathise			
drop (n)		easing (n)		empathising (n)			
drop (v)		east		empathy			
dropping (n)		eastern		empower			
drown		easy		empowered (a)			
drowning (a)		eat		empowering (a)			
drowning (n)		eating (n)		empowering (n)			
drunk		ecological		emptiness			
drunkard		ecology		empty (a)			
drunken		economical		empty (v)			
dry		economise		emptying (a)			
dryer		economising (n)		emptying (n)			
drying (a)		economy		enable			
drying (n)		edge		enabling (a)			

Appendix C — Index of Root and Augmented Syms

word		word		word		word	
enabling (n)		equal (v)		evil (a)			
enclose		equalise		evil (n)			
enclosed (a)		equality		examination			
enclosing (n)		equalling (n)		examine			
enclosure		equipment		examiner			
encourage		equitable		examining (n)			
encouragement		equity		example			
encouraging (a)		era		exceed			
encouraging (n)		erase		exceeding (n)			
end (n)		erasing (n)		except			
end (v)		erasure		exception			
ended (a)		eros		exceptional			
ending (a)		erroneous		excess (a)			
ending (n)		error		excess (n)			
enemy		escape (n)		excessive			
energetic		escape (v)		excite			
energise		escaped (a)		excited			
energised (a)		escapee		excitement			
energising (a)		escaping (a)		exciting (a)			
energising (n)		escaping (n)		exciting (n)			
energy		essence		exclude			
engine		essential		excluded			
enigma		establish		excluding (n)			
enigmatic		established		excluding (prep)			
enjoy		establishing (n)		exclusion (a)			
enjoyable		establishment		exclusion (n)			
enjoying (n)		eternal		execute (task)			
enjoyment		eternity		executing (n)			
enlarge		ethical		execution (task)			
enlarged (a)		ethics		executive (a)			
enlarging (n)		evaluate		executive (n)			
enmity		evaluating (n)		executor			
enough		evaluation		exemplary			
entity		even		exemplify			
entrance		even (adv)		exemplifying (n)			
environment		event		exit (n)			
environmental		eventful		expand			
equal (a)		every		expanded (a)			

word	symbol	word	symbol	word	symbol
expanding (a)		extra (a)		false	
expanding (n)		extra (n)		falsehood	
expansion		extraordinary		falsify	
expect		extreme		falsifying (n)	
expectation		extremism		fame	
expected		extremist		family	
expecting (a)		extrinsic		far	
expecting (n)		eye		farm	
experience				farmer	
experienced (a)		face		farming (a)	
experiencing (n)		face (person)		farming (n)	
expert		face (v)		fast (a)	
expertise		facet		fast (hunger)	
explain		facing (a)		fast (v)	
explaining (n)		facing (n)		fasten	
explanation		fact		fastener	
exploration		factor		fasting (n)	
explore		factor (v)		fat (a)	
explored		factored (a)		fat (bio)	
exploring (n)		factoring (n)		father	
expose		factory		fatherhood	
exposed (a)		factual		fathering (n)	
exposing (n)		fahrenheit		fatherly (a)	
exposure		fail		fatness	
express (v)		failed (a)		fattening (a)	
expressing (n)		failing (a)		fattening (n)	
expression		failing (n)		fatty	
expressive		failure		favour (n)	
extend		fair (just)		favour (v)	
extended (a)		faith		favoured (a)	
extending (a)		faithful (a)		favourite	
extending (n)		faithful (person)		fear (n)	
extension		faithfulness		fear (v)	
extent		fall (n)		feared (a)	
external (a)		fall (v)		fearful	
external (n)		fallen (a)		fearing (n)	
externalised (a)		falling (a)		fearless	
externalising (n)		falling (n)		fearlessness	

Appendix C — Index of Root and Augmented Syms

word		word		word		word	
feast (n)		filter (n)		flagged (a)			
feast (v)		filter (v)		flagging (n)			
feasting (n)		filtered (a)		flame			
feature (n)		filtering (n)		flash			
feature (v)		fin		flat			
featured (a)		final (a)		flatten			
featuring (n)		finalise		flattened (a)			
February		find (n)		flattening (n)			
feed (v)		find (v)		flavour			
feeding (a)		finding (n)		flavoured (a)			
feeding (n)		fine		flavouring (n)			
feel (n)		fineness		flesh			
feel (v)		finesse		fleshy			
feeling (n)		finger		flex (v)			
felt (a)		fingernail		flexibility			
female (a)		finish (n)		flexible			
female (n)		finish (v)		flexing (n)			
fence		finished (a)		flight			
fenced		finishing (a)		flip (n)			
fencing		finishing (n)		flip (v)			
ferry		finite		flipped (a)			
fertile		fire		flipping (n)			
fertility		firm (a)		float (v)			
few (a)		firm (v)		floating (a)			
few (n)		firming (n)		floating (n)			
field (object)		firmness		flood			
field (subject)		first (a)		floor			
fierce		first (n)		flow (n)			
fiery		fish+		flow (v)			
fight (n)		fisherman		flower			
fight (v)		fit (n - suit)		flowing (a)			
fighter		fit (v - suit)		flowing (n)			
fighting (a)		fitted (a)		fly (v)			
fighting (n)		fix (n)		flyer			
fill (n)		fix (v)		flying (a)			
fill (v)		fixing (n)		flying (n)			
filling (a)		flag (n)		focus (n)			
filling (n)		flag (v)		focus (v)			

201

word	symbol	word	symbol	word	symbol	word	symbol
focussed (a)		forgiving (n)		friendly			
focussing (a)		forgotten (a)		friendship			
focussing (n)		fork		fright (n)			
fog		form (n)		frighten			
fogged (a)		form (v)		frightened			
foggy		formation		frightening			
fold (n)		formed		from			
fold (v)		former		front (a)			
folded		forming (n)		front (n)			
folding (a)		fortitude		front (v)			
folding (n)		fortnight		fronting (a)			
follow		fortress		frost			
follower		forward		frosted (a)			
following (a)		foundation		frosty			
following (n)		founded (a)		frown (n)			
food		founder		frown (v)			
fooling (n)		founding (a)		frowning (a)			
foolish		founding (n)		frowning (n)			
foolishness		fraction		frozen			
foot		fragile		fruit			
foot (measure)		frail		fruit orchard			
for		frailty		fruiting (a)			
forbidden		frame		fruiting (n)			
force (n)		frame (v)		fruity			
force (v)		framing (n)		fry			
forced (a)		free (a)		fryer			
forceful		free (v)		frying (a)			
forcing (n)		freed (a)		frying (n)			
foreground		freedom		full			
forehead		freeing (n)		fullness			
forest		freeze		fun			
forget		freezer		function			
forgetfulness		freezing (a)		fungus			
forgetting (n)		freezing (n)		funnel (n)			
forgive		frequency		funnel (v)			
forgiven (a)		fried (a)		funnelling (n)			
forgiveness		friend		funny			
forgiving (a)		friendliness		fur			

Appendix C — Index of Root and Augmented Syms

word	sym	word	sym	word	sym
furious		gentleman		grass	
furnace		get		grateful	
furniture		getting (n)		gratitude	
fury		ghost		greed	
future		giant		greedy	
fuzzy		gift		green	
galaxy		give		grey	
gale		give not		grief	
gamble (n)		given (n)		grieve	
gamble (v)		giver		grieving (a)	
gambler		giving (n)		grieving (n)	
gambling (a)		glad		grievous	
gambling (n)		glass (material)		grill (n)	
game		glass (object)		grill (v)	
gap		glassy		grilled (a)	
garage		glide (n)		grilling (a)	
garden		glide (v)		grilling (n)	
gardener		gliding (a)		groin	
gardening (a)		gliding (n)		ground	
gardening (n)		go		group (n)	
garment		goal		group (v)	
garment (waist dn)		God		grouped	
garment (waist up)		god		grouping (n)	
gas		going		grove	
gaseous		good (a)		grow	
gate		good (n)		grower	
gather		goodness		growing (a)	
gathering		govern		growing (n)	
gauge (n)		governance		grown (a)	
gauge (v)		governing (a)		growth	
gauging (n)		governing (n)		guard (n)	
gender		government		guard (v)	
general		governor		guarded (a)	
generalisation		gradual		guardian	
generalise		grain (plant)		guarding (n)	
generalising (n)		grain (texture)		guess (n)	
generation		gram		guess (v)	
gentle		granular		guessing (a)	

guessing (n)	◇⁻	hate (n)	·ιχ	helper	⊁ᴵ		
guidance	⊤⁵	hate (v)	·ιχ´	helpful	⊁`		
guide (object)	⊤ᴴ	hated (a)	·ιχ"	helping (a)	⊁˜		
guide (person)	⊤ᴵ	hateful	·ιχ`	helping (n)	⊁⁻		
guide (v)	⊤´	hater	·ιχᴵ	her(s)	⊢`		
guided (a)	⊤"	hating (n)	·ιχ⁻	herb	⚲		
guiding (a)	⊤˜	hatred	·ιχ	here	∨`		
guiding (n)	⊤⁵	have	⌒´	hidden	⌓"		
guilt	ⓐ¹	have not	⌥´	hide	⌓´		
guilty	ⓐ¹`	hazard	▽¹	hiding (a)	⌓˜		
		hazardous	▽¹`	hiding (n)	⌓⁻		
hair	⊙	he	⊢	high	∧`		
half	⟨½⟩	head (a)	♀`	hill	△		
hammer	⊏	head (n)	♀	hilly	△`		
hammer (v)	⊏´	head (person)	♀ᴵ	him	⊢		
hammering (n)	⊏⁻	head (v)	♀´	hinge	⊛		
hand	∇	heading (n)	♀⁻	hinge (v)	⊛´		
handle (n)	⊐	heal	⚯´	hint (n)	◇¹		
handle (v)	⊐´	healing (a)	⚯˜	hint (v)	◇¹´		
handling (n)	⊐⁻	healing (n)	⚯⁻	hire in	▽´		
hang	ʖ¹	health	⚯	hire out	▽`		
hanging (a)	ʖ¹`	healthy	⚯`	his	⊢`		
hanging (n)	ʖ¹	hear	◯´	historic	⊠²		
happen	∽´	hearing	◯	historical	⊠˜		
happiness	♡	heart	♡	history	⊠¹		
happy	♡`	heartfelt	♡`	hit (a)	◉¹`		
harbour	✉ᵒ	heat (n)	⌢	hit (n)	◉¹		
hard	⌒`	heat (v)	⌢´	hit (v)	◉¹´		
harden	⌒´	heated (a)	⌢"	hitting (n)	◉¹⁻		
hardened (a)	⌒"	heater	⌢ᴴ	hold (n)	·ϒ·		
hardening (a)	⌒˜	heating (a)	⌢˜	hold (v)	·ϒ·´		
hardening (n)	⌒⁻	heating (n)	⌢⁻	holder (object)	·ϒ·ᴴ		
hardness	⌒	heaviness	⌒	holder (person)	·ϒ·ᴵ		
harmonious	⌽`	heavy	⌒`	holding (n)	·ϒ·⁻		
harmony	⌽	height	∧	hole	⌴		
has	⌒´	height (tall)	∆	hollow	⋎¹		
has not	⌥´	help (n)	⊁	hollowness	⋎¹		
hat	⊓¹	help (v)	⊁´	home	⧇		

Appendix C — Index of Root and Augmented Syms

word	sym	word	sym	word	sym
homely		hug (v)		image	
honest		hugging (n)		imaginary	
honesty		human		imagination	
honey		humble (a)		imaginative	
honour (n)		humble (person)		imagine	
honour (v)		humiliate		imagined	
honourable		humiliated		imaging (a)	
honoured (a)		humiliating (a)		imaging (n)	
honouring (n)		humiliating (n)		imagining (n)	
hook		humiliation		imbalance	
hook (v)		humility		immediate	
hooked (a)		humour		immoral	
hooking (n)		humourous		immorality	
hop (n)		hunger		impersonal	
hop (v)		hungry		importance	
hope (n)		hurried (a)		important	
hope (v)		hurry (n)		impossibility	
hopeful		hurry (v)		impossible	
hopefulness		hurrying (n)		impractical	
hopeless		hurt		imprecise	
hopelessness		hurt (a)		imprecision	
hoping (n)		hurt (v)		impress	
hopping (n)		hurting (n)		impressed (a)	
horizon		husband		impressing (n)	
horizontal		hut		impression	
hospital				impressive	
hot (spicy)		I		improbability	
hot (spicy) smell		ice		improbable	
hot (spicy) taste		iced		imprudent	
hot (temperature)		icon		impure	
hour		icy		impurity	
hourglass		idea		in	
hourly		idle (a)		in front	
house		idle (v)		in spite of	
housing (a)		idleness		inability	
housing (n)		if		inaccessible	
how		ill		inaccuracy	
hug (n)		illness		inaccurate	

word	symbol	word	symbol	word	symbol	word	symbol
inaction		industrialised (a)		inspire			
inactive		industrialising (a)		inspired (a)			
inch		industrialising (n)		inspiring (a)			
include		industrialist		inspiring (n)			
included		industry		instability			
including (n)		inequality		instinct			
including (prep)		inequitable		instinctive			
inclusion		inequity		instruct			
incomparable		infant		instructing (n)			
incomplete		infinite		instruction			
inconceivable		infinity		instructive			
increase (n)		inform		instrument			
increase (v)		information		integral			
increased (a)		informative		integrated (a)			
increasing (a)		informed		integrating (a)			
increasing (n)		informing (n)		integrating (n)			
incredibility		inherent		integration			
incredible		iniquity		integrity			
increment (n)		initial (a)		intellect			
increment (v)		initialise		intellectual (a)			
incremental		injure (v)		intellectual (person)			
indecision		injured (a)		intelligence			
indecisive		injuring (n)		intelligent			
indecisiveness		injury		interest (topic)			
indeed		inner		interest (v)			
index		inner garment		interested			
index finger		insect		interesting			
indicate		insecure		internal (a)			
indicated (a)		insecurity		internal (n)			
indicating (n)		insensitive		internalised (a)			
indication		insert		internalising (n)			
indicative		inserting (n)		internet			
indicator		insertion		intrinsic			
indirect		inside		intuition			
individual (a)		insight		invalid			
industrial		insipid		invalidate			
industrialisation		inspiration		invent			
industrialise		inspirational		invented			

Appendix C — Index of Root and Augmented Syms

word	sym	word	sym	word	sym
inventing (n)		judge (v)		kitchen	
invention		judgement			
inventor		judging (n)		kitchen knife	
invisible		jug		knee	
invitation		juice		kneel	
invite		July		kneeling (a)	
invited (a)		jump (n)		kneeling (n)	
inviting (a)		jump (v)		knife	
inviting (n)		jumper		knot	
irresponsible		jumping (a)		knotted (a)	
is		jumping (n)		know	
is not		June		knowing (a)	
issue		jungle		knowing (n)	
it		just (adv)		knowledge	
it all		just (fair)		knowledgeable	
item		justice		known (a)	
itemise		justification		label (n)	
itemised (a)		justified		label (v)	
itemising (n)		justify		labelling (n)	
its		justifying (n)		ladder	
				ladle	
jacket		keen		lady	
January		keeness		lake	
jar		keep		land	
jaw		key (a)		lane	
jetplane		key (n)		language	
job		keyed (a)		large	
join (v)		keying (a)		large intestines	
joining (a)		keying (n)		last night	
joining (n)		kick		late	
joint		kicking (n)		latter	
jointed (a)		kind		laugh	
joke		kindness		laugh (v)	
journey		king		laughing (a)	
joy		kingdom		laughing (n)	
joyful		kiss (n)		laughter	
joyous		kiss (v)		law	
judge (person)		kissing (n)		lawful	

lawfulness		letter B		linked (a)		
lawless		letter C		linking (n)		
lawn		level		lip		
layer (n)		level (measure)		liquid (a)		
layer (v)		library		liquid (n)		
layered (a)		lid		liquify		
laziness		lie down		list (n)		
lazy		life		list (v)		
lead		lifeform		listed (a)		
leader		lifetime		listen		
leading (a)		light (opp darkness)		listener		
leading (n)		light (opp heavy)		listening (a)		
leaf		light (v)		listening (n)		
lean (a)		light blue		listing (n)		
learn		light green		literal		
learned		lighted (a)		literary		
learner		lighten		literature		
learning (a)		lightening (a)		little (a - number)		
learning (n)		lightening (n)		little (a - size)		
least		lighting (n)		little (n - number)		
leave		lightness		little finger		
leaving (a)		like (a)		live (v)		
leaving (n)		like (v)		lived (a)		
left (opp right)		liked (a)		liveliness		
leg		likelihood		lively		
lend		likely		living (a)		
lender		liken		living (n)		
lending (n)		likening (n)		living (person)		
length		liking (n)		local (a)		
lengthen		limit (n)		locality		
lengthened (a)		limit (v)		locate		
lengthening (a)		limited		located (a)		
lengthening (n)		limiting (a)		locating (a)		
lens		limiting (n)		locating (n)		
less		limitless		location		
letter (character)		line		lock (n)		
letter (object)		link (n)		lock (v)		
letter A		link (v)		locked (a)		

Appendix C — Index of Root and Augmented Syms

word	sym	word	sym	word	sym	word	sym
locker		machine		mapping (n)			
locking (a)		machinery		March			
locking (n)		magic		marina			
logo		magical		marine			
loneliness		magician		marital (a)			
lonely		mail		mark			
long		main		market (n)			
look		maintain		market (v)			
looking (n)		maintaining (n)		marketing (a)			
loose		maintenance		marketing (n)			
loosen		major		maroon			
loosened (a)		majority		marriage			
looseness		make		married			
loosening (a)		make (n)		marry			
loosening (n)		make a mess		marrying (a)			
lose		maker		marrying (n)			
loss		making (n)		master			
lounge		male (a)		match (n)			
love (agape)		male (n)		match (v)			
love (v)		malice		matched			
loveable		malicious		matching (a)			
loved (a)		mammal		matching (n)			
loved (person)		man		material			
lovely		manage		matrix			
loving (a)		managed (a)		matter (issue)			
loving (n)		management		matter (object)			
low		manager		matter (v)			
lowered		managing (a)		May			
lowering (a)		managing (n)		may			
lowering (n)		mandate		may not			
lowness		mandatory		maybe			
loyal		manner		maybe not			
loyalty		mansion		me			
luck		manual (a)		meal			
lucky		many (a)		mean (v)			
lull		many (n)		meaning			
lunar		map		meaningful			
		mapped (a)		meaningless			

word	symbol	word	symbol	word	symbol
meant (a)		middle (n)		misunderstanding	
measure		middle finger		misunderstood	
measured		midnight		mix (n)	
measurement		mile		mix (v)	
measuring (a)		milk		mixed (a)	
measuring (n)		millennium		mixing (n)	
meat		mind		mixture	
mechanic		mind (n)		model (n)	
mechanical		mind (v)		model (person)	
mechanism		minder		model (v)	
medical		mindful		modelled (a)	
medical professional		minding (n)		modelling (a)	
medicine (object)		mine (a)		modelling (n)	
meet (v)		minor		moderate	
meeting (a)		minority		moderation	
meeting (n)		minute		moderator	
melodious		miracle		molecular	
melody		miraculous		molecule	
memento		mirror		moment	
memory		mirrored		momentary	
mess		mirroring (n)		money	
message		misfortune		month	
message (v)		misinform		monthly	
messaging (a)		misinformation		moon	
messaging (n)		misinformed (a)		moonlight	
messenger		misinforming (n)		moral (a)	
messy		miss (n)		morality	
metal		miss (v)		more	
metallic		missed (a)		moss	
metaphor		missile		most	
metaphorical		missing (a)		mother	
method		missing (n)		motherhood	
methodical		mist		mothering (n)	
metre		mistake (n)		motherly (a)	
micro-organism		mistake (v)		motion	
microscope		mistaken		motorcycle	
microscopic		misty		motorcyclist	
middle (a)		misunderstand			

Appendix C — Index of Root and Augmented Syms

word	sym	word	sym	word	sym	word	sym
mountain		narrow (a)		next			
mountainous		narrow (v)		nice			
mouth		narrowing (a)		niceness			
move (n)		narrowing (n)		night			
move (v)		narrowness		nightly			
moveable		nation		no			
moved (a)		national		noise			
movement		natural		noisy			
mover		nature		non-essential			
moving (a)		naughtiness		nonsense			
moving (n)		naughty		nonsensical			
much		near		noon			
mud		neat		north			
muddy		neatness		northern			
multiplication		necessary		nose			
multiply		neck		not			
multiplying (n)		need (n)		not enough			
muscle		need (v)		not even (adv)			
muscular		need not		not soon			
mushroom		needed		not very			
music		needing (n)		notice (n)			
musical		needle		notice (v)			
musician		needy		noticing (n)			
must		negative		November			
must not		negativity		now			
my		neither		nude			
mysterious		nerve		number (n)			
mystery		nervous		number (v)			
myth		nervousness		numbered (a)			
mythical		net		numbering (a)			
		network		numbering (n)			
nail		network (v)		nursery			
naked		networked		nut			
name (n)		networking (a)					
name (v)		networking (n)		obedience			
named (a)		new		obedient			
naming (a)		news		obey			
naming (n)		newspaper		obeying (n)			

211

Symese — Universal Symbolic Script

object (n)		operate		own not	
obvious		operated (a)		owner	
occur		operating (a)		ownership	
occurrence		operating (n)		owning (n)	
occurring (n)		operation			
ocean		operational		pack (n)	
October		operator		pack (v)	
odd		opinion		package	
odourless		opp of change		packed (a)	
of		opponent		packing (n)	
off		opportunity		page	
offer (n)		oppose		pain	
offer (v)		opposer		painful	
offering (n)		opposing (a)		painfulness	
office (a)		opposing (n)		paint (n)	
office (n)		opposite		paint (v)	
official (a)		opposition		painted (a)	
official (person)		option		painter	
often		optional		painting	
oil (n)		or		pair	
oil (v)		orange (colour)		palace	
oiled (a)		order		palm (of hand)	
oiling (n)		orderly		paper	
oily		ordinary		parallel	
old (of person)		organ		parcel	
old (of thing)		organism		park (n)	
old age		other		part	
old person		ounce		particular	
on		our(s)		partner (n)	
once		out		partner (v)	
one-tenth		outer		partnership	
one-third		outer garment		passenger	
only		outside		passive	
open (a)		oval		passivity	
open (v)		oven		past (conjunction)	
opened		over		past (time)	
opening (a)		own (a)		path	
opening (n)		own (v)		pattern	

212

Appendix C — Index of Root and Augmented Syms

word	sym	word	sym	word	sym	word	sym
pause (n)	◁ᵛ	phase	⋈	plant	⚭		
pause (v)	◁ˇ	philia	⊃	plastic	⌀		
paused (a)	◁ˇˇ	philosopher	⊐¹ᵢ	plate	|◠|		
pausing (n)	◁⁼	philosophy	⊐¹	platform	⌐		
peace	✂	phone (a)	θˋ	play (n)	▷		
peaceful	✂ˋ	phone (n)	θ	play (v)	▷ˊ		
peak (a)	△ˋ	phone (v)	θˊ	player	▷⁻ᴵ		
peak (n)	△	phoning (n)	θ⁻	playground	▷ᵛ		
pebble	⌽ᵛ	photograph	⊙¹	playing (a)	▷⁼		
peer	╫	phrase	⌊·⁼	playing (n)	▷⁻		
peg (n)	◁]¹	picture	⊙	plea	↑¹		
peg (v)	◁]ˊ	picturesque	⊙ˋ	plead	↑ˊ		
pegged (a)	◁]ˇ	pierce	⌊ˊ	pleading (n)	↑⁼		
pegging (n)	◁]⁼	piercing (a)	⌊⁼	please	٩ˊ		
pen	⊽	piercing (n)	⌊⁻	pleasurable	☒·		
pencil	⊼	pile	‖¹	pleasure	☒·		
people	⊥⁺	pillow	⊟¹	pocket	⌊		
perceive	◇ˊ	pin (n)	⌊	poet	⊢⁻ᴵ		
perceived (a)	◇ˇˇ	pin (v)	⌊ˊ	poetic	⊢⁻ˋ		
perceiving (n)	◇⁻	pining (n)	⌊⁻	poetry	⊢⁻		
perception	◇	pink	|②|	point	[·]		
perceptive	◇ˋ	pinned (a)	⌊ˇˇ	pointed	[·]ˇˇ		
perceptiveness	◇⁼	pipe	⎯¹	poison	⊠		
perfume	⟨+⟩	piped (a)	⎯¹ˇˇ	poisonous	⊠ˋ		
period	⊠̄	piping (n)	⎯¹⁻	pole	⌠		
periodic	⊠̄⁼	pit	↔ᴴ	political	⊗ˋ		
permission	⋊	pitch (sound)	♂	political party	⊗		
permissive (a)	⋊ˋ	place	⋈	politician	⊗ᴵ		
permissiveness	⋊¹	placid	⊛ˋ	politics	⊗		
permit (n)	⋊ᴴ	plain (ordinary)	⌑ˇ	pond	⊖⁴		
permit (v)	⋊ˊ	plan (n)	↬	poor (a)	⊡ˋ		
permitted (a)	⋊ˇˇ	plan (v)	↬ˊ	poor (person)	⊡ᴵ		
permitting (n)	⋊⁻	planet	⊖	port	⊠◌		
person	⊥	planetary	⊖ˋ	position	▷		
personal	⊥ˋ	planned (a)	↬ˇˇ	positive	+ˊ		
personality	⊥ᵛ	planner	↬ᴵ	positivity	+¹		
perspective	◌	planning (a)	↬⁼	possess	◡ˊ		
pharmacy	⊗¹	planning (n)	↬⁻	possessing (n)	◡⁻		

word	word	word	word
possession	pretence	processor	
possibility	pretend	produce (n)	
possible	pretending (n)	produce (v)	
pot	pretentious	producer	
potential	previous	producing (a)	
potential (a)	price (n)	producing (n)	
pound (weight)	price (v)	product	
poverty	priceless	production	
powder	pricing (n)	program (n)	
power	pride	program (v)	
power (v)	principal	programmable	
powered	principle	programmed (a)	
powerful	principled	programmer	
powering (n)	print (n)	programming (a)	
powerless	print (v)	programming (n)	
practical	printed (a)	progress (n)	
practice	printing (a)	progress (v)	
practise	printing (n)	progressing (n)	
practised (a)	privacy	progression	
practising (a)	private	progressive	
practising (n)	privatisation	project (n)	
pray	privatise	proof	
prayer	privatised (a)	proponent	
praying (n)	privatising (a)	propose	
precise	privatising (n)	proposed (a)	
precision	prize	proposer	
preparation	proactive	proposing (a)	
prepare	probability	proposing (n)	
prepared	probable	proposition	
preparedness	problem	proud (a)	
preparing (n)	problematic	proud (person)	
presence	proceed	prove	
present (now)	process (n)	proven	
present (opp absent)	process (v)	provide	
press (v)	process food	providence	
pressing (a)	processed (a)	provider	
pressing (n)	processing (a)	providing (n)	
pressure	processing (n)	proving (n)	

Appendix C — Index of Root and Augmented Syms

word	sym	word	sym	word	sym
provision		puzzling (n)		random	
prudence		pyramid		randomise	
prudent		pyramid-shaped		randomness	
public				range (n)	
publicise		qualification		range (v)	
publicised (a)		qualified (a)		ranging (a)	
publicising (n)		qualify		ranging (n)	
publicity		qualifying (a)		rare	
pull (n)		qualifying (n)		ratio	
pull (v)		quality		raw (natural)	
pulling (n)		quantification		raw (uncooked)	
pungent		quantified (a)		reach (n)	
pungent smell		quantify		reach (v)	
pungent taste		quantifying (n)		reachable	
punish		quantity		reaching (n)	
punishment		quarter		react	
purchase (n)		queen		reacting (a)	
purchase (v)		quest		reacting (n)	
purchased (a)		question (n)		reaction	
purchaser		question (v)		reactive	
purchasing (a)		questionable		read (n)	
purchasing (n)		questioned		read (v)	
pure		questioning (a)		reader	
purified		questioning (n)		readiness	
purifier		queue (n)		reading (a)	
purify		queue (v)		reading (n)	
purifying (a)		queueing (n)		ready (a)	
purifying (n)		quilt		ready (v)	
purity				readying (n)	
purple		racket		real	
purpose		rain (n)		realisation	
push (n)		rain (v)		realise	
push (v)		rainbow		realised (a)	
pushing (n)		raining (n)		realising (n)	
pushy		rainy		reality	
puzzle		raise (v)		reason	
puzzled (a)		raised (a)		reasonable	
puzzling (a)		raising (n)		reasoned	

reasoning (n)		reduction		relating (n)			
recap (n)		refer		relationship			
recap (v)		reference		relative (a)			
recapping (n)		referral		relative (person)			
receipt		referring (n)		release (n)			
receive		reflect		release (v)			
received (a)		reflecting (n)		releasing (n)			
receiver		reflection		relevant			
receiving (a)		reflective		relief (a)			
receiving (n)		reflector		relief (n)			
recent		refresh		relieve			
receptacle		refreshing (a)		relieved (a)			
recipient		refreshing (n)		relieving (n)			
recline		refreshment		religion			
reclining (a)		refrigerator		remember			
reclining (n)		region		remembering (n)			
recognise		regress		remind			
recognised (a)		regressing (n)		reminder			
recognising (n)		regression		reminding (n)			
recognition		regressive		removal			
record (v)		regular (even)		remove			
recorded		regular (norm)		removing (n)			
recorder		regulate (even)		repair (n)			
recording (a)		regulate (norm)		repair (v)			
recording (n)		regulated (norm)		repairing (n)			
recording studio		regulating (even)		repeat			
rectangle		regulating (norm)		repeated			
rectangular		regulation		repeating (a)			
rectification		regulator (person)		repeating (n)			
rectified (a)		regulatory		repel			
rectify		reject (n)		repellant (a)			
rectifying (n)		reject (v)		repelling (n)			
red		rejecting (n)		repetition			
red blood cell		rejection		repetitive			
reduce		rejoice		replace			
reduced (a)		rejoicing (n)		replacement			
reducing (a)		relate		replacing (n)			
reducing (n)		related (a)		report (n)			

Appendix C — Index of Root and Augmented Syms

word	sym	word	sym	word	sym	word	sym
report (v)		restricted (a)		richness			
reporter		restricting (n)		riddle			
reporting (a)		restriction		right (opp left)			
reporting (n)		restrictive		right (opp wrong)			
reptile		result (n)		right (v)			
reputation		result (v)		rightful			
require		resulting (a)		righting (n)			
required (a)		retreat (n)		ring (object)			
requirement		retreat (v)		ring (shape)			
requiring (n)		retreating (a)		ring finger			
research (n)		retreating (n)		ringed (a)			
research (v)		retry (n)		rise (n)			
researcher		retry (v)		rise (v)			
researching (n)		retrying (n)		risen (a)			
reside		return (n)		rising (a)			
resident (a)		return (v)		rising (n)			
resident (n)		returned (a)		risk (n)			
residential		returning (a)		risk (v)			
residing (n)		returning (n)		risking (n)			
resource		reveal		risky			
resourceful		revealed (a)		river			
resourcefulness		revealing (a)		road			
resourcing (a)		revealing (n)		rock			
resourcing (n)		revelation		rocket			
respond		reversion		role			
responding (a)		revert		roll (n)			
responding (n)		reverting (n)		roll (v)			
response		review (n)		rolled (a)			
responsibility		review (v)		rolling (a)			
responsible		reviewer		rolling (n)			
responsive		reward		roof			
rest (n)		reward (v)		room			
rest (v)		rewarding (a)		root			
rested (a)		rewarding (n)		rot (n)			
resting (a)		rhythm		rot (v)			
resting (n)		rhythmic		rotten			
restless		rich (a)		rotting (a)			
restrict		rich (person)		rotting (n)			

word	symbol	word	symbol	word	symbol	word	symbol
rough		salty		seated			
roughness		salty smell		seating			
route (n)		salty taste		second (a)			
route (v)		same		second (position)			
router		sameness		second (time)			
routing (a)		sample		secrecy			
routing (n)		sample (v)		secret (a)			
row		sampled (a)		secret (n)			
royal		sampling (n)		section			
royalty		sand		secure (a)			
rule (n)		sandal		secure (v)			
rule (v)		sandy		secured			
ruled (person)		save		securing (n)			
ruler (person)		saver		security			
ruling (a)		saving (a)		see			
ruling (n)		saving (n)		seed			
run (n)		saviour		seeing (a)			
run (v)		savoury		seeing (n)			
runner		savoury smell		seek			
running (a)		savoury taste		seeking (n)			
running (n)		say (v)		seem			
rush (n)		scalp		seldom			
rush (v)		scare (n)		self			
rushed hurried (a)		scare (v)		selfish			
rushing hurrying (n)		scared		sell			
		scary		seller			
sacrifice (n)		school		selling (a)			
sacrifice (v)		science		selling (n)			
sacrificial		scientific		send			
sacrificing (n)		scientist		sender			
sad		scissors		sending (n)			
sadness		scope		sense (n)			
safe (a)		screw		sense (v)			
safe (object)		screwdriver		senseless			
safety		sea		sensibility			
sale		season		sensible			
saliva		seasonal		sensing (a)			
salt		seat		sensing (n)			

Appendix C — Index of Root and Augmented Syms

sensitive		shaping (n)		shorts			
sensor		share (n)		should			
sensuous		share (v)		should not			
sent (a)		shared (a)		shoulder			
sentence		sharing (a)		shrink			
separate (a)		sharing (n)		shrinking (a)			
separate (v)		sharp		shrinking (n)			
separated (a)		sharpen		shutter			
separating (n)		sharpened (a)		sibling			
separation		sharpening (a)		sick			
September		sharpening (n)		sight			
sequence (n)		sharpness		sign			
sequence (v)		she		silence			
sequencing (n)		shelf		silent			
series		shell		similar			
serious		shelve		simple			
seriousness		shelving (n)		simplicity			
servant		shine		since			
serve		shining (a)		sing			
server		shining (n)		singer			
service		ship		singing (a)			
serving (a)		shirt		singing (n)			
serving (n)		shoe		single (a)			
set		shop (n)		single (n)			
sex (act)		shop (v)		singlet			
sex (gender)		shopper		singling (n)			
sexual		shopping (a)		sink (v)			
sexuality		shopping (n)		sinking (a)			
shadow		shopping mall		sinking (n)			
shall		short (opp excess)		sit			
shall not		short (opp long)		sitting (a)			
shallow		short (opp tall)		sitting (n)			
shallowness		shortage		situation			
shame		shortened (a)		size			
shameful		shortening (a)		skill			
shape (n)		shortening (n)		skilled			
shape (v)		shortness (height)		skin			
shaped		shortness (quantity)		skinny			

219

skirt		sneaker		sorting (n)			
sky		snow (n)		soul			
slant (n)		snow (v)		sound			
slant (v)		snowing (n)		sour			
slanted		snowy		sour smell			
slave		so		sour taste			
sleep (n)		so that		source (n)			
sleep (v)		social		source (v)			
sleeping (a)		societal		sourcing (a)			
sleeping (n)		society		sourcing (n)			
sleepless		sock		south			
sleepy		soft		southern			
slope (n)		soften		space (astronomy)			
slope (v)		softening (a)		space (physical)			
sloped		softening (n)		spark			
slow (a)		softness		sparked			
slow (v)		solar		sparking (n)			
slowing (a)		sold (a)		speak			
slowing (n)		sole (of foot)		speaking (a)			
slowness		solid (a)		speaking (n)			
small		solid (n)		special			
small intestines		solidify		specialisation			
smallness		solitary		specialise			
smell (n)		solitude		specialised (a)			
smell (v)		solution		specialising (n)			
smelling (a)		solve		specialist			
smelling (n)		solved (a)		specialty			
smelly		solver		specific			
smile (n)		solving (n)		specified			
smile (v)		some		specify			
smiling (a)		son		specifying (n)			
smiling (n)		song		spectacles			
smog		soon		spectrum			
smoke (n)		sorrow		speech			
smoke (v)		sorrowful		speed (n)			
smoking (a)		sorry		speed (v)			
smoking (n)		sort (v)		speeding (a)			
smoky		sorted (a)		speeding (n)			

Appendix C — Index of Root and Augmented Syms

word	sym	word	sym	word	sym	word	sym
sphere		standard (a - class)		step (n)			
spherical		standard (a - norm)		step (v)			
spice		standard (n - norm)		stepped (a)			
spiral (a)		standardise		stepping (a)			
spiral (n)		standardised (a)		stepping (n)			
spiral (v)		standardising (a)		sterile			
spiralling (a)		standardising (n)		stew (n)			
spiralling (n)		standing (a)		stew (v)			
spirit		standing (n)		stewed (a)			
spiritual		star		stewing (n)			
split (a)		star (person)		stick (n)			
split (n)		starring (a)		still (a)			
split (v)		starring (n)		stillness			
splitting (a)		starry		stolen (a)			
splitting (n)		start (n)		stomach			
spoon		start (v)		stone			
sport(s)		started (a)		stop (n)			
sporting (a)		starter		stop (v)			
sporting (n)		starting (a)		storage			
sports person		starting (n)		store (n)			
spotted		state (n)		store (v)			
spring (object)		state (v)		stored (a)			
spring (season)		stated (a)		storge			
springy		statement		storing (n)			
square (a)		static		storm			
square (n)		stating (n)		stormy			
squared (a)		station		story			
squaring (n)		status		stove			
stability		steadiness		straight			
stable (a)		steady		straighten			
staff		steal		straightened (a)			
stage (phase)		stealing (n)		straightening (n)			
stage (place)		steam		strange			
stake (claim)		steamed (a)		strategic			
stakeholder		steaming (a)		strategise			
staking (n)		steaming (n)		strategising (n)			
stand (n)		steamy		strategist			
stand (v)		stench		strategy			

stream		substantive		surface (a)			
street		subtle		surplus			
strength		subtract		surprise			
strengthen		subtracting (n)		surprised (a)			
strengthening (a)		subtraction		surprising (a)			
strengthening (n)		suburb		surprising (n)			
stretch (n)		succeed		swap (n)			
stretch (v)		succeeding (n)		swap (v)			
stretched (a)		success		swapping (n)			
stretching (n)		successful		sweet			
string (n)		such		sweet smell			
string (v)		sudden		sweet taste			
string of letters		sugar		swim (n)			
stringing (n)		suitability		swim (v)			
stripe		suitable		swimmer			
striped		suited (a)		swimming (a)			
strong		summer		swimming (n)			
structural		sun		switch off			
structure		sung (a)		switch on			
structured		sunlight		switching off (n)			
structuring (n)		sunny		switching on (n)			
strung (a)		superficial		sword			
student		superset		symbol			
studied (a)		supplied (a)		symbolic			
studious		supplier		symbolise			
study (n)		supply		symbolising (n)			
study (v)		supply (n)		system			
studying (n)		supplying (a)		systematic			
stunted		supplying (n)					
stupid		support (n)		table (n)			
stupidity		support (v)		table (v)			
sub		supported		tablet (electrical)			
subconscious		supporter		tabling (n)			
subconscious (n)		supporting (a)		tabulate			
subject		supporting (n)		tabulated (a)			
subset		supportive		tabulating (n)			
substance		sure		tabulation			
substantial		surface		tactic			

Appendix C — Index of Root and Augmented Syms

word	sym	word	sym	word	sym
tactical		team (a)		the	
tactician		team (n)		theft	
tail		tear (n)		them	
take (n)		tearful		theme	
take (v)		tearing (n)		then	
take a chance		technical		theoretical	
take not		technician		theory	
taken		technique		there	
taker		technological		these	
taking (n)		technology		they	
talk		telescope		thick	
talk (n)		telescopic		thickening (a)	
talkative		tell (n)		thickening (n)	
talking (a)		tell (v)		thickness	
talking (n)		telling (n)		thief	
tall		temperature		thin	
tame		template		thing	
tap (object)		tempo		think	
tape (n)		temporal		thinker	
tape (v)		ten times		thinking (a)	
taped (a)		tent		thinking (n)	
taping (n)		term		thinness	
target		terrified (a)		thinning (a)	
taste (n)		terrify		thinning (n)	
taste (v)		terrifying (a)		third (a)	
tasteful		terrifying (n)		third (n)	
tastefulness		terror		thirst	
tasteless		test (n)		thirsty	
tasting (a)		test (v)		this	
tasting (n)		tester		those	
tasty		testing (a)		though	
taught		testing (a)		thought	
tea		testing (n)		thoughtful	
teach		text		thoughtfulness	
teachable		than		thoughtless	
teacher		thank		thoughtlessness	
teaching (a)		thankful		thrice	
teaching (n)		that		through	

223

word		word		word		word	
throw (n)		too (excess)		transacted (a)			
throw (v)		tool		transacting (a)			
throwing (n)		tooth		transacting (n)			
thumb		top		transaction			
tidiness		topic		transcend			
tidy (a)		torso		transcendence			
tidy (v)		touch (n)		transcendent			
tie (v)		touch (v)		transcending (n)			
tied (a)		touching (a)		transport			
tight		touching (n)		trap (n)			
tighten		towards		trap (v)			
tightened (a)		towel		trapped (a)			
tightening (a)		town		trapping (n)			
tightening (n)		townouse		travel (n)			
tightness		toxic		travel (v)			
timbre		toxin		traveller			
time (n)		toy		travelling (a)			
time (v)		trade (n)		travelling (n)			
timed		trade (v)		tray			
timely		traded (a)		tree			
timer		trader		trend			
timing (n)		trading (a)		trending (a)			
tin (object)		trading (n)		trending (n)			
tip		tradition		trendy			
tissue		traditional		trial			
to		traffic		trialling (n)			
to and fro		tragedy		triangle			
today		tragic		triangular			
toe		train (n)		triangulate			
toenail		train (v)		triangulating (n)			
together		train station		triple (a)			
togetherness		trained		triple (n)			
toilet		trainee		triplet (n)			
tomorrow		trainer		tripling (n)			
tomorrow night		training (a)		trough			
tone (sound)		training (n)		trough (a)			
tongue		training course		trousers			
tonight		transact		truck			

Appendix C — Index of Root and Augmented Syms

truck depot		unbeliever		uniting (a)			
true		uncaring (a)		uniting (n)			
truncate		uncertain		unity			
truncated (a)		uncertainty		universal			
truncating (n)		unchanged		universe			
truncation		unchanging (a)		unjust			
trust (n)		uncommon		unjustified			
trust (v)		unconscious		unkind			
trusted (a)		unconsciousness		unkindness			
trusting (a)		uncooked		unknowing (a)			
trusting (n)		uncover		unknown (a)			
trustworthiness		uncovered (a)		unknown (n)			
trustworthy		uncovering (n)		unlawful			
truth		undecided		unlike			
truthful		under		unlikelihood			
try (v)		underpants		unlikely			
tube		understand		unlimited			
tumbler		understandable		unlock (v)			
tunnel		understanding (a)		unlocked (a)			
turn (n)		understanding (n)		unlocking (n)			
turn (v)		understood (a)		unlucky			
turning (a)		undesirable		unnatural			
turning (n)		undoubted (a)		unnecessary			
twice		unequal		unneeded			
twin		unethical		unofficial			
two months		uneven		unpack			
two years		unexpected		unpacking (n)			
tying (n)		unexplored		unpowered (a)			
type		unfair		unprocessed			
		unfaithful		unquestionable (a)			
ugliness		unfaithfulness		unquestioned (a)			
ugly		unfriendly		unquestioning (a)			
umbrella		unhealthy		unreachable			
unappreciative		unhelpful		unreal			
unassuming (a)		unimportant		unreasonable			
unavailable		unit		unregulated			
unbalanced		unite		unresponsive			
unbelievable		united		unscientific			

unsecured		validate		villa		
unseen (a)		validated (a)		village		
unselfish		validating (n)		vinegar		
unskilled		validation		violet		
unspecified		valley		viral		
unstable		valuable		virtue		
unsteadiness		valuation		virtuous		
unsteady		value (n)		virulent		
unsure		value (v)		virus		
unteachable		valued (a)		visibility		
unthinking (a)		valuer		visible		
until		valuing (n)		visit (n)		
unusual		vapour		visit (v)		
unwanted		variable (a)		visiting (a)		
up		variable (n)		visiting (n)		
up and down		variance		visitor		
urgency		varied (a)		visual		
urgent		variety		voice		
urinate		various		volume (sound)		
urinating (n)		vary		vote (n)		
urination		varying (a)		vote (v)		
us		varying (n)		voter		
usage		vegetable		voting (a)		
use (n)		vegetarian (a)		voting (n)		
use (v)		vegetarian (person)				
used (a)		vehicle		wait		
user		vent		wait (n)		
using		vertical		waiter		
usual		very		waiting (a)		
utensil		vest		waiting (n)		
		vice		walk (n)		
vacancy		vicious		walk (v)		
vacant		viciousness		walker		
vacate		view (n)		walking (a)		
vacating (n)		view (v)		walking (n)		
vacuum		viewer		wall		
vague		viewing (a)		want (n)		
valid		viewing (n)		want (v)		

Appendix C — Index of Root and Augmented Syms

word		word		word		word	
want not		weapon		will close		wind	
wanted		weather (n)		will not		window	
wanting (a)		weather (v)		will open		windy	
wanting (n)		weathered		win (n)		wine	
war		weathering (n)		win (v)		wing	
warm (a)		week		wind		winning (a)	
warm (v)		weekly		window		winning (n)	
warming (a)		weight		windy		winter	
warming (n)		weird		wine		wire	
warmth		west		wing		wiry	
warring		western		winning (a)		wisdom	
wastage		wet (a)		winning (n)		wise	
waste (n)		wet (v)		winter		with	
waste (v)		wetting (a)		wire		within	
wasted (a)		wetting (n)		wiry		without	
wasting		what		wisdom		woman	
watch (device)		wheel		wise		wonder (n)	
water		wheeling (n)		with		wonder (v)	
water (v)		when		within		wonderful	
watering (a)		where		without		wondering (n)	
watering (n)		which		woman		wood	
watery		while (conjunction)		wonder (n)		wooden	
wave (n)		white		wonder (v)		word	
wave (v)		white blood cell		wonderful		work (n)	
waving (n)		who		wondering (n)		work (v)	
wavy (a)		whole		wood		worker	
wax (n)		why		wooden		working (a)	
wax (v)		wicked		word		working (n)	
waxed (a)		wickedness		work (n)		world	
waxy		wide		work (v)		worldly	
way		widen		worker		worried	
we		widening (a)		working (a)		worry (n)	
weak		widening (n)		working (n)		worry (v)	
weaken		width		world			
weakening (a)		wife		worldly			
weakening (n)		wild		worried			
weakness		will (n)		worry (n)			
wealth		will (v)		worry (v)			

227

worrying (a)	⊚↥ˣ	writing (n)	⩑⁻	young	⌣ˋ	
worrying (n)	⊚↥ˣ	written	⩑ˋˋ	young person	⌣ᴵ	
worse	⤬	wrong (a)	✝ˋ	your(s)	⊤ˋ	
worst	⤬	wrong (v)	✝´	youth	⌣	
worth (n)	$	wrongful	✝ˋˋ	youthfulness	⌣⁻	
worth (v)	$			yucky	⌓ˣ	
wound (n)	⋈ᴴ	yard (measure)	A⁴			
wound (v)	⋈ᴴ	year	⨉³	zip (n)	◁²	
wounded (a)	⋈ᴴ	yearly	⨉³	zip (v)	◁²	
wounding (n)	⋈ᴴ	yellow	④	zipped (a)	◁²	
wrath	⋈·	yes	+	zipping (n)	◁²	
write	⩑´	yesterday	⊠	zone	⌒	
writer	⩑ᴵ	you	⊤			
writing (a)	⩑ˉ	you all	⊤			

Appendix D – Index of Headwords

word		word		word		word	
a		agree		annual			
able		agriculture		another			
about (approx)		ahead		answer (n)			
about (relating to)		aid (n)		antidote			
above		aim (n)		anxiety			
absent		air		any			
accept		aircraft		apart			
access (v)		airport		apartment			
accident		alcohol		apology			
accord		align		app			
account		alike		apparent			
accurate		alive		appear			
ache		all		appetite			
achieve		allow		apply			
across		almost		appreciation			
act		alone		April			
active (a)		along		arc			
actor		alphabet		arch			
adapt		also		are			
add		altitude		area			
address		altruism		arena			
administer		amaze		arm			
adornment		amid		around			
adult		among		arrange			
advance (n)		an		arrive			
advantage		analog		arrogance			
advice		analogy		art			
affect		analysis		artificial			
afraid		ancestor		as			
after		ancient		ascend			
again		and		ascertain			
against (oppose)		anger		ash			
against (space)		angle		ask			
age		angry		asleep			
ago		animal		aspire			

Symese — Universal Symbolic Script

word	symbol	word	symbol	word	symbol
assemble		balance (parity)		below	
assess		ball		belt	
assume		balloon		bench	
at		band (object)		bent	
atmosphere		bank		beside	
atom		barrel		bespectacled	
attach		barren		best	
attack (n)		base		better	
attempt (v)		basement		between	
attend		basic		beyond	
attic		basin		bicycle	
attract		basis		big	
audience		basket		bin	
audio		bat (object)		bind (v)	
August		bathroom		bird	
aural		battle		bit	
author		battlefield		bite (n)	
authority		be		bitter smell	
automatic		be not		bitter taste	
autumn		be still		black	
available		beam (object)		blade	
avenue		beard		blame (n)	
average (a)		beast		blanket	
awake		beat (v)		blind (a)	
away from		beauty		block (n)	
axe		because		blood	
		become		blouse	
baby		bed		blow (v)	
back (opp front)		bedroom		blue	
back of body		beer		blunt (a)	
back of head		before		board (n)	
background		befriend		boat	
backward		begin		body	
bacteria		behind		boil (v)	
bad		being (n)		bond	
bag		belief		bondage	
bake		bell		bone	
balance (harmony)		beloved (a)		book	

230

Appendix D — Index of Headwords

word		word		word		word	
book collection		but		ceiling		chain	
boot		butter		cell (bio)		chair	
border		buttock		centigrade		chance	
boredom (n)		button		centre		change (n)	
borrow		buy		century		chaos	
bottle		by		certain		character	
bottom				chain		charity	
bound (a)		cabin		chair		chasm	
boundary		cage		chance		check (n)	
bow (v)		calendar		change (n)		cheek	
bowl		call (v)		chaos		cheese	
box		callous		character		chemical	
bra		calm		charity		chest	
brain		camera		chasm		chew	
branch		can (able to)		check (n)		child	
brave		can (object)		cheek		chin	
break (v)		candy		cheese		choose	
breast		cane		chemical		chopper	
breath		cannot		chest		chopsticks	
breeze		cap		chew		circle	
bridge		car		child		city	
bright		card		chin		claim (v)	
brilliant		cardboard		choose		clarity	
bring forward		care (n)		chopper		clause	
broken		career		chopsticks		clay	
broom		careful		circle		clean (a)	
brown		careless		city		cleanse	
brush (n)		carriage		claim (v)		clear (uncluttered)	
bubble		carry		clarity		clear (unobscured)	
bucket		cart		clause		clever	
bud		case		clay		click (n)	
build		cash		clean (a)		climate	
bulb		castle		cleanse			
bundle (n)		casual		clear (uncluttered)			
burn (v)		catalog (n)		clear (unobscured)			
bus		catch (v)		clever			
business (n)		category		click (n)			
busy		cause (n)		climate			

231

word	symbol	word	symbol	word	symbol
climb (v)		confident		crash (n)	
clinic		confuse		crawl	
clock		conscious		create	
close (a)		consider		creature	
cloth		consult		credible	
clothes		consume		creek	
cloud (n)		contain		creep	
coat		content		crew	
code		context		criminal (n)	
coffee		continent		critical	
cognition		continue		crooked	
coil (n)		contract (deal)		crop	
cold (a)		contract (shrink)		cross (shape)	
collect		control (v)		crowd	
colour		converge		cruel	
colourless		converse (v)		cry (v)	
column		cook (v)		cube	
come		cooktop		cuddle (n)	
comfort (n)		cool (a)		culture	
command (n)		cooler (object)		cup	
comment (n)		cooperate		cupboard	
common (frequent)		copulate		curious (a)	
common (shared)		copy (n)		curl (n)	
communicate		core (n)		currency	
community (n)		corner		current (time)	
companion		corpse		curve (n)	
company (n)		correct (v)		customer	
compare		cost (n)		cut (v)	
compete		count (n)		cutlery	
complete (a)		country		cyan	
complex		couple		cycle (n)	
compound		courage		cyclist	
computer		court		cylinder	
concept		cover (n)			
concern (n)		covering (foot)		daily	
condition		covering (head)		damage (n)	
cone		crack (n)		damp (a)	
confide		craft		dance (n)	

Appendix D — Index of Headwords

danger	destitute	dislike (v)	
data	destroy	disloyal	
date (n)	detail (n)	disorder	
daughter	develop	disperse	
day	device	distance	
dead	diagram	distress (n)	
deadly	diamond	district	
deaf	diamond shape	disunity	
death	die (v)	diverge	
decade	differ (v)	divide	
decay (n)	difficult	divine	
December	diffident	do (v)	
decentralise	dig	do not	
decide	digital	door	
decorate	diligent	doorway	
decrease (n)	dining room	dot	
deduce	dip	double (a)	
deep	direct (a)	doubt (n)	
defecate	direction	down	
defend	director	drain	
defer	dirt	draw	
delay (n)	disable	drawer	
delicious	disadvantage	dread (n)	
deliver	disagree	dreadful	
demand (n)	disappear	dream (n)	
depart	disbelief	dress	
depot	discard (v)	dried (a)	
depressed	discern	drink (n)	
depth	discontinue	drive (n)	
descend	discourage	drop (n)	
descendant	discover	drown	
describe	discuss	dry	
desert	disease	dull	
design (n)	disguise (n)	duration	
desire (n)	disgust	during	
desk	dish	dust	
despise (v)	dishonest	duty	
despite	dishonour (n)	dynamic	

word	word	word	word
eager	entrance	external (a)	
ear	environment	extra (a)	
early	equal (a)	extraordinary	
earn	equipment	extreme	
earth (world)	equity	extrinsic	
east	era	eye	
easy	erase		
eat	eros	face	
ecology	error	facet	
economy	escape (n)	fact	
edge	essence	factor	
effect (n)	establish	factory	
effort	eternity	fahrenheit	
egg	ethics	fail	
ego	evaluate	fair (just)	
either	even	faith	
elated	even (adv)	fall (v)	
elbow	event	false	
electric	every	fame	
element	evil (a)	family	
email (n)	examine	far	
emergency	example	farm	
emotion	exceed	fast (a)	
empathy	except	fast (hunger)	
empower	excess (a)	fasten	
empty (a)	excite	fat (a)	
enable	exclude	father	
enclose	execute (task)	favour (n)	
encourage	exit (n)	favourite	
end (n)	expand	fear (n)	
enemy	expect	feast (n)	
energy	experience	feature (n)	
engine	expert	February	
enigma	explain	feed (v)	
enjoy	explore	feel (v)	
enlarge	expose	female (a)	
enough	express (v)	fence	
entity	extend	ferry	

Appendix D — Index of Headwords

word		word		word		word	
fertile		flower		frost			
few (a)		fly (v)		frown (n)			
field (object)		focus (n)		fruit			
field (subject)		fog		fruit orchard			
fierce		fold (n)		fry			
fight (n)		follow		full			
fill (n)		food		fun			
filter (n)		foolish		function			
fin		foot		fungus			
final (a)		foot (measure)		funnel (n)			
find (v)		for		funny			
fine		forbidden		fur			
finesse		force (n)		furnace			
finger		foreground		furniture			
fingernail		forehead		fury			
finish (n)		forest		future			
finite		forget		fuzzy			
fire		forgive					
firm (a)		fork		galaxy			
first (a)		form (n)		gale			
fish+		formation		gamble (n)			
fisherman		former		game			
fit (n - suit)		fortitude		gap			
fix (n)		fortnight		garage			
flag (n)		fortress		garden			
flame		forward		garment			
flash		foundation		garment (waist dn)			
flat		fraction		garment (waist up)			
flavour		fragile		gas			
flesh		frail		gate			
flex (v)		frame		gather			
flexible		free (a)		gauge (n)			
flight		freeze		gender			
flip (v)		frequency		general			
float (v)		friend		generation			
flood		fright (n)		gentle			
floor		from					
flow (n)		front (a)					

235

word	symbol	word	symbol	word	symbol	word	symbol
gentleman		hair		hire out		his	
get		half		history		hit (n)	
ghost		hammer		hold (v)		hole	
giant		hand		hollow		home	
give		handle (n)		honest		honey	
give not		hang		honour (n)		hook	
glad		happen		hop (n)		hope (n)	
glass (material)		happy		horizon		horizontal	
glass (object)		harbour		hospital		hot (spicy) smell	
glide (v)		hard		hot (spicy) taste		hot (temperature)	
go		harmony		hour		hourglass	
goal		has		house		how	
God		has not		hug (n)		human	
god		hat		humble (a)		humour	
good (a)		hate (n)		hungry		hurry (n)	
govern		have		hurt		husband	
gradual		have not		hut		I	
grain (plant)		hazard		ice		icon	
grain (texture)		he		idea			
gram		head (n)					
grass		heal					
grateful		health					
greed		hear					
green		heart					
grey		heat (n)					
grief		heavy					
grill (n)		height					
groin		help (n)					
ground		her(s)					
group (n)		herb					
grove		here					
grow		hide					
guard (n)		high					
guardian		hill					
guess (n)		him					
guide (v)		hinge					
guilt		hint (n)					
		hire in					

Appendix D — Index of Headwords

idle (a)	industry	is not	issue
if	inequality	it	it all
ill	inequity	item	its
image	infant		
imagine	infinity	jacket	January
imbalance	inform	jar	jaw
immediate	inherent	jetplane	job
immoral	iniquity	join (v)	joint
impersonal	initial (a)	joke	journey
important	injure (v)	joy	judge (v)
impossible	inner	jug	juice
impractical	inner garment	July	jump (v)
imprecise	insect	June	jungle
impress	insecure	just (adv)	just (fair)
improbable	insensitive	justice	justify
imprudent	insert		
impure	inside	keen	keep
in	insight	key (n)	kick
in front	insipid	kind	king
in spite of	inspire	kiss (n)	kitchen
inaccessible	instinct		
inaccurate	instruct		
inactive	instrument		
inch	integrating (a)		
include	integrity		
incomparable	intellect		
incomplete	intelligence		
inconceivable	interest (topic)		
increase (n)	internal (a)		
incredible	internet		
increment (n)	intrinsic		
indecisive	intuition		
indeed	invalid		
index	invent		
index finger	invisible		
indicate	invite		
indirect	irresponsible		
individual (a)	is		

237

word	symbol	word	symbol	word	symbol
kitchen knife	◁¹	level	[=]ˇ	loyal	✽`
knee	⋏	level (measure)	×¹	luck	⇀ˇ
kneel	☐´	library	◫ᴴ	lull	⊘
knife	✕¹	lid	⊜	lunar	⌑`
knot	⌒	lie down	⊏¹		
know	◇´	life	⊘	machine	⬠
		lifeform	8	magic	✸
label (n)	⊥ᴴ	light (opp darkness)	△	mail	♡¹
ladder	⊨	light (opp heavy)	⛉`	main	⋈
ladle	◁²	like (a)	╲`	maintain	▱
lady	(⊧	likely	⋀`	major	⌒
lake	⊖³	limit (n)	⊥	majority	⌒
land	⊖	line	⊐	make	⌇
lane	⌐¹	link (n)	⊚	make a mess	∢ˣ
language	♡	lip	⊖	male (a)	)`
large	⌒`	liquid (n)	⛉	malice	✕¹
large intestines	⊚	list (n)	-|-	mammal	⊗
last night	⋈	listen	0ˇ	man	)ᴵ
late	>`	literal	∥²	manage	⊆´
latter	ⅅ\`	literature	⊢	mandate	⊻³
laugh	⊙	little (a - number)	▽`	manner	⌐ˇ
law	⋈	little (a - size)	∪`	mansion	⊟⌒
lawn	⚲ˇ	little finger	⊻⁵	manual (a)	⊃`
layer (n)	F	live	⊘´	many (a)	△
lazy	⊬ˣ	local (a)	⊃ˇ	map	⊃²
lead	⊳´	locate	⊃ˇ	March	×²₃
leaf	⚲	lock (n)	⊓	marina	⊠ˇ
lean (a)	∞ˣ	locker	⊓ᴴ	marine	⊖²
learn	◁´	logo	⊢²	mark	⊢³
least	⋁°	lonely	∥²	market (n)	⋈
leave	>´	long	⋀`	maroon	⊚
left (opp right)	←`	look	⊙´	marriage	⊠
leg	⋏	loose	⊳`	master	⋈
lend	⊃¹	lose	⟆´	match (v)	⌐`
lens	∞	lounge	⊟¹	material	▽
less	⋁`	love (agape)	♡	matrix	⟨⟩
letter (character)	⋅|	lovely	♡`	matter (issue)	⋀
letter (object)	♡¹	low	⋁`	matter (object)	⊡ᴴ

Appendix D — Index of Headwords

May		miracle		myth		
may		mirror				nail
may not		misfortune		naked		
maybe		misinform		name (n)		
maybe not		miss (n)		narrow (a)		
me		missile		nation		
meal		mist		nature		
mean (v)		mistake (n)		naughty		
measure		misunderstand		near		
meat		mix (n)		neat		
mechanic		mixture		necessary		
mechanism		model (n)		neck		
medical professional		moderate		need (v)		
medicine (object)		molecule		need not		
meet (v)		moment		needle		
melody		money		negative		
memento		month		neither		
memory		moon		nerve		
mess		moral (a)		net		
message		more		network		
messy		moss		new		
metal		most		news		
metaphor		mother		next		
method		motion		nice		
metre		motorcycle		night		
micro-organism		mountain		no		
microscope		mouth		noise		
middle (n)		move (v)		nonsense		
middle finger		much		noon		
midnight		mud		north		
mile		multiply		nose		
milk		muscle		not		
millennium		mushroom		not enough		
mind		music		not even (adv)		
mine (a)		must		not soon		
minor		must not		not very		
minority		my		notice (n)		
minute		mystery				

November		orange (colour)		pattern	
now		order		pause (n)	
nude		ordinary		peace	
number (n)		organ		peak (n)	
nursery		organism		pebble	
nut		other		peer	
		ounce		peg (n)	
obey		our(s)		pen	
object (n)		out		pencil	
obvious		outer		people	
occur		outer garment		perceive	
ocean		outside		perfume	
October		oval		period	
odd		oven		permit (v)	
odourless		over		person	
of		own (v)		perspective	
off		own not		pharmacy	
offer (n)				phase	
office (n)		pack (n)		philia	
often		package		philosophy	
oil (n)		page		phone (n)	
old (of person)		pain		photograph	
old (of thing)		paint (n)		phrase	
old person		pair		picture	
on		palace		pierce	
once		palm (of hand)		pile	
one-tenth		paper		pillow	
one-third		parallel		pin (n)	
only		parcel		pining (n)	
open (a)		park (n)		pink	
operate		part		pipe	
opinion		particular		pit	
opp of change		partner (n)		pitch (sound)	
opportunity		passenger		place	
oppose		passive		placid	
opposite		past (conjunction)		plain (ordinary)	
option		past (time)		plan (n)	
or		path		planet	

Appendix D — Index of Headwords

word		word		word		word	
plant		pride		queen		racket	
plastic		principal		quest		rain (n)	
plate		principle		question (n)		rainbow	
platform		print (n)		queue (n)		raise (v)	
play (v)		private		quilt		random	
playground		prize				range (n)	
plea		proactive		racket		rare	
please		probable		rain (n)		ratio	
pleasure		problem		rainbow		raw (natural)	
pocket		proceed		raise (v)		raw (uncooked)	
poetry		process (n)		random		reach (v)	
point		process food		range (n)		react	
poison		produce (v)		rare		read (v)	
pole		program (n)		ratio		ready	
politics		progress (n)		raw (natural)		real	
pond		project (n)		raw (uncooked)		realise	
poor (a)		proof		reach (v)		reason	
port		proponent		react		recap (v)	
position		propose		read (v)		receive	
positive		proud (a)		ready		recent	
possess		provide		real		receptacle	
possible		prudent		realise		recline	
pot		public		reason		recognise	
potential		pull (v)		recap (v)		record (v)	
pound (weight)		pungent smell		receive		recording studio	
powder		pungent taste		recent		rectangle	
power		punish		receptacle		rectify	
practice		purchase (v)		recline		red	
pray		pure		recognise		red blood cell	
precise		purple		record (v)		reduce	
prepare		purpose		recording studio		refer	
present (now)		push (v)		rectangle		reflect	
present (opp absent)		puzzle		rectify			
press (v)		pyramid		red			
pressure				red blood cell			
pretend		quality		reduce			
previous		quantity		refer			
price (n)		quarter		reflect			

241

Symese — Universal Symbolic Script

refresh		review (v)		same	
refrigerator		reward		sample	
region		rhythm		sand	
regress		rich (a)		sandal	
regular (even)		riddle		save	
regular (norm)		right (opp left)		savoury smell	
reject (v)		right (opp wrong)		savoury taste	
rejoice		ring (object)		say (v)	
relate		ring (shape)		scalp	
release (n)		ring finger		scare (n)	
relevant		rise (v)		school	
relief (n)		risk (n)		science	
religion		river		scissors	
remember		road		scope	
remind		rock		screw	
remove		rocket		screwdriver	
repair (n)		role		sea	
repeat		roll (n)		season	
repel		roof		seat	
replace		room		second (a)	
report (n)		root		second (time)	
reptile		rot (n)		secret (n)	
reputation		rough		section	
require		route (n)		secure (a)	
research (n)		router		see	
reside		row		seed	
resource		royal		seek	
respond		rule (n)		seem	
responsible		run (v)		seldom	
rest (v)		rush (n)		self	
restless				sell	
restrict		sacrifice (n)		send	
result (n)		sad		sense (n)	
retreat (n)		safety		sensible	
retry (n)		saliva		sentence	
return (v)		salt		separate (a)	
reveal		salty smell		September	
revert		salty taste		sequence (n)	

Appendix D — Index of Headwords

series	simple	son	
serious	since	song	
serve	sing	soon	
set	single (a)	sorrow	
sex (act)	singlet	sorry	
sex (gender)	sink (v)	sort (v)	
shadow	sit	soul	
shall	situation	sound	
shall not	size	sour smell	
shallow	skill	sour taste	
shame	skin	source (n)	
shape (n)	skirt	south	
share (v)	sky	space (astronomy)	
sharp	slant (n)	space (physical)	
she	slave	spark	
shelf	sleep (v)	speak	
shell	slope (n)	special	
shine	slow (a)	specific	
ship	small	spectacles	
shirt	small intestines	spectrum	
shoe	smell (n)	speed (n)	
shop (n)	smile (v)	sphere	
shopping mall	smog	spice	
short (opp excess)	smoke (n)	spiral (n)	
short (opp long)	sneaker	spirit	
short (opp tall)	snow (n)	split (a)	
shortage	so	spoon	
shorts	so that	sport(s)	
should	social	spring (object)	
should not	society	spring (season)	
shoulder	sock	square (n)	
shrink	soft	stable (a)	
shutter	solar	staff	
sibling	sole (of foot)	stage (phase)	
sick	solid (n)	stage (place)	
sign	solitude	stake (claim)	
silence	solve	stakeholder	
similar	some	stand (v)	

243

Symese — Universal Symbolic Script

word	symbol	word	symbol	word	symbol
standard (a - class)		study (n)		tactic	
standard (a - norm)		stunted		tail	
star		stupid		take (v)	
star (person)		sub		take a chance	
start (v)		subconscious		take not	
state (n)		subject		talk (n)	
state (v)		subset		tall	
static		substance		tame	
station		subtle		tap (object)	
status		subtract		tape (n)	
steady		suburb		target	
steal		success		taste (n)	
steam		such		tea	
stench		sudden		teach	
step (n)		sugar		team (n)	
sterile		suitable		tear (n)	
stew (n)		summer		technical	
stick (n)		sun		technique	
still (a)		superficial		technology	
stomach		superset		telescope	
stone		supply		tell (v)	
stop (v)		support (v)		temperature	
store (n)		sure		template	
storge		surface		tempo	
storm		surplus		temporal	
story		surprise		tent	
stove		swap (v)		term	
straight		sweet smell		terror	
strange		sweet taste		test (n)	
strategy		swim (v)		text	
stream		switch off		than	
street		switch on		thank	
stretch (n)		sword		that	
string (n)		symbol		the	
string of letters		system		theft	
stripe				them	
strong		table (n)		theme	
structure		tablet (electrical)		then	

Appendix D — Index of Headwords

theory		tonight		try (v)	
there		too (excess)		tube	
these		tool		tumbler	
they		tooth		tunnel	
thick		top		turn (v)	
thief		topic		twice	
thin		torso		twin	
thing		touch (n)		two months	
think		towards		two years	
third (a)		towel		type	
thirst		town			
this		townhouse		ugly	
those		toxin		umbrella	
though		toy		unassuming (a)	
thought		trade (n)		unbelievable	
thrice		tradition		uncertain	
through		traffic		uncommon	
throw (v)		tragedy		unconscious	
thumb		train (n)		uncover	
tidy (a)		train (v)		under	
tie (v)		training course		underpants	
tight		transact		understand	
timbre		transcend		uneven	
time (n)		transport		unexpected	
tin (object)		trap (n)		unfair	
tip		travel (v)		unit	
tissue		tray		unity	
to		tree		universe	
to and fro		trend		unjust	
today		trial		unknown (n)	
toe		triangle		unlike	
toenail		triple (a)		unlikely	
together		trough		unlimited	
toilet		trousers		unlock (v)	
tomorrow		truck		unlucky	
tomorrow night		true		unnatural	
tone (sound)		truncate		unnecessary	
tongue		trust (n)		unreal	

Symese — Universal Symbolic Script

unreasonable	⟡ˣ	virtue	⌣	white	①
unseen (a)	⌒ˣ	virus	∞²	white blood cell	∞
unsure	⟨ˋ	visible	⌒"	who	?
until	⟩	visit (n)	<	whole	⊓
unusual	⌣ˣ	voice	♡	why	⟨
up	↑ˋ	volume (sound)	♡	wicked	⌣²
up and down	⋄	vote (n)	{¹	wide	⩓ˋ
urgent	△¹			wife	⊥
urinate	⊙ˊ	wait	⟨ˊ	wild	⩓
us	⊥	waiter	⟨ᴵ	will (n)	8
usage	⌢⁻	walk (v)	人ˊ	will (v)	⟩ˊ
use (v)	⌢ˊ	wall	▭	will not	⟩ˣ
usual	⌣ˋ	want (v)	⟩ˊ	win (v)	兀ˊ
utensil	◁	want not	⟩ˣ	wind	①
		war	⋈	window	▭
vacancy	⩔ˢ	warm (a)	⌒⋅	wine	⊻²
vacuum	⩔²	waste (n)	⟩ˢ	wing	⟆
vague	⌢ˣ	watch (device)	⋈ᴴ²	winter	⊖
valid	↓ˋ	water	⊖	wire	⌢
valley	∇	wave (n)	⊡ᴴ	wise	◇ˋ
value (n)	$	wax (n)	⊙¹	with	⊓
vapour	⊙	way	⊤	within	⌒
various	⌢ˋ	we	⊥	without	⌐
vary	⌢ˊ	weak	⋃ˋ	woman	⟨ᴵ
vegetable	⧫	wealth	⌢	wonder (n)	◇
vehicle	▱	weapon	⋈	wood	⊖
vent	⌐	weather (n)	⊙	word	⋅
vertical	[ǀ]ˋ	week	⋈¹	work (v)	⊞
very	∧ˋ	weight	⌒⁻	world	⊖
vest	⊔³	weird	⌣ˣ	worry (n)	⊙ˣ
vice	⌣	west	←	worse	⌣ˢ
vicious	⌣ˋ	wet (a)	⊖ˢ	worst	⌣ˢ
view (v)	⌒ˊ	what	⟨	worth (n)	$ˢ
villa	⊟¹	wheel	[⊙]ᴴ	wound (n)	⊠ᴴ
village	⊖⁷	when	⟨ˋ	wrath	⊙⋅
vinegar	③⁻	where	⟩ˋ	write	⊻
violet	⑦ǀ	which	?	wrong (a)	✝ˋ
viral	∞ˢ	while (conjunction)	⌣		

Appendix D — Index of Headwords

yard (measure)	⩟ ⁴	you	⊤	youth	⌣
year	⨯ ³	you all	⊤̄	yucky	⌑ˣ
yellow	④	young	⌣ `	zip (n)	◁• ²
yes	+	your(s)	⊤ `	zone	⌒
yesterday		⨯				

APPENDIX E – INDEX OF COMPOUND SYMS

account (narrative)	⊲	⌓▫
afternoon	⋈	˃`
afternoon tea	[|⌒|	⋈	)|`]
algebra	[|◇ˢ	ξ]₃
aluminium	⊲|₁₃	
always	[⋈	|||]
angel	⌀	∨`
ankle	[⊖	⋀]
anniversary	⊼	⋈³`
ant	∞	-for
anyhow	[⌐|	⊡]
anyone / anybody	[⊥	⊡]
anything	[⊢	⊡]
anytime	[⋈	⊡]
anywhere	[⌇`	⊡]
apple	⚲	-mal
arithmetic	[|◇ˢ	ξ]₂
artificial intelligence	⟐ˢ	⊽▫
athletics	[▷¹	人]
badminton	[▷¹	ᒣ¹]₃
banana	⚲	-mus
barley	⚲	-hor
barrister	[⌒ᴴˢ	⋈]₂
baseball	[▷¹	ᒣ¹]₅
basic (easy to learn)	=`	|◇▫
basketball	[▷¹	[⊙]⁻	⍯]₁
battery	[△	w¹]
beach	[⌐	⊖²]
bean	⚲	-pha
bear	⚲	-urs
beat (music)	[⋋	♂`]
bedsheet	[⌣	⊟]

Appendix E — Index of Compound Syms

bee	∞	-apo		
big hearted	∩ `	♡ ▫		
biologist	[∞ ᴴˢ	8]		
biology	[◊ ˢ	8]		
birth	[⊗	▷ `	⌐]	
blood or blood-forming organs disease	8₃			
blunt (speech)	⋁ `	☺ ▫		
boat driver	[D $\frac{1}{I}$	✉]		
born (v)	[⊗	▷ `	⌐] ″	
boy	⊥	) `		
bracelet	[✕ ²	⊖	▽]	
branch (place)	⚲	⋈ ▫		
bread	[⚘	-tri	ε ']₁	
break (work)	≈	⊡ ▫		
breakfast	[|⌒|	⊠		
		♀ ▫		
bright (clever)	△ ˢ	) `		
brother	Ⅱ			
bus driver	[D $\frac{1}{I}$	Σ]		
butterfly	∞	-lep		
cabbage	⚘	-cap		
calculus	[◊ ˢ	ε]₄		
calm (emotion)	⊙ `	◇ ▫		
camp (n)	[‖	[△]¹]		
camp (v)	[‖	[△]¹] ′		
camper	[‖	[△]¹] ᴵ		
camping (n)	[‖	[△]¹⁻] ⁻		
camping (a)	[‖	[△]¹⁻] ˋ		
candle	[△	⊖]		
capital	⊖ ⁵	⋈ `		
car driver	[D $\frac{1}{I}$	◁]		
carbon	♂₆			
card game	[▷ ˢ	→	⊞]	
carpet	[⌑ ¹	⊟	∩ `]	
carrot	⚘	-car		

Symese — Universal Symbolic Script

cat	♀	-cat	
caterpillar	[∞	-lep	亖]
cave	[⌴	△]	
centimetre	[A¹	⟨10⟩¹]	
chapter	[⊔	⊓]	
chase	大 ´	)| `	
cheap	◁	▽ `	
chemist	[∞ ᴴˢ	⋃¹]	
chemistry	[|◇ ˢ	⋃¹]	
chicken	⚥	-gal	
chili	⚇	-cap	
chocolate candy	[⟐¹	⚲	-cac]
chocolate drink	[⊙	⚲	-cac]
cinema	[⊟	⊙	⊃ ⁻]
circulatory system disease	8 1 1		
circus	[⊞	8]²	
class	[☱	|◇ ᴴˢ]	
classroom	[☱	|◇ ᵛ]	
cliff	[⌐	△ ^]	
closed minded	⌒ `	♀ ▫	
clown	[♀|	⟰ ¹=	♡¹ `]
clue	[↑	◇¹]	
cockroach	∞	-bla	
cocoa	⚲	-cac	
coconut	⚱	-coc	
coin	[⚮	⊖]	
cold hearted	⋃ `	♡ ▫	
collar	[⊔	⊓	⚥]
computer network	⊞	▽ ▫	
cool headed	⋃ `	♀ ▫	
copper	⚶ 2 9		
corn	⚱	-zea	
corn flour	[⟨∴⟩	⚱	-zea]
cough	[⊙ ^	♡]	

Appendix E — Index of Compound Syms

cousin brother	[☺	II	♡	♡]
cousin sister	[☺	II	♡	♡]
cow / bull	♀	-tau		
crab	∞	-bra		
cream	⊼	⌣`		
cricket	[▷¹	⁀¹]₄		
crocodile	∝	-cro		
cucumber	ϕ	-cuc		
currency note	[⸸	⫿]		
cycling	[▷¹	∞]		
daisy	⍾	-bel		
dawn	⨯	|(`		
deer	♀	-cer		
demon / devil	⌀	⤩		
dentist	[⨁¹	♡]		
diary	[⨯″	⩒]		
dictionary	[-|-	Σ	⌊·⌋]	
digestive system	⑧₁₃			
dinner	[|⌾|	⨯	▷`]	
dinosaur	∝	⩯`		
disappointment	[⍾ˣ	⌃]		
disaster	[≋^	⟨⟩ˢ]		
doctor	⨁¹ ₁			
dog	♀	-can		
doll	[⨀	II]		
domesticated animal	⨀	⨺`		
drag	⤙´	⩯`		
drop (liquid)	⟨·⟩	⏚□		
duck	⍥	-pla		
dull (stupid)	△ˣ	♀□		
dusk	⨯	|(`		
eagle	⍥	-acc		
ear or mastoid process disease	⑧₁₀			

Symese — Universal Symbolic Script

echo	[⌓	⊙]		
electric bicycle	[⚭	ᴡ¹ˋ]		
electric light	[△	ᴡ¹]		
electron	[⊔	⌐¹]³		
elephant	⚲	-ele		
endocrine, nutritional, metabolic disease	⚯₅			
engineer	[⌒⌒ ᴴ ˢ	⇥]		
engineering	[◌◇ ˢ	⇥]		
enhance	[∽ˋ	⌵ˢ]¹		
enter	[▷ˋ	⊏]		
evening	⨯	⟩ˋ		
ever	[⨯	+]		
every time	[⨯	⦙]		
everyone / everybody	[⊥	⦙]		
everything	[⊢	⦙]		
everywhere	[ↄˋ	⦙]		
excellent	⌵ˋ	∧ˇ		
excuse	⟡	⨯ˋ		
exercise	[ᴅˋ	ᴡ]		
exit (v)	[▷ˋ	⌐]		
expensive	⊲	△ˋ		
extensive	∩ˋ	⋈ˌ		
extract	[ꜱˋ	⌐]		
fairy	⌀	◇ˋ		
feather	[⊟	⚭]		
fever	[⌒̄	⚯	∧ˋ]	
firefighter	[⟩ᴴ	⏉₁	⊖]	
fireworks	[⊣	⊖]		
flux / oscillate	[ᴅˋ	⬦]		
forenoon	⨯	⎛ˋ		
forever	⨯	⟡ˋ		
frog	∝	-anu		

Appendix E — Index of Compound Syms

garlic	⌀	-sat	
gem / jewel	[⌀	◁	△`]
genitourinary disease	⊗ 1 6		
geography	[|◇ˢ	⋈]	
geometry	[|◇ˢ	{]₅	
ginger	⌀	-zin	
girl	⊥	(·`	
give birth	[⊚	▷`	⊐]´
glove	[▱	▽]	
go in	[△´	⊏]	
go out	[△´	⊐]	
goat	⚲	-cap	
gold	⌀₇ ₉		
granddaughter	⌣	)|`	
grandfather	⌢	|(`	
grandmother	⌣	|(`	
grandson	⌢	)|`	
graph	[⊙	◇ˢ]	
great-granddaughter	⌣	)|‡	
great-grandfather	⌢	|(‡	
great-grandmother	⌣	|(‡	
great-grandson	⌢	)|‡	
hairpiece / wig	[✕²	⚇]	
handbag	[⊙	▽]	
heavy hearted	⌒`	♡▫	
heel	[△	◁]	
helium	⌀₂		
helmet	⊓¹	⌒`	
heptagon	△₇		
hexagon	△₆		
historian	[⌒ᴴˢ	|⊠¹]	
hockey	[▷¹	[⊙]⁻	⌒]₁
holiday / vacation	[▫	⊕]	
hoof	[△	⚭	⌒`]

253

Symese — Universal Symbolic Script

horse	♀	-equ	
huge / enormous / massive	⌒`	∧‡	
hunt	人´	)|`	
hydrogen	♂$_1$		
ice hockey	[▷¹	[⊙]⁻	⌐]$_2$
ice-cream	[⊼	⌣`	⊖¹]
immune system	8$_4$		
improve	[∼´	∨ʃ]	
indoor	[⊏	⊟]	
infectious or parasitic disease	8$_1$		
ink	[▽	⊻]	
interrupt	[◁ᵛ	⊙]´	
interrupted (a)	[◁ᵛ	⊙]"	
interrupting (n)	[◁ᵛ	⊙]⁻	
interruption	[◁ᵛ	⊙]	
iron	♂$_{2\,6}$		
island	[⊖	⊓	⊖]
just (legal)	⋈`	⋈□	
kettle	⌣⌒	⊖³	
kill	[⫯⌒	⊘]	
kilogram	[⌂¹	⟨10⟩²]	
kilometre	[∧¹	⟨10⟩²]	
kite	[⍟	人¹	⌣]
knock	[⊙¹	⊖	⊻]
knuckle	[⊖	⊻]	
lawyer / solicitor / attorney	[∞ᴴˢ	⋈]$_1$	
leave (work)	△	⊞□	
lemon	⍟	-lim	
lettuce	⌽	-lac	
lifeguard	[>ᴵ	⌣⌒$_1$	⅄]
light hearted	▽`	♡□	

254

Appendix E — Index of Compound Syms

lightning	[W¹	⊙ ⌢]		
lightning storm	[⊙ ⌢	W¹]		
lion	♀	-leo		
lotion	[⚱¹	∪]		
lower arm	Y	∨ `		
lower leg	人	∨ `		
lunch	[|⌒|	⨯	◡]
lust	↑ ¯	⚱ ▫		
machine learning	|◇ ¯	⩔ ▫		
magazine	[▯	⊙¹]		
magnet	[⌿₂ ₆	⊣ ⌢]		
mango	⚲	-man		
mask	[⊖	♀|]		
mat / rug	[⌑¹	☐]		
mathematics	[|◇ ⌢	⧘]₁		
medicine (subject)	[|◇ ⌢	⚱ ⌢]		
melt	[∪ ´	⌒]		
mental, behavioural, neurodevelopmental disease	8 6			
mercy	⌇²	⚱ ▫		
metric ton	[⌓¹	⟨10⟩ ⁵]		
milligram	[⌓¹	⟨10⟩ ²]		
millimetre	[A¹	⟨10⟩ ²]		
morning	⨯	< `		
mouse	♀	-rod		
movie	[⊙	D ¯	⌒ `]	
murder	[⚯ ⌢	⚱	⨯ ⌣]	
musculoskeletal, connective tissue disease	8 1 5			
musical instrument	⌂ ⌢	◌ `		
necklace	[⨯²	⊤̇]		
neoplasms or cancers	8 2			
nephew	[⍵	Ⅱ]		
nervous system disease	8 8			
netball	[▷¹	[◉] ¯	▽]₃	

255

Symese — Universal Symbolic Script

neutron	[⊔	ᓂ¹]²	
never	[⊠	×]	
niece	[ઉ	ⅠⅠ]	
nitrogen	ᓂ₇		
nobody	[⊥	×]	
nonagon	△₉		
none	[⊢⊣	×]ˇ	
noodle / spaghetti	[♀	-tri	ε´]₃
northeast	[⇑	↔]	
northwest	[⇑	←]	
nothing	[⊢⊣	×]	
nowhere	[⊃	×`]	
nuclear	[⋎	ᓂ¹]`	
nuclear energy	[⋎	ᓂ¹]	
nurse	⊗¹ᵢ ₂		

octagon	△₈		
octopus	∝	-oct	
oil lamp	[△	⊕]	
old man	≡	)`	
old woman	≡	(·`	
onion	⊕	-cep	
open minded	⌣`	♀▫	
ophthalmologist	[⊗¹ᵢ	⊙]	
optician / optometrist	[⌒ˢ	⊙]	
orange (fruit)	♀	-aur	
orchid	♀	-orc	
outdoor	[⊐	⊟]	
oxygen	ᓂ₈		

paramedic	[>ᴵ	⏝¹	⊗]
parent	[♡	♡]	
pasta	[♀	-tri	ε´]₂
patient	[▽ᴵ₁	⊗¹ᵢ 1]	
paw	[△	8]	

Appendix E — Index of Compound Syms

pay	[⌒ ´	▷]	
peel / skin (v)	[→▷ ´	⌂]	
pentagon	△5		
pepper	⌀	-pip	
pet	[8	◁ `]¹	
pharmacist	[⌒ᴴₛ	▫	◯¹ `]
photo album	[▱	⊙]	
pie	[⌀₄	-tri	ℰ ´]
pig	⌀	-sui	
pill	[◯¹	⌂]	
pillow case	[⌓	⊡¹]	
pilot	[▷¹ᴴ	⊠]	
pizza	[⌀₅	-tri	ℰ ´]
platinum	⌀ ₇ ₈		
point (subject)	[·]	⊓▫	
police	[>ᴵ	▽⌒₁	⌒]
		⌀▫	
positive (mind)	+``		
potato	⌀	-tub	
praise	[◯²	◉]	
proton	[⊔	◯¹]¹	
psychiatrist	[◯¹ᴴ	⋈]	
psychiatry	[◇ₛ	◯ₛ	⋈]
psychologist	[⌒ᴴₛ	⋈]	
psychology	[◇ₛ	⋈]	
put / take in	▽ ´	⌐ `	
put / take out	▽ ´	⌐ `	
quilt cover	[⌓	⊡³]	

rabbit	⌀	-lep	
respiratory system	8 1 2		
rice	⌀	-ory	
rice flour	[⋰	⌀	-ory]
roll of dice	[▷ₛ	→	[▫]]
rose	⌀	-ros	
rotate	▷ ´	[○] `	
rugby	[▷¹	[⊙]⁻	△]²

Symese — Universal Symbolic Script

word	symbol 1	symbol 2	symbol 3
salmon	∞	-sal	
satiated	⌒	⋏ `	
scale	[⊖	∞]	
seagull	⚲	-lar	
selfish	⌒ `	⊘ ▫	
selfless	⌣ `	⊘ ▫	
shake	[D ´	⇢]	
sheep	⚲	-ovi	
silicon	⊲ 1 4		
silver	⊲ 4 7		
sister	⊥	(·`	
skeleton	[8	8]	
skin	8 1 4		
slap	[⊙ ´¹	△]	
sleep-wake disorders	8 7		
sleeve	[⊔	⟐	Υ]
sloth	⊐⊓ˣ	⊘ ▫	
snake	∝	-ser	
sneeze	[⊙ ⌒	⌗]	
soccer	[▷¹	[◎] ⁻	△]₁
somehow	[⌐	≡]	
someone / somebody	[⊥	≡]	
something	[⊢	≡]	
sometimes	[⊠	≡]	
somewhere	[⊃ `	≡]	
southeast	[↓	↣]	
southwest	[↓	↤]	
soybean	⚲	-gly	
spider	∞	-ara	
start of week	[⊠ ¹	▷]	
substantial	⌒ `	N ▫	
sunflower	⚲	-hel	
surgeon	⊘ ¹ᵢ 3		
swan	⚲	-cyg	
swimming	[▷¹	Ψ ´]	

Appendix E — Index of Compound Syms

table tennis	[▷¹	ꝗ ¹]₂	
tasteless (cultural)	⌔ˣ	♡□	
television	[▲]	⊙	D⁻]
tennis	[▷¹	ꝗ ¹]₁	
terrible / horrible	⌵ `	∧ ‡	
thesaurus	[-|-	Σ	╲ `]
thread	⌐	⊙ `	
thunder	[⊙	⊙ ⌒]	
thunderstorm	[⊙ ⌒	⊙]	
tiger	♀	-tig	
tin (metal)	♂₅ ₀		
tiny / minute / miniscule	∪ `	∧ ‡	
tomato	⌀	-esc	
torrent	⌐ ´	⌒ `	
tortoise	∝	-tes	
touched (emotion)	♡ `	♡ □	
train driver	[D ¹ᵢ	⊠]	
trickle / drip	⌐ ´	⌒	
truck driver	[D ¹ᵢ	⊠]	
uncle / aunt (maternal)	[∏	♡]	
uncle / aunt (paternal)	[∏	♡]	
upper arm	Y	∧ `	
upper leg	⋏	∧ `	
very bad	⌵ `	∧ `	
very big	⌒ `	∧ `	
very good	⌵ `	∧ `	
very small	∪ `	∧ `	
vibrate	[D ´	⇢◇]ᵛ	
video	[⊙	D⁻]	
visual system disease	⌾ ₉		
volcano	[▲ ⌒	⊖]	
volleyball	[▷¹	[⊙]⁻	▽]₂

wallet	[⊙	⌐.]	
warm hearted	⌒˙ `	♡ ▫	
weekend	[⊼ ¹	◁ ˜]	
whale	⋈	-cet	
wheat	⚲	-tri	
wheat flour	[⊙⋯	⚲	-tri]
whisper	♡	⌣˙ `	
whistle	[⊘ ¹	⚲]	
wild animal	⚭	⊳ `	
wrist	[⊖	⏀]	
zinc	ɑ₃₀		
zoo	[⊟	⚭] ¹	

Appendix F – Design Principles

1. There is a logical link between sym and concept, eg an upward- or right-pointing shape is used to denote a more active or perceptible concept – ⊓ for *on*, ⊐ for *out* – and a similar downward- or left- pointing shape for its converse – ⊔ for *off*, ⊏ for *in*.

2. Where a shape has parts pointing in opposite directions, the direction of the left or upper part of the shape indicates the concept denoted, eg ∽´ with its left part pointing up and ⟩´ with its upper part pointing right denote the more active concepts *do* and *give* while their mirror image syms ∽´ and ⟨´ denote the more passive concepts *be* and *take*.

3. A symmetry of sym pairs is achieved by flipping and rotating the glyphs.

4. Particles and nouns are the default parts of speech and do not need a superscript to denote them as such – particles by virtue of their frequent occurrence in sentences and nouns for the reason that, consistent with the basic mental process of perceiving objects with our senses, they are used as tangible gateways to intangibles.

5. Superscript ` (adjective qualifier or) s added for adjectives and adverbs and superscript ´ (verb qualifier or VQ) is added for verbs.

6. Where a word has divergent meanings, the most common parallel meanings are assigned to a sym, eg ⊓ denotes *on*, with the parallel meanings 'at a given time' and 'in contact with'. Similarly, ⊓ denotes 'next to' and 'in the manner of' as parallel meanings of *with*.

7. Modifiers are added to basic shapes to denote related concepts, eg a dot or line is added to ∩ and ∪ to make ∩˙ and ∪˙ for *hard* and *soft*, △ and ▽ for *solid* and *liquid*, A` and ∀` for *strong* and *weak*, A` and ∀` for *wide* and *narrow*, △` and ▽` for *heavy* and *light*, A` and ∀` for *firm* and *flexible*, A` and ∀` for *thick* and *thin*.

8. Based on the convention (eg buttons on a tape recorder) of arrows pointing left and right to indicate backward and forward, we denote *back, be still, before, previous, present* and *near* by left-pointing shapes ⊲`, ⊲´, ⎸⎨, ⎸⎨`, ⎸⎨` and <` and the opposite concepts by their mirror image shapes.

9. The symmetry of symbols fills conceptual gaps in natural languages.

10. A numeral is used as a number or sym qualifier but not as a standalone sym. Besides 0-9, we also retain the conventional usage of the following common symbols:

.	:	'	!	(	#	&	-
,	;	"	?	)	*	%	=

11. Noun qualifier (NQ) superscript ⁻ is used for a noun, opposite qualifier (OQ) superscript ˣ for the opposite of a concept, numeric qualifier (#Q) superscripts ¹ ² ³ etc for a derivative or extension of a concept, device/substance qualifier (DQ) superscript ᴴ for the device or substance formed from a concept and essence/nuance qualifier (EQ) superscript ˘ for the essence or nuance of a concept. The superscript is doubled or tripled where the root sym already has a superscript for the same part of speech.

12. Where multiple superscripts are added to a sym, the topmost one indicates the primary derivative while the bottommost one indicates the part of speech. For example, NQ at the top and AQ at the bottom of A˘⁻ indicate an adjective augmentation of the noun *widening*.

13. As an extension of DP 4, NQ is left out for the most basic noun extension of a base verb or adjective, a single NQ is added for the next most basic noun, a double or triple NQ is added for less basic nouns, eg *thickness* as the most basic noun extension of *thick* needs no NQ while *thickening* as the next most basic noun has a single NQ.

The most basic nouns are those that use the same base word, the second most basic nouns are formed by adding a suffix like *-ness, -ty, -tion* or *-ing* indicating the action or quality of something, eg ⌒ for *heat* and ⌒⁻ for *heating*.

Appendix F — Design Principles

14. A single AQ is added for the most basic adjective or adverb extension of a base noun or verb, a double or triple AQ is added for less basic adjectives or adverbs. The most basic adjectives are those that use the same base word or are formed by adding suffix -ing to a base word indicating the quality of something relating to its action, the next most basic adjectives are those formed by adding suffix -ed to a base word indicating the state of something, eg ⟨glyph⟩ for *heated*. Adjectives formed by adding -ed are always denoted with double AQ.

15. A single VQ is added for the most basic verb extension of a base noun or adjective, a double or triple VQ is added for less basic verbs. The most basic verbs are those that use the same base word as the noun or adjective, eg ⟨glyph⟩ for *firm* as verb.

16. For #Qs, ¹ is added for the most basic noun derivative of a base noun, verb or adjective and ², ³, ⁴ etc are added for less basic nouns.

17. A line across certain sym shapes denotes its negative, eg a line across ⟨glyph⟩ (for *do*) makes ⟨glyph⟩ (for *do not*).

18. Extending part of a sym shape indicates an extension of a concept, eg extending the horizontal line in ⟨glyph⟩ for *success* makes ⟨glyph⟩ for *achievement.*

19. As an extension of DP 6, which established the principle of keeping the associations between sym and concept at a basic level to make the script less language specific, certain concepts are represented by a shared sym, eg *staff* and *cane* by a glyph that looks like a walking stick with a handle on the right, reflecting the prevalence of right-handedness.

20. =Q and -Q indicate a bigger (or otherwise more advanced case) and smaller (or otherwise less advanced case) – for example, added to *house* to make *mansion* and *hut* respectively. IQ indicates person – added to *male* to make *man*. PQ indicates a place of – added to *money* to make *bank*. GQ indicates group – added to *person* to make *crowd*.

21. SQ indicates plural where the noun number is relevant – added, for example, to *age* to make *ages*. RQ indicates repeated action – added to *try* to make *retry*. UQ indicates upper case – added to *earth* to make *Earth*. +Q and *Q indicate more and most – added to *good* to make *better* and *best*, with the redundant adjective superscript left out. <Q and >Q indicate past and future tenses – added to *close* to make *closed* and *will close*, with the redundant verb superscript left out.

22. Some numeric qualifiers are embedded within the sym, eg adding Embedded Qualifier (~Q) to ⌒ for *taste* makes ①, ② and ③ for *sweet, salty* and *sour taste*, to ▱ for *smell* makes ①, ② and ③ for *sweet, salty* and *sour smell*.

23. A noun sym is placed before its qualifying adjective sym, eg ⊥ for *child* + ⟨˙ for *female* = ⊥ ⟨˙ for *girl*, ⊥ + ⟩˙ = ⊥ ⟩˙ for *boy*. ☰ for *old person* + ⟨˙ = ☰ ⟨˙ for *old woman*, ☰ + ⟩˙ = ☰ ⟩˙ for *old man*.

24. PO (parcel open) and PC (parcel close) are square brackets that enclose two or more glyphs denoting a single concept. Having appropriated [and] for use as qualifiers, we denote square brackets in common usage by ⟦ and ⟧.

25. Using a combination of basic syms as a synonym for a more complex sym presents a choice between elegance of expression (and precision) and having fewer root syms to memorise. Examples include *coconut*: the more precise ⚘ -coc vs ⚘ ⊙˙ ⌒˙ (big spherical fruit), *hug*: ⊖¹ vs [♡ Y] (love with arms) and *fun*: ♡¹ vs [♡ ▷] (love with play).

26. A fuzzy qualifier (FQ) indicates a close synonym of a sym.

27. A field mark (FM) qualifies a word parcel with its communication context.

QUALIFIERS

AQ	Adjective / Adverb	\	-Q	Mini	∪	*Q	Most	⟩
VQ	Verb	/	IQ	Person	I	<Q	Past tense	☽
NQ	Noun	−	PQ	Place	v	>Q	Future tense	☾
OQ	Opposite	x	GQ	Group	||	~Q	Embedded	▱
#Q	Derivative	1	SQ	Plural	+	PO	Parcel open	[
DQ	Device / substance	H	RQ	Repeat	‡	PC	Parcel close	]
EQ	Essence/nuance	∽	UQ	Upper case	∧	FQ	Fuzzy	◇
=Q	Maxi	∩	+Q	More	⟨	FM	Field mark	▫

APPENDIX G – GLOSSARY

augmented sym	sym formed by adding one or more qualifiers to a root sym
basic concept	one of a set of concepts on which Symese is built
compound sym	sym formed by combining two or more root syms
derivative sym	sym formed by modifying a root sym
design principle	aspect of the architectural logic of Symese
etymology	historical roots of a word
flexion	modified form of a word with a different ending
glyph	symbol or icon representing a word or concept in a pictographic language
hieroglyphics	system of writing with pictorial symbols to denote meanings or sounds
homographs	words with the same spelling but different meanings
homonyms	words with the same sound and spelling but different meanings
ideogram/ideograph	symbol denoting a concept but not its sound
logogram/logograph	symbol denoting a spoken word but not its sound
mentalese	language-like representation of concepts without words
modifier	stroke added to a basic shape to denote a related concept
natural language	language that came about organically in a historical cultural context
particle	article or preposition or conjunction
phonetic	representing speech sounds
phonograph	symbol that denotes the sound of a syllable or word
pictogram/pictograph	pictorial symbol that denotes a word, phrase or concept
pictographic logic	pictorial link between a symbol and the concept it represents
pictographic roots	pictographic logic at the root of a symbol
qualifier	symbol (usually a superscript) that modifies a sym
rebus word	pictorial symbol that denotes the sound of a word
root sym	sym that denotes a basic concept
script	writing system for a language
semantics	relationship between words and their meanings
sym	Symese symbol
sym seeds	root syms and qualifiers that make up augmented or compound syms
syntax	elements of sentence structure

APPENDIX H – INDEX

A

abstract concepts 35, 49, 62

active concepts 19

alphabet 8

Arika Okrent 8

articles 17

associated concept 30, 34

augmented definitions 56

augmented sym 64

B

Babel 5

baggage of word connotations 87

basic concepts 9–10, 17, 39

blank canvas 20, 64

Blissymbols 7

C

calculus of thought 17

capitalisation of nouns 17

caveman symbols 8

cerebral palsy 7

Charles Bliss 7

compound concepts 92

compound sym 9, 17, 25, 64–65, 87

conceptual gaps 23, 31

conjunctions 17

critical mass of users 9

cultural context 5, 8

D

default part of speech 29

derivative concepts 8

derivative sym 17

design principles 19, 25

divergent meanings 20, 37, 85, 89

doodle 39, 86, 94

E

embedded qualifiers 60

emoji 5, 7, 39, 84, 94

encapsulated metaphors 92

Esperanto 17

etymology 20

extension of a concept 25, 37

F

flexions 7

G

    geometric shapes 11, 30

    glyphs 6, 8–9, 18–19, 39, 41, 61–62, 64–65

    glyphs derived from images 6

H

    hieroglyphics 6

    homographs 89

    homonyms 89, 91

    hybrid of several languages 17

I

    iConji 7

    ideographic 6

    ideographic language project 7

    Interlingua 17

J

    John Wilkins 17

L

    Leibniz 6

    logic of Symese 25, 33

    Loglan 17

    logographic 6

M

    mentalese 17, 33

    modifiers 21, 30

    multiple superscripts 26

N

    natural languages 8, 23, 39, 84, 87, 93–94

    niche synonyms 85, 87

    noise of words 8

    non-superscript qualifiers 58

O

    object genders 17

P

    parallel meanings 20

    particles 7, 17, 20, 85

    passive concepts 19

    pedantry of syntax and semantics 84

    phonetic 6, 9

    phonographic 6, 8

    pictogram 6–7, 9, 93

    pictographic 3, 6, 8–11, 17, 25, 32

    pictographic logic 12, 31, 39

    pictographic roots 6, 9, 30, 34, 52

    pictographic-rooted radical 6

prepositions 17

primal utterances 8

primary derivative 26

Q

qualifiers 20, 24–25, 56, 58, 60, 64–65, 87–88, 93

R

rebus words 6

Rongorongo 6

root sym 17, 25, 33, 49, 86, 93

S

semantics 5, 8, 14, 33, 39, 84, 94

sound of silence 8–9

superscript qualifiers 58

syllabic 6

sym seeds 25

symmetry of sym pairs 19

syms 11, 14, 17, 19–20, 24, 26, 33, 35, 41, 56, 61, 64, 86–87, 89

syntax 5, 39, 84

T

tangible gateways to intangibles 20

tapestry of cultural virtue and vice 5

U

unwieldy precision 85, 87

V

verb inflections 17

visual aid 84

visual gateway to thought 39

W

word frequency lists 7

word parcel 65–66, 88, 91

About the Author

Tim Lee speaks three languages – his mother tongue (Chinese), the language of his country of birth (Malay) and English, the closest thing there is to a global language. He also speaks the language of the heart (music) – self-taught, with no formal music education.

As a Business Analyst, he discovered the elegance of capturing business logic and processes in computer code. Finally, his grandchildren taught him to speak *babese* and *toddlese*.

Integrating his experience of language into a whole that is more than the sum of its parts, he embarked on a decade-long quest to invent a universal symbolic script – *Symese* (pronounced "sai-mees") – the language of symbols. Tim thinks he has succeeded in developing a logical framework for a script that can become a living universal language.

Such a labour of love is an age-old quest with hundreds of offspring and Esperanto coming closest to maturity but without achieving the critical mass needed to become self-sustaining. Has Tim succeeded? You be the judge.

Notes

www.ingramcontent.com/pod-product-compliance
Lightning Source LLC
Chambersburg PA
CBHW061110070526
44583CB00027B/3244